Black College Sport

BLACK COLLEGE SPORT

Ocania Chalk

ILLUSTRATED WITH PHOTOGRAPHS

Dodd, Mead & Company · New York

Library of Congress Cataloging in Publication Data

Chalk, Ocania.
    Black college sport.

    Includes index.
    1. Negro athletes. 2. College sports—History.
3. Sports—United States—History. I. Title.
GV583.C45   796'.092'2   [B]   75-43833
ISBN 0-396-07023-X

831407 ∨

Foreword

The black female athlete has not been discussed in the pages that follow. Any effort possibly would have been presumptuous, and certainly would have been inadequate.

A work of quality, backed by in-depth research, has long been needed. To have treated the black woman athlete cursorily would have compounded the sins of the past as has too often been done with the black male athlete.

The writer awaits a definitive treatment on the accomplishments of black women in sports.

Ocania Chalk
Washington, D.C.

Contents

The Oberlin baseball team of 1881. Moses Fleetwood Walker (6) and Weldy Wilberforce Walker (10) were probably the first black players on a college baseball team.

1

Black Stars on White College Baseball Teams

The first intercollegiate baseball game was played on Friday, July 1, 1859, between Williams College and Amherst College in Pittsfield, Massachusetts.

At a meeting after chapel at Amherst, a motion had been made that the college would challenge Williams to a friendly game. Williams accepted the challenge, and the agreement was made that thirteen men would be picked to represent each school.

The game started at eleven o'clock on the grounds of the Pittsfield baseball club.

Amherst batted first. At the end of the second inning (called "rounds") the score was Amherst, 1, Williams, 9. By the end of the third inning, Amherst had tied the score, 9–9. They then took the lead in the next inning and held it.

After four hours and twenty-six rounds, Amherst was declared the winner, 73–32.

Special messengers relayed Amherst's victory to the campus about eleven that night. The students, who had retired, were roused, and bells were rung, bonfires were lighted, and the night was spent in a victory celebration.

It might be noted that in this first intercollegiate game, no gloves were worn, and Amherst's players were not dressed in uniforms.

It is believed that the first Negro to play on a college varsity baseball team was Moses Fleetwood Walker, at Oberlin College, Oberlin,

Ohio, in 1881. Walker entered Oberlin in 1878, having been registered in its preparatory department in 1877. Oberlin College was founded in 1833 and from its early days had always admitted students without regard to race, creed, or color, beginning with its first Negro student, James Bradley, in 1840. In 1880 Oberlin did not have a varsity baseball team, but intramural games were in vogue. The Alpha Deltas played the Phi Kappa Pis, the freshmen played the preps, and the juniors played the seniors.

Amherst and Williams had been the pioneers, but Harvard, Yale, and Princeton quickly assumed command once they took up the game in 1868. At first players were selected at random, without regard to class. Harvard won a single game from Princeton and Yale to gain the first intercollegiate baseball championship in what became a run of five victorious Harvard seasons, until 1873 when Princeton won its first title. Dual series existed in 1869, 1871, and 1872, when Princeton failed to field a team. The championship was at first decided by single-game matches between all competitors; two games were played starting in 1872.

By 1880 the game of "base ball" (as it was first spelled) was spreading to other colleges. The *Oberlin Review* of October 9, 1880, reported that Walker had been elected captain of the nine.

On October 15 Oberlin featured a game between the seniors and the juniors on its new baseball field. The *Review* noted that the field and stands were the best in the land. About two hundred enthusiasts attended, and fittingly for the nation's first coeducational college, a large number of young women were present. The *Oberlin Review* of October 23 reported:

In the third the juniors tied the game, by hits by Matter, Hotchkis, Walker, and Burket. In the fourth the seniors made one run and for four innings after that both sides were blanked. In the eighth the juniors scored seven runs, Walker making a superb hit over Cabinet Hall bringing in three men and coming home himself. In the ninth the seniors secured three runs more, the score standing at the close 11–8 for the juniors. Burket's pitching, the catching of Walker and Bellows, and the fine fielding of Day were especially noticed.

In 1881, Walker's younger brother, Weldy Wilberforce Walker, entered Oberlin's preparatory department, which prepared students for college in the absence of adequate academies and high schools.

Weldy quickly established his athletic prowess. The *Review* of May 14 stated:

The preps won their second game last Saturday, this time over the freshmen, by a score of 9–6. Some beautiful fly catches were made by Walker and Slater.

As far back as December 6, 1879, delegates from Harvard, Yale, Brown, Amherst, Princeton, and Dartmouth, met at Springfield, Massachusetts, and formed the American College Baseball Association, the first college league.

It was not until 1881, however, that Oberlin organized a varsity team which played in a modest number of intercollegiate contests. Intramural play continued. On May 21, the varsity beat the preps, 12–3, with Weldy Walker now a member of the varsity squad.

Oberlin's first varsity lineup included Moses Fleetwood Walker, catcher; Harlan Fessenden Burket, pitcher; Charles D. Harrison, shortstop; Josiah H. Bellows, first base; Willis F. Day, second base; Edward D. Burwell, third base; Charles D. Green, left field; Weldy Wilberforce Walker, right field; and Merton E. Thompson, center field.

On May 19 the varsity played a practice game against a pickup team and lost, 27–6. The only bright spot for Oberlin was Moses Walker's home run, two doubles, and single. Oberlin's varsity nine then defeated Hudson, 4–0.

Finally came the big game, a contest against the University of Michigan, on June 12, on Oberlin's home grounds. The rains fell on Monday, the seventh, and continued on into Thursday, the tenth. It was both wet and cold. But Friday was a lovely day with sunshine beckoning each team. A good contest was eagerly awaited by all.

Members of the athletic association began scurrying about in preparation for the big event. There was no end of volunteers to help them. They even mended fences, to make sure that all paid to see the contest. Nothing, however, could be done about students looking out of the windows of Cabinet Hall.

Saturday was clear and the stadium was jammed with six hundred fans, including at least two hundred young women. The attendants, paying $0.50 "at the door," or $0.25 before the event, would insure that the $100 expenses for the Ann Arbor team's travel could be made.

At two o'clock the Michigan team alighted from their carriages, and at precisely two-thirty the band struck up and the game began.

Oberlin proved too powerful for its opponents and the final score was 9–2. Michigan's two runs were the result of an error by Moses Walker when he made a high throw over second base that rolled almost all the way to Cabinet Hall. The home team was overjoyed with its victory, and the athletic association found itself in the possession of $128.26 in gross receipts, with a net of $28.26 after Ann Arbor's traveling expenses were deducted.

When school closed in 1881, Moses Walker joined an amateur team in Cleveland called the "Whites." In a game scheduled between the Whites and Louisville, the Kentucky team objected to Walker's participation. He was ordered off the grounds, but sober heads prevailed and he was allowed to "remain" with his teammates.

On October 1, the *Oberlin Review* noted:

'82—Mr. M. F. Walker will complete his course at Ann Arbor.

Walker enrolled in the University of Michigan Law School, the class of 1884, where he formed a battery with Arthur T. Packard on the baseball team.

In 1882 Oberlin returned to intramural play exclusively. Weldy Walker, then a freshman, played second base. The *Oberlin Review,* on November 12, 1881, published statistics showing that Weldy Walker was the second leading batter of the championship season. Of twenty-eight listed players, Walker batted .307 and had a fielding average of .805 to rank eleventh.

The freshmen, sophomores, juniors, and seniors played nine games each. The sophomores won the championship with six wins against three losses. The freshmen, with Walker, won five and lost four. The seniors won four and lost five. And the juniors won three and lost six.

In March 1882 the *Review* reported that Moses Walker had passed through the city on his way to Ann Arbor to finish his course.

In April the *Review*, keeping tabs on its outstanding former star, reported that Moses Walker and Packard were the battery for the Michigan varsity, and in a game against the sophomores, both players turned in outstanding performances, with Walker making a home run, scoring J. C. Moore.

In the summer of 1882 Moses Walker and Harlan Burket played baseball with a team in New Castle, Pennsylvania.

In September 1882, when Moses Walker returned to Ann Arbor, he was joined by his brother Weldy. The Michigan campus paper cheered the action:

We are glad to welcome Weldy, and are willing to harbor any more [Walkers] if they are as good a base-ballist as Weldy's brother.

Neither brother graduated. In May 1883 Moses Walker and Harlan Burket were reportedly seen passing through Oberlin on their way to Toledo. Both turned professional and joined the Toledo Mudhens, at that time a minor-league team in the Northwestern League.

When Toledo opened the home season on May 5, Walker debuted behind the plate. He had one hit—a double—in five at-bats and scored a run. On defensive play, he had eight put-outs and two assists. He also made two errors.

Weldy Walker, never far from his brother, also left the University of Michigan and had an abbreviated minor-league baseball career. He later became the business manager of his brother's numerous enterprises.

The next black to play on a white college baseball team was James Francis Gregory, a freshman at Amherst College in 1895. Gregory played both infield and outfield.

During the 1896 season Amherst won nine exhibition games and lost nine. Amherst also won four league games and lost four as a member of the Tri-Collegiate League, which included Dartmouth and Williams.

Williams College won the Tri-Collegiate League championship with a 6–2, won-lost, record, and Dartmouth finished last with a 2–6, won-lost, record.

In the 1896 season Gregory played shortstop, and batted eighth. On May 12 his defensive work was acknowledged in the *Boston Globe*:

GREGORY MAKES BRILLIANT PLAYS FOR VISITORS

However, Harvard beat Amherst, 8–3. Gregory had nine assists and one put-out. He also scored a run, contributed a triple, and made an error.

On May 15 Dartmouth beat Amherst, 7–2. Gregory went hitless. But on May 16 Amherst turned the tables on Dartmouth. Amherst won, 9–5. Gregory played shortstop and hit a home run. He was still batting eighth in the lineup.

In the eight league games Amherst played in 1896, Gregory batted .061. But in 1897 he would be shifted to center field and moved up in the batting order.

In the 1897 season, Amherst played sixteen exhibition games, winning five, losing ten, and tying one. In eight league games, Amherst won two and lost six.

In the 1897 season, Gregory was moved to the number three and lead-off batting spot. On May 21 he had one of his biggest days. Batting cleanup, he had three hits, scored two runs, and stole two bases as Amherst beat Dartmouth, 10–8. The *Boston Globe* told of another game on May 26:

CUBAN GIANTS[1] 5, AMHERST 1

Amherst, May 25—The Cuban Giants defeated Amherst today 5 to 1. . . . Fletcher's stops at third and Gregory's throw to the plate were pretty plays.

[1] The Cuban Giants was the first fully salaried Negro professional baseball team. It was organized in 1885.

In eight league games, Gregory batted .203.

In the 1898 season, Amherst played fifteen exhibition games, and won seven and lost eight. In league games, Amherst won one and lost seven. Dartmouth finished first with an 8–0 record, followed by Williams, with a three win and five loss record.

Gregory had been elected captain. It was not one of the better Amherst teams, but Gregory had his moments. The *Boston Globe* of May 4 disclosed that some eight hundred fans showed up to see Williams beat Amherst, 6–5. However, Gregory had three hits and stole a base. He was playing center field and batting first in the lineup.

In eight league games, Gregory batted .223. After graduation in 1898, Gregory entered Yale's Divinity School, and earned his degree in 1901.

James Francis Gregory was born in Washington, D.C., on April 10, 1876. He did his preparatory work at Howard Academy in Washington. After graduation from Amherst and Yale, he became associate pastor of the Central Presbyterian Church in Philadelphia before turning to the field of education. Between 1902 and 1906 he was the

The Amherst College baseball team of 1898. Back row, left to right: Foster, Fisher, DeWitt, Mitchell (Assistant Manager), Watson, and Rushmore. Middle row, left to right: Thompson, Fosdick, Gregory, Tinker, and Messinger. Front row, left to right: Moore and Whitney.

director of the Training and Industrial School, in Bordentown, New Jersey. Besides a varied career as minister and educator, during World War I he served as YMCA field secretary for the Army, and as demobilization secretary for the YMCA after the war.

Gregory also found time to continue his baseball career, first with a summer resort team, and later for about ten years in the Burlington County League in New Jersey. It was shortly after the turn of the century, but Gregory stated that "during all these years we never met with any embarrassing experience from players or spectators." Gregory played second base and outfield, as he had done at Amherst. His brother, Eugene, also played in the Burlington County League. Eugene pitched and played third base.

Ever the optimist that a Negro would break into the major leagues, James Gregory correctly predicted that a college man would crack the major-league color barrier. Like many other black pioneers, however, James Francis Gregory did not live quite long enough to see his prediction come true.

Eugene Gregory was the next black to play on a white college baseball team. In 1897 Eugene was a member of Harvard's freshman, or second team. The *Harvard Book of Athletes* does not confirm his ever having attained membership on the varsity team. The pitcher-infielder played on May 19 at Exeter, New Hampshire. The *Boston Globe* of May 20 reported:

EXETER 5, HARVARD 2D, 3

ACADEMY BOYS HAVE IMPROVED A LOT SINCE THEIR DEFEAT TO HARVARD
FRESHMEN EARLY IN THE SEASON

After leaving Harvard, Eugene Gregory became an outstanding educator in Bordentown, New Jersey.

Frank Armstrong was another early black athlete to play white college baseball. He was born in Marion, Iowa, and graduated from Cornell College, in Mount Vernon, Iowa, on June 14, 1900. In his senior year he alternated between playing first and second base, and was elected team captain.

Frank Armstrong played three years on the Cornell (Iowa) College baseball team from 1898 to 1900. He is shown above on June 14, 1900 at graduation exercises. (Courtesy Cornell College)

The scholar-athlete, at Cornell's forty-third commencement exercises, spoke on "The Future of the American Negro."

As a sophomore he played first base in a game against Luther College in May 1898. It was Luther College's home-season opener, at Decorah, Iowa, and Cornell won, 10–6.

The Scarlett and Black, the Grinnell College student newspaper, covered the University of Iowa's encounter against Cornell on May 14. Cornell won, 4–3. As the paper reported: "Cornell's best batting was done by Armstrong, the colored first baseman, and Moser." On Friday, June 10, Cornell beat Grinnell, 4–1. Armstrong drove in two runs, resulting in the following newspaper account:

Cornell scored in the fourth inning. Millere got a single into left field, and Williams flew out to Fiske. White hit to Higgs, who threw to second for a double play. Blatherwick muffed and both men were safe. Armstrong came up and lined out a single and both runs counted.

By beating Grinnell, Cornell took possession of the "Silver Bat," emblematic of the championship of the state. *The Scarlett and Black* of June 11 stated:

The Silver Bat for next year goes into possession of Cornell. Iowa College is sorry to see it go, but will live in the hope of "getting a crack at it" next year.

In the next year, on April 26, Cornell opened its home season against Luther College. Cornell won, 17–6. On Tuesday afternoon, May 29, at Athletic Park, Iowa City, Armstrong and his teammates edged out the University of Iowa, 2–1. Cornell College's first black varsity athlete looked forward to his senior year in 1900, as the 1899 baseball season ended.

In 1900 Cornell won five games and lost nine. The *Vidette-Reporter*, student newspaper of the University of Iowa, covered the game played on April 21:

In the seventh, A. Miller for Cornell singled, and in squaring the diamond was caught at the plate. K. Millere also singled. Kelly went out from pitcher to first, Armstrong, the man of color, who holds the initial bag, lined out a double scoring Miller. But was caught when he tried to stretch it into a three-bagger by a pretty throw by Parsons.

Iowa won, 12–5, in a game played in one hour and a half.

Frank Armstrong, the fifth black athlete to play on a white baseball team in the nineteenth century, earned his varsity letter for three years. He was also a member of the Adelphian Literary Society, and served on the executive committee of the athletic association.

In 1900, Booker T. Washington made a speech on campus, and Armstrong was in charge of the preparations committee for the great educator's visit. After graduation, Armstrong went on to earn an M.D. from the University of Illinois. He later served as the assistant secretary to Dr. Washington, who had been impressed with the young Armstrong at Cornell. After a stint with the U.S. Public Health Service, Armstrong took up private practice in Chicago, in 1919.

William Clarence Matthews, of Harvard, followed Armstrong. He prepared at Phillips Academy in Andover, Massachusetts, where he played on the baseball, football, and track teams, and in his senior year was elected captain of the baseball team.

Matthews was born on January 7, 1877, in Selma, Alabama. He attended grade school at Tuskegee Institute. A great admirer of Tuskegee's president and founder, Booker T. Washington, Matthews worked his way through school. He said: "Mr. Washington taught us at Tuskegee that the best help a man can get is an opportunity to help himself."

Matthews entered Harvard College in 1901. He worked in hotels, in Memorial Hall, on campus, and taught in one of the North Cambridge night schools. The only financial assistance he had throughout his college career was the $200 Price Greenleaf Aid he received in his freshman year.

Matthews may have been the best of the early Negro stars. He was good enough to make the Harvard College varsity as a freshman.

Harvard opened its 1902 season on Saturday, April 5, at Boston's Soldiers' Field. Seven hundred cheering Harvard partisans saw the Crimson beat the University of Maine, 8–2. Matthews' debut was auspicious. Playing shortstop, he had two hits, scored two runs, and stole a base. But in an era when segregation was the "law of the land," Matthews did not play in the next two Harvard games, one against the University of Virginia, to be played in the nation's capital, and the other against the U.S. Naval Academy, to be played at Annapolis, Maryland.

Matthews played in the next two games, at West Point and against Bates College, at Lewiston, Maine. He was missing from the lineup in the next ten games. In some cases players refused to play against a Negro in the lineup, and in some cases the coach or manager would threaten to cancel the game if a Negro was not removed.

On May 24 Matthews, now at second base, returned to the lineup against Holy Cross at Soldiers' Field, and he played in the remaining eight games. He also played right field and third base.

When Matthews had returned to the lineup in April against West

William Clarence Matthews on the 1902 Harvard baseball team.

Point, Harvard ran roughshod over the Cadets, 14–4. Harvard made a total of seventeen hits, and Matthews got two hits, stole two bases, and scored three runs. The Cadets had a twenty-one-year-old player in center field who got one hit. His name was listed as "McArthur."

In the 1902 season, Harvard played twenty-four games, and won twenty-one. Matthews played in ten games, and batted .233. He saved his best performance for the last game of the season against Harvard's arch-rival, Yale. *The New York Times* of June 29 reported:

HARVARD DEFEATS YALE
IN DECIDING GAME OF THE CHAMPIONSHIP SERIES
BIG CROWD AT POLO GROUNDS

MATTHEWS, RIGHTFIELDER FOR THE CRIMSON TEAM, BROUGHT
IN WINNING RUN IN NINTH INNING

Harvard won a thrilling contest, 6–5, before nine thousand on-lookers. (Each team had previously won one game on the home grounds of the other.) Walter Clarkson, Harvard's ace pitcher, held Yale to one hit for seven innings, while Harvard had scored two runs in the first inning. In the seventh, Yale tied the score. In the last of the seventh, Harvard again scored to regain the lead, 3–2. In the top of the eighth, Yale captured the lead by earning three runs. The score now stood, 5–3. Harvard bounced back in its half of the eighth inning and tied the score, 5–5. In the top of the ninth, Yale went down in 1–2–3 order. Then Matthews hit the first pitch for a single. Milne hit a slow grounder to short, and Miller tried to throw out Matthews at second, but Matthews beat the throw. Carr then sacrificed Matthews over to third base. When Coolidge lofted a long fly ball to right field, Matthews scored the winning run after the catch by Wear.

Having won the rubber game of the three-game series, Harvard won the championship.

Another black baseball player, Merton P. Robinson, had also played on a white college team—Oberlin—in 1902. Oberlin was defeated on April 19 against the Case School of Applied Science, 7–6, with Robinson serving as catcher.

On Tuesday, June 10, before over nine hundred and fifty fans, Oberlin defeated Ohio Wesleyan University, 11–10, thereby winning the Ohio State Collegiate Baseball Championship. Oberlin closed the season the next week with a 5–1 loss to Cornell University.

Six years later, Merton's brother, Howard N. Robinson, also played on the Oberlin baseball varsity as an infielder-outfielder. But neither

Merton P. Robinson on the Oberlin College baseball team of 1902. (Third from left, front row)

W. C. Matthews on the 1903 Harvard baseball team.

Robinson's talents approached the Harvard wonder, William Clarence Matthews.

In Matthews' second season, as a sophomore, his acceptance was still marginal. In a game against Georgetown University, played on the Georgetown campus in Washington, D.C., Harvard won, 3–0. A turnout of twenty-five hundred was on hand. The account in the *Washington Star* of April 20 stated:

Sam Apperious, Georgetown's captain and catcher, was not in the contest Saturday. He declined to go into the game because the Harvard men played Matthews, the colored shortstop, who comes from the same town in Alabama from which Apperious hails. Matthews displayed the abilities of a first-class ball player and conducted himself in a gentlemanly manner. Notwithstanding, there were hisses every time he stepped up to bat and derisive cheers when he failed to connect with the ball. The little shortstop took no notice of these demonstrations occasioned by the prejudice of a number of the spectators.

Matthews reached on a hit, stole second, and came home on a passed ball by the catcher. Meanwhile, Clarkson was limiting Georgetown to two hits. The Boston papers did not play up the incidents against

Matthews. But Washington's other major daily followed the *Star*'s coverage:

CRIMSON'S DUSKY SHORTSTOP PLAYED FINE BALL, ALTHOUGH THERE WERE
MILD DEMONSTRATIONS AGAINST HIS APPEARANCE ON THE TEAM

In a game on June 13, 1903, Harvard beat the University of Pennsylvania, 9–0. The game was played in one hour and fifty minutes. Matthews, playing shortstop, got two hits, including a double. Clarkson struck out twelve.

Walter Clarkson, Harvard's top pitcher, had only lost five games in four years, three to Princeton, one to Georgetown, and one to Williams College. But in the next season—his last—he was barred from further participation in college athletics. It was June 13, 1904, and five games remained to be played.

On May 6 it had been discovered that Clarkson had signed a contract to play ball with the New York Highlanders (later the New York Yankees) of the American League. He had been paid $500 in addition to a reputed $8,000 season contract. There had been a verbal agreement that Clarkson would make his major-league debut after the college season ended on July 2. But somehow the athletic committee at Harvard got wind of the "deal" and, in a four-and-one-half-hour meeting, voted to bar Clarkson.

Matthews did not have any such problems. The major leagues had a definite policy against signing "colored" players. All were sharp-eyed guardians. When Matthews first appeared in the Polo Grounds, *The New York Times* reporter was color conscious. He told his readers:

Matthews, by the way, has a deeper dye to his skin than was put there by the rays of the sun.

In the 1903 season, Harvard played twenty-four games and won nineteen. Matthews played in twenty-one games, batting .315. He hit four home runs, scored sixteen runs, hit one triple, and stole twelve bases.

W. C. Matthews on the 1905 Harvard baseball team.

In the 1904 season, Harvard played twenty-two games, of which it won seventeen. Matthews played in nineteen, batting .300. He hit three home runs, and stole eight bases.

In 1905, Harvard played twenty-five games, and won eighteen, lost six, and tied one. Matthews played in all twenty-five games. The schedule did not list any "southern" climes to visit, as explained in the *Freeman* of March 11, 1905:

The Harvard College baseball team has declined to arrange games for the coming season with the Georgetown baseball club, because that club refused to permit Matthews, the Negro member of Harvard's batting team, to play in a game last season.

On April 27, 1905, Matthews got five hits, scored three runs, and stole a base in Harvard's 12–1 win over Bates College. On May 4, another big day was reported:

MATTHEWS GETS TWO HOMERS, A DOUBLE AND A SINGLE IN FOUR TIMES UP

Harvard beat Colby, 16–5. One of Matthews' homers was a grand-slammer. The *Boston Globe* further commented on his batting surge:

Matthews has been making a pretty good batting record since the Harvard nine has been back from the Southern trip. In the five games played he has made 14 hits in 21 at-bats. In the Bates game . . . he got a hit every time he came up.

Matthews continued his onslaught against the pitchers. In Harvard's 6–1 victory over Princeton on May 20, he earned seven bases, including a home run and a triple. Some six thousand fans looked on.

Then came the longest slump of his college baseball career. He failed to get a hit in games against Brown, Dartmouth, Bowdoin, and the University of Pennsylvania. But on June 14, Matthews broke out of his slump with a bang. He got four hits, scored one run, and stole two bases, as Harvard beat Columbia, 5–1. The game lasted one hour and forty minutes.

Matthews played his last college game against Yale on June 27, a losing cause, 7–2. Twelve thousand fans saw him get one hit and play errorless ball. Altogether, he batted .400 and stole twenty-two bases, which made his last season, 1905, the best. Had he been white, the majors would have been fighting to sign up this awesome talent.

Matthews completed his requirements for a degree and in September 1905 entered Harvard Law School, where his academic proficiency continued. Before his enrollment, however, and with no further amateur standing to protect, Matthews joined the ten-week Burlington, Vermont, Summer Baseball League. Other Ivy League players with Matthews were Cote of Yale and Wells of Princeton.

The man who would make it possible more than forty years later for blacks to enter the white major leagues was also playing college baseball in 1902.

Wesley Branch Rickey was born in Lucasville, Ohio, on December 20, 1881. In 1902 he was a catcher on the Ohio Wesleyan University baseball team, but left to become Wesleyan's baseball coach when charges of professionalism were hurled against him. Rickey's minor-league baseball career had run virtually concurrent with his college baseball career. To his credit he never denied playing professional baseball, even when it was suggested that it would be his word against unsubstantiated charges.

In July 1904 Rickey played with the Dallas club of the Texas League. On August 22 he was sold to the Cincinnati Reds of the National League. After a brief trial, Cincinnati released him unconditionally. In the fall of 1904 he became a coach, student, and instructor at Allegheny College. In 1905 and 1906 he played with the St. Louis Browns of the American League. In 1907 he was traded to the New York Yankees, then called the New York Highlanders because the team was located in Washington Heights. Rickey saw very little action, because of illness. He played in 119 major-league games and batted .238. In 1908 he retired to become athletic coach at the University of Michigan, where he guided the Wolverines baseball team until 1913.

But it was 1903. A young black athlete, Charles Lee Thomas, had graduated from Zanesville, Ohio, High School in 1902, and entered Ohio Wesleyan University. Rickey assigned Thomas to his former catching position. Thomas's bat became "feared all over the State of Ohio." On April 18, 1903, Western Reserve went down to defeat before Wesleyan, 9–3. Thomas got two doubles and four hits.

On May 16, 1903, Thomas earned two hits in Wesleyan's 10–2

Charles Lee Thomas on the 1903 Ohio Wesleyan University baseball team. At the extreme left in the back row is the coach, Branch Rickey. In front is the team's mascot, Ernest Settles.

In 1903 Branch Rickey had coached Charles Lee Thomas on the Ohio Wesleyan baseball team. Forty-two years later, the sixty-four year old Rickey signs twenty-six year old John "Jackie" Roosevelt Robinson to a contract in organized professional baseball.

victory over Case Institute of Technology. He also stole a base. On May 23, before one thousand fans on Wesleyan's home grounds at Delaware, Ohio, Wesleyan beat Oberlin College, 2–1.

In the 1904 baseball season, Wesleyan opened the home season on Saturday, April 16, by beating Otterbein College, 12–4. In his batting cleanup, Thomas got two hits and stole two bases as six hundred fans cheered.

On April 29 Ohio Wesleyan University scheduled a practice game in Columbus, Ohio, against East High School. Ohio Wesleyan won, 8–3. Thomas, now playing first base, hit a home run with the bases loaded. On May 7, Ohio Wesleyan returned to Columbus and defeated Ohio State University, 9–4, before 1,117 fans. Thomas got one hit, a triple, and scored two runs. But the *Ohio State Journal* was upset over the antics of Ohio Wesleyan's twenty-two-year-old coach:

Wesleyan has the worst lot of bench coaches ever turned loose. Coach Rickey did his talking to Webb and fellow players through an improvised megaphone. And a couple of Methodist subs did more than their share of howling . . . bench coaching is illegal and not true baseball.

The *Boston Globe* remarked on May 22 that Case was an easy victim to Wesleyan, but that "Thomas, the colored first baseman, was obliged to warm the bench this afternoon, having fallen below grades in some studies."

Thomas did not remain out of the lineup for long. Wesleyan was now in the thick of the fight for the Big Six state championship. The Big Six teams were Wesleyan, Oberlin, Western Reserve, Kenyon, Case, and Ohio State. Ohio State got revenge by beating Wesleyan, 9–7, on May 25 on the Wesleyan field. Thomas, back in the lineup as catcher, was held hitless. But on May 27 Thomas made four hits in five at-bats as Ohio Wesleyan beat Western Reserve, 9–3. Thomas also stole a base. On May 28 Wesleyan beat Case, 11–1. Thomas, now playing center field, got two hits and stole a base as five hundred fans looked on. The *Boston Globe* observed:

Wesleyan has a good team, well balanced in every department and looks like the probable winner of the state championship this season.

Ohio Wesleyan went on to win the state championship for the 1904 season.

Wesleyan opened the 1905 baseball season at Ada, Ohio, on April

Charles Lee Thomas as a member of the 1904 Ohio Wesleyan University state champion baseball team. (Courtesy Ohio Wesleyan University)

22 against Ohio Northern University and won, 2–1, in sixteen innings. Thomas was again catching and batting in the cleanup spot.

In a conference game on May 6 at Delaware, Ohio Wesleyan beat Kenyon College, 6–4, before the "largest crowd of the year." Seven hundred and thirty fans were in attendance.

On May 13 Thomas had fifteen put-outs and an assist in Wesleyan's win over Western Reserve, 5–0. He also had two singles and a double in five at-bats. Near the end of the 1905 season, Ohio Wesleyan had won fourteen of nineteen games and would finish in the runner-up spot to Oberlin College, which was the Big Six champion for the 1905 season. The coach was now Ben Davis.

Like Matthews, Thomas would have made an excellent major-league player. Instead, he went on to receive his diploma from the Ohio Medical College at Columbus in 1908. He began the practice of dentistry in St. Louis in 1912 and moved to New Mexico in 1921.

Branch Rickey, his one-time coach, and the man who over forty years later signed Jackie Robinson to a major-league contract, graduated from Ohio Wesleyan on June 11, 1908. Rickey later obtained a law degree and, of course, went on to play major-league baseball.

William Clarence Matthews became a distinguished attorney, Charles Lee Thomas, a prominent dentist. But neither black man could become a major-league baseball player.

The colleges were trying to avoid further incidents. The *Boston Globe* of April 15, 1905, reported in reference to Harvard:

Manager Thornton is endeavoring to arrange two games to fill the dates with Annapolis and Trinity College of North Carolina which have been canceled.

Significantly, the first college on Harvard's 1905 schedule was the University of Vermont, which also had a Negro player at shortstop.

The University of Vermont lost the opener to Harvard on April 5 in a game limited to five innings because of rain. George Walter Williams, Vermont's Negro shortstop, played in all of their nineteen games.

On April 25 Vermont opened its home schedule with the University of Maine and won, 9–6, to start a winning streak of ten straight games.

In Vermont's 9–4 win over Lehigh on May 11 Williams got four hits, including two doubles, and stole a base. The *Burlington Daily Free Press* remarked:

Williams had on a full suit of batting togs. Four hits in five times up. That's stinging the ball some.

On May 13 Williams had moved up to second place in the batting averages. He was now batting .375 to Campbell's .424.

The season ended on June 8. Vermont won fourteen and lost five with two rain-outs.

Soldiers' Field was the site of the 1906 opening game between Harvard College and the University of Vermont. Williams was still at shortstop as Harvard won, 9–4, on April 4.

On April 28 Vermont thrashed Norwich, 22–2. For the first time since the Walker brothers, two black athletes were in the line-up of a white college baseball team. Fenwich Henri Watkins, then a substitute player, was the right fielder for several innings. Williams played in all of the sixteen games, and Watkins played in eight games, one behind the plate, two in center, and five in right field. The season's record for Vermont was eight wins, seven losses, and one tie game.

In 1906 Beloit College in Wisconsin had also discovered the game of baseball. One of that school's black pioneers in sports was a member of the first team. Samuel Ransom was a star of the basketball and football teams before playing third base in the game Beloit won against Northwestern, 6–1, in May.

In 1907 Vermont's first game was against Harvard. Vermont lost, 11–6. Williams was now playing second base, and Watkins was a starter at first base. In the opener, Watkins went hitless, but scored two runs. Williams got three hits, and stole a base. Vermont had won ten and lost seven of its seventeen games up to June 4. In fact its season had ended on June 1, and a game was scheduled against a local team.

Then John H. Pollard came seeking games. John Pollard, a

graduate of Dartmouth, class of 1895, was the coach of the University of Alabama's baseball team. Pollard's team was the king of the South. The *Boston Globe* of June 6, 1907, remarked:

DRAW THE COLOR LINE

ALABAMA CANCELS ITS GAME WITH VERMONT—REFUSES TO PLAY

WITH WATKINS AND WILLIAMS

Burlington, Vt., June 5—Manager Pollard of the University of Alabama baseball team was in the city today and canceled the two games with the University of Vermont scheduled for tomorrow and Friday because his team refuses to play against colored men. The men objected to are first baseman Watkins and second baseman Williams of the Vermont aggregation. Alabama pays a forfeit of $300 for canceling the game.

Williams departed in the 1908 season.

On Saturday, April 11, 1908, Vermont played its fourth game of the season on the road against Harvard and won, 9–5. Watkins, playing first base, had no hits, but played errorless ball and had ten put-outs.

On April 27 Vermont played its first game on its home field. It beat the University of Maine, 3–0, on Centennial Field. Watkins batted eighth in the order and doubled and stole a base.

On May 2 Vermont journeyed to Hanover, New Hampshire, to play Dartmouth College. The team was accompanied by three hundred students and the band, whose members were bedecked in their bright new uniforms. Vermont shut out Dartmouth, 3–0. Watkins, still batting in the eighth slot, got one hit—a double.

In the Holy Cross game at Worcester, Massachusetts, on May 12, Watkins scored a run, collected two hits—and was still batting eighth. Vermont won, 6–5.

On May 22 Watkins was shifted behind the plate in a game against St. Lawrence College. Vermont won, 6–2.

The University of Vermont's season came to a close—and with it, Watkins's collegiate baseball career—on June 4, when Vermont defeated Manhattan College, 6–4.

The 1908 schedule reflected the programs that Harvard and Vermont were accepting to avoid racial embarrassment to their Negro players. In 1908 Fenwich Henri Watkins played in all but two games. Vermont's season record was: 13 won, 5 lost, and 2 tied.

As 1910 approached a few other black baseball players were seen on white college teams.

Henry Beckett in 1906 played at Springfield College (then the Springfield Young Men's Christian Association Training School) in Massachusetts. Oscar Brown was at Syracuse in 1908. Other pioneers as the succeeding decades unfurled were Oberlin's F. M. Sheffield and John W. Copeland, Northwestern's Sam Taylor, Western Reserve's Booker T. Spencer, Harvard's Earl Brown, the University of Washington's John Prim, Dartmouth's Harry Thompson, Norwich's Harold Martin, Columbia University's Manuel Riviero, and Rutgers' ubiquitous Paul Leroy Robeson.

Robeson was on Rutgers' baseball team as a twenty-year-old junior in 1918. Five varsity members of the 1917 team had enlisted in the service, as the 1918 season opened on April 19 in New Brunswick, New Jersey. Rutgers lost, 6–4, to Cornell University. On May 4 Robeson was held hitless as Rutgers lost, 8–7, to Fordham University; nevertheless, he played errorless ball and had nine put-outs.

Rutgers opened the 1919 baseball season on April 19 in "regular football weather," and defeated Cathedral College, 3–0, Robeson going one for four.

On April 12 Rutgers beat NYU, 6–2. Robeson scored two runs, stole a base, and slammed out a triple. His college baseball career ended May 31 with the big catcher's team losing to Georgetown University, 10–4.

One of the black athletes who pioneered in white college sports— and one of the greatest influences in Negro professional baseball—was Cumberland Willis Posey. "Cum," as he was called, was named after his father, Cumberland Willis Posey, Sr. The elder Posey was born in Charles County, Maryland, on August 13, 1858. He was the eldest of three children and was always called "CW."

CW's father, Alexander Posey, was a slave. After the Civil War he became a preacher in Washington, D.C. In 1867 the Reverend Posey moved his family to Virginia, where young CW worked on the farm along with the other family members. Not long thereafter, the Reverend Posey moved to Belfry, Ohio, and young CW went to work for the Payton family, owners of a large riverboat, *Magnolia*. It was while working on the boat that CW decided to become an engineer. He was encouraged by Mr. Payton and the other workers.

With startling aptitude, the young CW quickly grasped his duties, and in a few years, rose to assistant engineer on the steamer *Striker*. He mastered all the machinery aboard and filled his position so well, that after only one year he was made chief engineer for Stewart Hayes, a prominent river man who owned several steamboats, becoming the first black man in the United States to be licensed as chief engineer. He was twenty years old and held this position for fourteen years.

In 1882 CW married Ann Stevens of Athens, Ohio, a school teacher in an all-white school.

In 1892, a year after Cum was born, CW moved into his new home in Homestead, Pennsylvania, one of the city's largest houses.

The young Cum was the youngest of a family that included a brother, Seward Hays, and a sister, Beatrice. Beatrice was born in 1885, and Seward in 1888. Seward, also an athlete, was on the Monticello basketball team in 1911 with Cum.

In 1892 Captain (CW) Posey made his first investment in coal boats. He organized the Delta Coal Company, of which he was general manager and treasurer for seven years. He then sold his share in the company and organized the Posey Coal Dealers and Steamboat Builders. All the steamboats were constructed under his supervision.

CW later sold his controlling share in this company to the Marine Coal Company and remained as manager and a minority stockholder. He also owned real estate in Homestead and was director of one of the city's largest banks. The enterprising CW had recognized that the bosoms of three great rivers—the Ohio, the Monongahela, and the Allegheny—bore away millions of tons of coal. And CW had simply supplied the solution.

This also afforded the family the means to give its offspring the finest available education. W. Rollo Wilson, writing in the *Pittsburgh Courier* of January 20, 1934, noted this:

Because he was born beyond the pale of want, Cumberland has had every educational advantage and at various times he was a student at Penn State, Holy Ghost, and Pitt. But an adventurous and turbulent spirit brooked no faculty interference with his desires and he never stayed anywhere long enough to get the recognition which might have been his.

It was at Duquesne University—formerly Holy Ghost College—that the twenty-five-year-old Cum Posey was a member of the college baseball team in 1916. In April he had been one of forty candidates trying out for the eighteen positions on the varsity squad. His name was listed: Charles W. Cumbert.[2] On April 18 the Duquesne candi-

---

[2] It was thought that the fair-skinned Posey had changed his name in order to "pass." It is more likely, however, that he was using an assumed name because of the popularity of the "Posey" name in Western Pennsylvania sports circles. He was in effect a pro athlete, and playing under an assumed name was rather common in those early days of collegiate sports.

The 1916 Duquesne baseball team. Top Row, left to right: John Doran, Andrew Marsula, Charles Cumbert (Posey), James Sweeney, Leo Zitman, Andrew Harenski, William O'Malley, and Ellsworth Schaffer. Sitting, from left to right: Michael Morrissey, Joseph Harenski, Rev. C. B. Hannigan (Graduate Manager), Nicholas Popoff, and Michael Obruba. In front, (Mascot) William Egan.

dates were down to fourteen, and Cumbert had made the squad.

On April 20, in the first game, Cumbert was in center field in Duquesne's 5–2 loss to the University of Buffalo. Batting in third position, he did not get a hit, but played flawlessly afield. In the next game, against Juniata College, Duquesne started a streak of nine straight wins. However, Cumbert did not play in the Juniata game on April 29, won by Duquesne, 4–2.

Cumbert returned to the lineup against Wynesburg College on May 5. He had one hit, scored two runs, and had one put-out in center. Duquesne won, 12–10.

Cumbert did not play in the game against Grove City College, on May 12, won by Duquesne, 15–6. But he returned to the lineup as Duquesne won, 5–3, against Westminster College on May 17. In the game against Muskingum College, Cumbert played in center field and at second base. Michael Obruba injured his leg in the first inning, and Cumbert replaced him. He handled five chances without error. On June 10, Cumbert was out of the lineup with a sprained ankle.

All in all, Cumbert played in seven of the twelve games and batted .224 to rank tenth of the twelve players listed. He had six hits in twenty-eight at-bats.

On June 20, as part of commencement exercises, members of the varsity baseball team were awarded their *D* letters and commended for "one of the most successful baseball seasons in the history of the school," eight wins and three losses.

In 1973 Cum Posey's daughter, Ethel Posey Maddox, acknowledged that her father had attended Duquesne University.

Cum Posey did attend (Holy Ghost College) Duquesne University. Since the Posey family was known to be black in race if not in colour, I believe he was enrolled under the name of Cumbert.

It is not known why Posey chose to enroll under the name of Charles Willis Cumbert. But it is known that in 1911 and afterward he played basketball for pay with the Monticello team and later with the Loendi Big Five. In this period, around 1912, he was also playing baseball with the Homestead Grays as outfielder. His playing days lasted until 1929; later he was owner and co-owner of the Homestead Grays, becoming the most successful executive of a Negro franchise.

For nearly thirty years, Posey's teams were competitive and financial successes. As a manager and owner, he fielded and helped develop some of the foremost black stars of the day, including Joe "Cyclone" (or "Smokey") Williams, Willie Foster, Vic Harris, Oscar Charleston, Josh Gibson, Leroy "Satchel" Paige, and Walter "Buck" Leonard.

From 1911 to 1913 Cumberland Posey was enrolled at the University of Pittsburgh. The *Pittsburgh Post* of April 4, 1912, reported:

Summer baseball is still being discussed by the college reformers who are divided in their opinions as to where the line should be drawn upon professionalism in athletics. On account of the inability to control the situation, a number of institutions have canceled the National sport from their list. The eastern universities have been loud in their disapproval of the practice, but nevertheless it exists. In many sections of the West professional ball is played openly by students.

Cumberland Posey enrolled under his true name at Pittsburgh. He did not play on the University of Pittsburgh's varsity baseball team.

New York University opened its 1923 season on April 3, beating Columbia University, 12–4. NYU had a Negro athlete in left field named Joe Washington. Columbia had an athlete at first base named Lou Gehrig, who got two hits. Gehrig would enter the New York Yankees lineup on June 1, 1925, and play in 2,130 straight games at first base—or until May 2, 1939.

In right field, on May 4, 1923, Washington played his fourth position in NYU's sixth straight victory, an 8–4 win over Amherst College.

On May 8, 1923, Trinity fell before NYU, 8–2. Washington played shortstop. Fordham lost its second game to NYU, 2–1, on May 12, 1923. Then, on May 18, 1923, Dartmouth was defeated by NYU, 2–1.

After completing an undefeated home season, NYU departed on a southern tour. It had played all its home games at Ohio Field. When NYU departed, Joe Washington was left behind.

Historically, Harvard College usually had a winning baseball team. In 1924 Harvard won its opening game against Boston University, 10–3. Then on April 9, Harvard beat Seton Hall, 12–1, at Cambridge, and *The New York Times* announced:

Earl Brown, Harvard's colored twirler, made his first start on the mound and in five innings allowed three hits.

On April 23 Harvard beat Bates College, 11–8. Brown pitched seven innings and gave up six hits. Nash relieved him and gave up four hits in the last two innings.

The University of Georgia came to Cambridge for two games on April 24 and 25. Earl Brown, of course, did not play against the southern college. Harvard won the first game, 6–2. The second game was won by the University of Georgia, 5–3.

Brown returned to the mound against Middlebury on April 30. Harvard won, 11–4. Brown gave up six hits in seven innings, and Toulman relieved him. He gave up one hit in two innings.

In Harvard's 11–1 loss to Cornell on May 3, Brown pitched two innings and allowed one hit. Spaulding started and gave up seven hits in four and two-thirds innings. Toulman gave up one hit in two and one-third innings.

The New York Times reported on Brown's next start on May 22:

BROWN HOLDS OPPONENTS TO SIX HITS

Harvard beat Amherst, 12–3. The game was played at Cambridge's Soldiers' Field. Earl Brown walked six, and struck out twelve.

Brown played his last college baseball game on June 18, 1924, against Yale University, won by Yale, 8–7. Brown allowed three hits in the one inning he pitched.

Harvard's record for the 1924 season was nine wins and six defeats.

Earl Brown was born in 1900, received his degree from Harvard in

The 1924 Harvard University baseball squad. Earl Brown, shown in first row on left. Note small glove of the era on his right hand.

1924, and entered government service. He also played several seasons of pro baseball with the New York Lincoln Giants. The *Chicago Defender* of July 12, 1924, took note of his signing:

EARL BROWN, HARVARD STAR JOINS LINCOLN

Brown joined manager Judy Gan's Lincoln Giants on July 11, 1924.

It had been a long time since John Brown Russwurm had been the first Negro to graduate from college,[3] (Bowdoin; in Brunswick, Maine; class of 1826). Born in Jamaica on October 1, 1799, to a white father and Jamaican mother, Russwurm was sent to Canada by his father to be educated under an assumed name. When his father died, his mother allowed him to resume his father's name and financed his education in America.

After the First World War, and during the postwar boom, athletic programs mushroomed on Negro college campuses. They placed high priority on the black athlete who had already performed at the white colleges.

[3] Some sources maintain that Edward A. Jones graduated from Amherst College a few days prior to Russwurm's graduation from Bowdoin.

Beginning with tennis great Charles C. Cook, a Cornell graduate who was the first football coach at Howard University in 1893, there were Charles Drew at Morgan, Charles West at Howard, Matthew Bullock at Morehouse, Frederick Douglass at Lincoln (Pa.) University,[4] Cleveland Abbott at Tuskegee, and Manuel Rivero at Lincoln (Mo.) University.

Rivero, a Negro Cuban, played on Columbia's varsity baseball team for three seasons. *The New York Times* of April 23, 1931, observed:

RIVERO DRIVES HOME RUN

Only three extra-base hits were made in the contest, two by the losers. However the home run by Manuel Rivero, Columbia third baseman, in the third inning, accounted for half of the Lions total.

Columbia won over Fordham, 4–3.

The next year, on Saturday, April 2, Rivero made his pitching debut when Columbia beat City College of New York, 10–7.

On April 16 Rivero played center field and earned one hit, in the Lions' 4–3 victory over Harvard.

On May 6, 1932, *The New York Times* sports page blared:

RIVERO'S DOUBLE COUNTS 3

Rivero stole a base, went two for three, and scored a run as Columbia beat Navy, 7–2.

Manuel Rivero ended an outstanding collegiate baseball career in 1933. On May 5 of that year he went two for four as Columbia defeated Fordham, 8–3.

Forty-five hundred fans gave the center fielder an ovation. Rivero headed for Lincoln University, Jefferson City, Missouri, and a long and distinguished coaching career.

---

[4] Pollard was listed as the coach of Lincoln's football team in 1926, while he was also receiving a reputed "$10,000" for playing with the Akron Pros of the NFL. He also played with the Gilberton Pennsylvania Catamounts of the Eastern Professional League in 1926.

The 1890 census showed a black population of 7,470,040, with all but 580,888 in the South and the District of Columbia.

From 1826, when the first Negro graduated from college, until 1909, there were approximately ten Negro graduates from West Coast colleges.

In 1910 blacks began a migration north, which by the end of 1920 brought almost half a million Negroes to the states in the North and the West.

Ralph Johnson Bunche was born in Detroit on August 7, 1904. He was orphaned at thirteen and went to live with relatives in Los Angeles, where he entered Jefferson High School.

In September 1923 young Bunche enrolled at UCLA, where he pioneered the way in football and basketball for a glittering array of black athletes who would follow over a decade later.

Bunche played varsity basketball for three years under Coach Caddy Works before graduating in 1927. Two decades later Bunche became UN mediator in the Palestine dispute, and, later, deputy secretary general for special political affairs and the winner of the 1950 Nobel Peace Prize for his work in Palestine. He was an able precursor of the black athlete on the West Coast.

Mallie Robinson joined the westward migration of 1920, leaving a plantation near Cairo, Georgia, for Pasadena, California, with her

Manuel Rivero, on end at right, on the 1932 Columbia University baseball team. (Courtesy of Columbia University)

Rivero, second from right, on the 1933 Columbia University baseball team.

five children: nine-year-old Frank, eleven-year-old Edgar, seven-year-old Matthew, five-year-old Willa Mae, and sixteen-month-old Jackie.

In the 1930s, the black athlete on the West Coast vied for greater recognition.

Kenneth Stanley Washington was one of the first to gain national acclaim as a football All-American in 1939. But in the baseball season of 1938, the *Los Angeles Times* of April 9 could observe:

Ken Washington, UCLA's Negro shortstop, whammed out a home run over the right field fence in the seventh inning.

UCLA defeated Stanford, 5–2, at Palo Alto.

After ten games, Kenny Washington was the leading batter in the California Intercollegiate Baseball Association.

Meanwhile, nineteen years old, Jackie Robinson could not report for spring football practice with the other seventy-six candidates at Pasadena Junior College because in April, Ray Bartlett, an end, and he, a quarterback, were on the baseball team.

The next month, Jackie Robinson was on the track and field team. The *Los Angeles Times* of May 8, 1938, reported:

It was Jackie Robinson of Pasadena who soared 25 ft. 6½ in. to break his brother Mack's accepted record.

Matthew "Mack" Robinson, then attending the University of Oregon, had leaped 25 feet 5½ inches.

The article continued:

Jackie, a versatile lad who has starred in four major sports over the past year, had one jump of 24 ft. 5 in. before sailing forth on his record smashing leap.

Among the many talented black athletes on the coast around this period were Bryant Allen, Wilbur Miller, Raleigh Blepso, Joe Batiste, Harry Thompson, Brice Taylor, Ray Bartlett, William Steele, William Laceford, Joe Lillard, Len Jones, Henry Daniels, Bill Duffy, and Woodrow Wilson Strode.

Woody Strode had once tossed the discus 165 feet in a practice throw and had a shot-put competition of 51 feet 5½ inches.

Strode, Washington, and Jackie Robinson would all meet as teammates on the gridiron in fall 1939.

But in spring 1939 sportswriter Bill Henry explained on May 15 that "the sensational Jackie Robinson wasn't yet eligible" to report for football practice at UCLA, being still in his last year at Pasadena.

Kenny Washington had not reported for spring football drills either —nor had he played baseball in 1939, having instead obtained after-class employment.

In the 1940 baseball season, Robinson escaped unscathed. The day was Saturday, April 8; the teams, UCLA *vs.* Stanford; and the headlines read the next day:

BRUINS SHADE INDIANS, 3 TO 2

UCLA got only one hit, but defeated Stanford, as:

Jackie Robinson, safe on a fielder's choice, scored later on a passed ball, while Bill Guyer and Bob Null walked and tallied on errors by infielder Dan Boone and outfielder Bob Templeton.

On April 15 UCLA's seventeen-man traveling squad played at

St. Mary's and won, 5–2, Robinson going one for five and stealing a base.

Ray Bartlett stole two bases.

On Monday, April 15, Ray Bartlett and Jackie Robinson enjoyed their best day. UCLA defeated the San Diego Marines, 15–3.

Jackie beat out three bunt singles and stole a base. He also slammed a double to top off his spree. Bartlett, who was Jackie's best friend, and the left fielder, slugged two home runs.

On May 6, the season ended with a 6–1 defeat of UCLA by the University of Southern California.

The final standings of the California Intercollegiate Baseball Association follow:

	Won	*Lost*	*Pct.*
St. Mary's	11	4	.733
California	9	6	.600
Southern California	8	7	.533
Santa Clara	7	8	.463
UCLA	6	9	.400
Stanford	4	11	.267

Later in May, before Robinson started spring football practice, he won the National Collegiate Athletic Association's broad jump mark with a leap of 24 feet 10¼ inches.

After the 1940 football season, Jackie was eligible for one more season of baseball and track during his senior year in 1941. Then suddenly the *Los Angeles Times* on March 4, 1941, announced:

BASKETBALL OVER, ROBINSON CHECKS OUT OF WESTWOOD

Jackie Robinson, the only athlete ever to win letters in four sports at the University of California at Los Angeles, withdrew from the University, yesterday, it was announced by the Registrar's Office. . . . Reasons given for his abrupt withdrawal were financial. Robinson is said to be considering offers to play with the Broadway Clowns, Negro basketball touring squad now in Hawaii, and with a Colored baseball team this Spring. . . .

At John Muir Technical High School, Robinson earned letters in football, basketball, baseball, and track. Later, at Pasadena Junior College, he duplicated this feat, breaking all school records in his two years as the quarterback on the football team.

When Jackie Robinson left school, two days after playing in his last basketball game, he became assistant athletic director at the National Youth Administration's (NYA) work camp in Atascadero, California.

In the early 1940s there were no Negroes playing in major professional sports. So when the NYA discontinued the work camp, Robinson signed on with a semipro team, the Honolulu Bears, playing on Sundays and working for a construction company during the week.

The football season ended in November, and Robinson left his job near Pearl Harbor on Friday, December 5, 1941.

Sunday, December 7, the Japanese attacked Pearl Harbor, and Jackie five months later enlisted in the U.S. Cavalry at Fort Riley, Kansas. These events would have a historic effect upon college baseball in general, and professional baseball in particular, as they would on all of major professional sports.

The halcyon days of baseball had long ago ended. The college game was no longer played in serene rustic settings. Yet the roots of black athletes who played on white college baseball teams can be traced to the Southland.

They were the sons of the Mallie Robinsons who did not go West— or North. They were Benedict College's Charles Taylor, Wiley's Grady Orange, Livingstone's Laymon Yokeley, and Howard's Melvin "Doc" Sykes. They went to Negro colleges, and played on all-black baseball teams. Their beginnings and emergence can be seen on the Negro college baseball team.

2

Stars on Black College
Baseball Teams

American baseball is thought to have evolved rather than to have been "invented" as was basketball. The first baseball club was organized in New York in 1845. After 1851 other amateur clubs were formed. In 1857 a convention of delegates from sixteen clubs in and around New York and Brooklyn was held. The College Baseball Association was started in 1862. At the annual Association meeting in 1866, two hundred and two baseball clubs from seventeen states and the District of Columbia were represented.

In 1860 there were nearly four million slaves and almost half a million free Negroes. Negroes born free in the nonslave states or freed through manumission had played baseball almost from the onset of the game as it developed in this country. But the slaves' lot was one of toil, not play. If baseball had not originated in the East it is doubtful that the black would have been able to pursue the sport, for neither recreation nor education was available for the displaced African natives brought to these shores as slaves.

In 1832 the State of Alabama declared that any person attempting to educate a person of color, upon conviction, would be fined a sum of not less than $250 nor more than $500. The exception to this law were the colored Creoles in Mobile to whom these restrictions did not apply under the terms of the Treaty of 1803 with France.

In Georgia, in 1831, a Negro instructing another Negro to read or write was liable to a fine and a whipping. A white person might be sentenced to a fine of $500 and imprisonment for the same "offense." In 1832 a young Quaker teacher, Prudence Crandall, was jailed for maintaining a "nigger-school" in Canterbury, Connecticut.

With the end of the Civil War, the Thirteenth Amendment to the Constitution was ratified in 1865, declaring:

Neither slavery nor involuntary servitude, except as a punishment for a crime whereof the party shall have been duly convicted, shall exist within the United States, or any place subject to their jurisdiction.

Morehouse College was founded in 1867 under the name of Augusta Institute. In 1879 it moved to Atlanta and incorporated under the name Atlanta Baptist College and Seminary.

In 1890 baseball was the first intercollegiate sport played at the Atlanta Baptist College. Some members of the first team included D. D. Crawford, Alfred D. Jones, James Bryant, W. E. Rainwater, and J. R. Epps. Atlanta University and Clark University—two nearby black colleges—were the chief opponents.

In 1896 the first city (Atlanta) baseball league was formed. The league was composed of Atlanta University, Clark University, Morris Brown College, and, of course, Atlanta Baptist College.

The period from 1890 to 1895 was characterized by a lack of institutional control over athletics.

Baseball was the only sport that Morris Brown College played from 1895 through 1910. Willie Lane, a student, organized the first team and served as the coach. Some of the first players included E. K. Nichols, Charles L. Harper, and Riley, a standout pitcher.

The Atlanta Baptist College won the city championship in 1896, 1897, and 1898. The college was led by such outstanding players as Zackary T. Hubert, James Carmichael, Charles Willis, H. P. McClendon, and James M. Nabrit. In 1892, Nabrit's first season, the team won four of the six games played. The regulars were George Darden, pitcher; Charles Robinson, catcher; William Maxwell, second baseman; Henry Darden, shortstop; Cornelius S. Johnson, right fielder;

The 1897 Atlanta Baptist College (later Morehouse) baseball team. From left to right: J. Brown, Charles Robinson, H. P. McLendon, C. Carey, C. McLarin, Charles Willis, Zackary T. Hubert, James Carmichael, and E. Lester. (Courtesy of Milt Roberts)

Lucius Jones, center fielder; Timothy Williams, left fielder; and James M. Nabrit, first baseman. The substitutes were: Henry Martin, W. C. Lawrence, and James Foster.

Nabrit was Atlanta Baptist College's great star during this period. He ended his college baseball career in 1899, with two home runs, a triple, and a double. His son, James Madison Nabrit, Jr., born in Atlanta on September 4, 1900, would become president of Howard University in 1960.

On Saturday, November 17, 1866, at the Columbia Law Building —opposite Judiciary Square in Washington, D.C.—the first words from which Howard University evolved were spoken. During a prayer meeting, the Reverend Benjamin A. Morris proposed that an institution of theology be started to train Negro ministers. Later, Reverend Morris' idea was expanded to include preparatory and college departments.

On May 1, 1867, five students gathered in a rented frame building and started a normal and preparatory school on Georgia Avenue, just below "W" or Pomeroy Street, in northwest Washington, D.C. Six months later it was incorporated under the name of a thirty-six-year-old commissioner of the Freedman's Bureau, Major General Oliver Otis Howard. The Freedman's Bureau (shorthand for the Bureau of Refugees, Freedmen, and Abandoned Land) was established in 1865. The Bureau assisted the newly freed slaves in obtaining supplies, medical services, and an education. One school receiving financial assistance was Howard University, of which Oliver Otis Howard served as president from 1869 to 1873.

In 1868 Howard University had 238 students in its college division, 402 in the high school—or preparatory department—and 592 students in its professional schools.

Number 70 of "Regulations of Howard University" for 1872 states:

From time to time, certain portions of the University grounds will be designated for purposes of recreation for each sex, and all out-door recreation will be confined to these limits.

Intramural competition probably evolved from this proclamation, with varsity competition starting in the 1890s.

James Francis Gregory states that as early as 1894, when he was a senior in the preparatory department, he played "first base on the varsity nine at Howard University."

During this early period, of course, all Negro institutions of higher learning maintained both a preparatory school and a college department. Some had grade schools as well. An athlete in the preparatory department—if good enough—might play on the varsity before actually entering the college department.

Later, when regional conferences came into being, a three-year eligibility limit was established to prohibit seven and eight years of varsity competition.

The *Washington Post* of April 19, 1894, reported on the outcome of one of Howard's early games:

KENDALLS MEET THEIR FIRST DEFEAT

The game between Kendall Green and Howard University on the grounds of the former yesterday was interesting. In the sixth inning, with two men on base, O. H. Cook of the Howards made a home run, making the score 10 to 11 in favor of the Howards. The Kendalls refusing to accept the decision of the umpire on the last ball, which was declared fair, and also refusing to play the game out. It was decided, according to the rules, in favor of the Howards. It was the first defeat of the season for the Kendalls.

Kendall Green College (now Gallaudet College) is the only undergraduate institution in the nation devoted to the education of the deaf. Kendall's "loss" to Howard was further clarified by the *Washington Post* of April 22, 1894:

The Kendalls, instead of being defeated by the Howards, as was reported several days ago, took that team into camp by a score of twelve to nine. The umpire, a student at Howard, who is also a manager of the team representing that institution, called a ball that struck a tree and rolled into fair ground a fair ball . . . after some kicking, the umpire gave the game to the Howards by the reported score.

Trinity College, of Hartford, Connecticut, came to Washington to play a series against Georgetown University and later consented to a game against Howard. The *Washington Post* of April 24, 1894, reported:

TRINITY WINS FROM HOWARD IN A GAME REPLETE WITH HITS AND ERRORS

Trinity won, 34–17, and the *Washington Post* informed its readers that:

The error column, perhaps never showed larger totals in a game between clubs of the caliber of Trinity and Howard.

There were a total of thirty-one errors, ten by Trinity and twenty-one by Howard. In the early days of baseball competition, when basic skills were being developed, scores were astronomical.

James Francis Gregory says that the 1894 season "was the last time that Howard played baseball with clubs of the other group." But in 1898, when Gregory was playing at Amherst with the "other group,"

Howard had a scheduled game against the Yale Law School. The *New Haven Register* of April 4 reported:

The Yale Law School nine was scheduled to play its first game this afternoon, meeting Howard University, the celebrated Negro institution. This is the first time that a Yale nine ever played a colored school. The game was booked by manager John Knox Blake before the Law School nine left.

The game was played on Good Friday, April 8, instead of as previously scheduled. The *New Haven Register* of April 9 commented:

VARSITY SHUTS OUT HAMPTON AND LAW SCHOOL
DEFEATS HOWARD UNIVERSITY

The Yale Law School beat Howard, 11–7, while Yale's varsity beat the Hampton, Virginia, Athletic Club (not the Negro college), 12–0.

Howard's 1901 squad was composed of the following players: R. S. Scott, catcher; Young, catcher; Jackson, shortstop; Bundy, first base; Nutter, second base; Williams, pitcher; Scott, pitcher; Southern, third base; Turner, second base; Watkins, second base; Holmes, center field; Carper, right field; and Shorter, left field.

There were, of course, activities of more cosmic concern than either baseball or sports in the Negro's world of the turn of the century. The 1900s kaleidoscope shows Negro Americans in all its variations.

In 1904 William Edward Burghardt DuBois, thirty-seven-year-old professor of sociology, saw his $1.20-a-copy book, *Souls of Black Folk*, go into a third printing. The *New York Age, Philadelphia Tribune*, and *Cleveland Gazette*, Negro newspapers, ran "before and after" advertisements. Fifty cents could buy skin whiteners, skin bleachers, and hair straighteners. "Wonderful results" were promised by Original Ozonized Ox Marrow.

The U.S. Census registered a population of 8,833,994 Negroes.

On April 17, 1903, Andrew Carnegie, industrialist-philanthropist, gave a $600,000 endowment fund to Tuskegee Institute, mainly on the basis of his admiration for the school's president and founder, Booker T. Washington. Carnegie said, "To me he seems one of the greatest of living men because his work is unique, this modern Moses, who leads his race and lifts it through education. History is to tell of two Washingtons, one white, the other black, both fathers of their people."

Tuskegee was founded in 1881 with thirty students and a converted chicken coop. Two decades later, Tuskegee had 1,200 students, 56 buildings, 86 instructors, 2,300 acres, and property worth over half a million dollars.

In October 1901 Booker T. Washington, forty-five, dined in the White House with Theodore Roosevelt, forty-three, shortly after the youngest President in United States history took office.

Washington, in a speech at the Berkeley Lyceum on West Forty-Fourth Street, in New York, on March 15, 1902, said, in part: "The Negro must have the element of progress and civilization which can only be acquired by education. That education is being furnished and appreciated, is evidenced by the fact that while there were no colored schools in the South fifty years ago, every County has them now."

In 1900 there were thirty-four institutions providing college training, 28,566 Negro teachers, and more than a million and a half Negro children in the public schools, nearly a thousand being in colleges.

On March 30, 1904, the Reverend John Gordon, former president of Tabor College, Iowa, was inaugurated as president of Howard University. President Roosevelt sent his best wishes:

Permit me to extend to President Gordon and to Howard University my congratulations on this occasion. I wish I could be with you in person, for I appreciate to the full all the work that Howard University has done for the education and uplifting of our colored fellow-Americans, whose struggle for spiritual and intellectual development is of necessity so different and often so painful.

In 1906 Washington called on Andrew Carnegie again at his Fifth Avenue home. Washington had a copy of his book *Up From Slavery*.

Later Tuskegee Institute received a $250,000 grant from Carnegie. It is also believed that Dr. and Mrs. Washington were granted a "pension for life" from the industrialist.

In 1906 President Roosevelt addressed the thirty-ninth annual graduation class at Howard University. The Harvard graduate, class of 1880, said in part: "I do not wish to see any college graduate leave an institution like this with his eyes so firmly fixed upon the stars that he forgets that he has got to walk on the ground."

The kaleidoscope shifts to the athletic field to view the life in microcosm on the diamond world.

On May 4, 1907, at three o'clock, Fisk and the National Baptist baseball team met in Nashville. Fisk beat the local amateur team, 13–2. The *Nashville Globe* observed:

Fisk has a strong team, one that can give any amateur aggregation a run for the money, and, too, they have been at work since February, so the Baptist boys should compliment themselves on not being shut out.

On April 4, 1908, Morris Brown College beat Atlanta Baptist College, 5–1. Later, Atlanta Baptist College, on a seven-game winning streak, avenged the loss to Morris Brown, 11–1, thereby winning the city league championship.

In 1909, with baseball coming more under the control of the college administration, Alfred D. Jones became Atlanta Baptist College baseball coach.

In 1909 an intercollegiate baseball league was formed in Nashville, including teams from Fisk University, Roger Williams University, Walden University, and Pearl High School.

In the first game on Saturday, March 9, Pearl High School defeated Fisk, 6–4. The game was called after six innings because of rain.

Fisk withdrew from the league, and Roger Williams was unable to complete its schedule because of a fire that destroyed several buildings on campus. Pearl High School and Walden University had played four games each, Pearl High winning three and losing one, with Walden winning two and losing two. Pearl High School was awarded the Silk Pennant, emblematic of winning the championship.

On March 19, 1910, in the first game of the season, Pearl High School beat Walden University, 13–9. This would be Walden's only defeat, as it finished with a 5–1 won-lost record. Pearl High School was second with a 5–5 record. Roger Williams, back in league play, finished with a 0–4 won-lost record.

On Saturday, April 1, 1911, Lincoln University opened its baseball season against Oxford Academy and won, 6–1. Jamison pitched four innings and struck out ten batters and Duckrey pitched five innings and struck out eight batters. Redd and Ogburn also starred for Lincoln.

On Saturday, April 8, 1911, Claflin College defeated Shaw University, 1–0, at Orangeburg, South Carolina. Thomas, who had a triple,

The 1911 Lincoln (Pa.) University baseball team. (1) Wesley Redd, Manager, (2) Leon Frazier, (3) Frank Goss, (4) Francis Jamison, (5) Harold Grim, (6) Frank Wheaton, (7) George Bullock, (8) George F. Cherry, (9) Wayne Maxwell, (10) George Cherry, (11) John Barnum, (12) William Jamison, and (13) Henry Goss.

and McDonald starred for Claflin. The *New York Age* on April 13, 1911, noted:

The names of Clifford McDonald and Benson Parks are familiar to Eastern fans as they played last season with the Philadelphia Giants.

From the beginning, college baseball had operated informally. For example, in the nineteenth century, a Charles C. Cook, while Howard's coach and professor, played on the varsity baseball team.

When conferences came into being, the same approach generally prevailed. A common anomaly would see a player perform with a professional team and also play openly with a college team.

The "national pastime" was the last sport on the yearly calendar—and without a regular stable budget. If the entertainment value could be heightened by a professional or two, so be it. Because of the early closing of Negro colleges, the players were not usually under the aegis of their alma maters.

In 1911 Shaw finished its home season on April 21 and 22, by beating Howard University twice, the first game, 7–4, and the second game, 1–0. "Big Chief" Lytle shut out Howard with five hits in the second game, and struck out fifteen batters.

The *New York Age* commented upon Shaw's 1911 season:

The Shaw team has just returned from its Southern trip, where out of eleven games played they lost only one, that being to Claflin, which has enlisted some professional players.

In 1911 Hampton Institute won two and lost one. Lincoln University won eight and lost six. Virginia Normal and Industrial Institute of Petersburg won four and lost none in 1911. Tuskegee Institute's mighty machine rolled over seventeen opponents in eighteen games, the single loss being to Clark University, 4–3. But Tuskegee avenged this defeat with a 10–2 victory in the very next game. (Members of Tuskegee's team follow: Captain Watson, catcher; Sampson, pitcher; Sloan, pitcher; Nave, pitcher; Howard, first base; Sullins, second base; Miranda, short stop; Peek, third base; Gilmore, left field; Jones, center field; and Washington, right field.)

The 1911 Howard University baseball team. (1) Bell, (2) Marshall, (3) Murphy, (4) Gray, (5) Toby, (6) Young (7) Westmoreland, (8) Hightower, (9) Slaughter, (10) Brice, (11) Jones, (12) Turner, (13) Hunt, (14) Oliver, Captain.

On April 12, 1912, at the Raleigh State Fair Grounds, Shaw beat Lincoln, 3–0. "Big Chief" Lytle pitched a two-hitter and struck out eleven batters. Lincoln's Burnett gave up five hits and struck out seven batters.

Tuskegee laid claim to the southern championship in 1911 with a 17–1 record. The next year, Atlanta University won the honors. The *New York Age* of May 23, 1912, reported:

ATLANTA UNIVERSITY WINS LOCAL CHAMPIONSHIP

Morris Brown's 3–1 win over Atlanta Baptist College on May 18, 1912, gave the Atlanta University baseball team the Georgia championship. In the deep South, Tuskegee still reigned supreme. In 1912 it won fifteen and lost only one game, again to Clark University. Tuskegee now had a record of thirty-two wins and two losses over two years.

Booker T. Washington's return to his alma mater for Founders Day was marred as Lincoln beat Hampton, 11–2, in 1912.

In 1913 Livingstone College finished with a record of twelve wins and five losses. In a game against Lutheran College, McCorkle of Livingstone pitched a no-hit, no-run game. Livingstone won, 21–0.

The 1913 Livingstone College baseball team. (1) McCain, (2) Michael, (3) Locke, (4) Jacobs, (5) Robinson, (6) McCorkle, (7) Pryor, (8) Henderson, (9) Platt, and (10) Lloyd.

The 1913 Lincoln University team won five of seven games, including a 15–9 win over Oxford High School.

In 1913 Arkansas Baptist College finished with a perfect 17–0 record. Although the game was spreading, it was slow in getting started at some schools. Charles H. Williams, director of physical education at Hampton Institute, reported that:

Baseball has not taken place at Hampton the way the other sports have,

The 1913 Arkansas Baptist College baseball team. (1) Little, (2) Young, (3) W. Wiley, (4) Love, (5) Dolphin, (6) Wilson, (7) Booker, (8) Patterson, (9) Horton, (10) Miller, (11) Gardner, (12) McGrue, (13) Henderson, (14) A. Wiley, (15) J. A. Hibbler, (16) Proffitt, (17) Moore, and (18) Miles Albert Hibbler, and (19) John Arthur Hibbler, mascots.

especially intercollegiate baseball, owing to the early closing of school and our busy Spring. There are, however, baseball leagues which play through the Spring and Summer seasons playing four games each week. At the close of the Summer season the winning team is awarded a pennant.

Biddle University reported that its 1911 season record was 10–1.

The 1913 Hampton Institute baseball team. (1) Gurnoe, (2) Easley, (3) Wolfe, (4) Coons, (5) Vaughn, (6) Johnson, (7) Beauchamp, (8) Manning-ton, (9) J. Williams, (10) V. Brown, (11) P. Brown, (12) Young, (13) Davis, and (14) C. Williams, Coach.

And in 1912 the National Religious Training School (now North Carolina Central) won fourteen games and lost five.

In 1912 Lincoln sent its baseball team South under the leadership of Captain George Frazier and the management of George H. W. Bullock. Lincoln won seven of the thirteen games played on that trip.

Penson of Shaw pitched a no-hit game in March 1913 against Oxford of Eastern North Carolina, and won, 2–1. He struck out ten batters. On Friday, March 28, Shaw beat the National Religious Train-

The 1913 National Religious Training School baseball team (now named North Carolina Central at Durham, N. C.). (1) Jones, (2) Henderson, (3) Dunn, (4) Bess, (5) Bynum, (6) Kittrel, (7) Borden, (8) Eaton, (9) Mallet, and (10) Saunders.

ing School, 25–10. And on Saturday, March 29, Shaw beat Greensboro Agricultural and Mechanical College, 15–2.

On April 25, Shaw beat Livingstone, 12–3. In the second game of the series, on Saturday, April 26, Livingstone beat Shaw, 8–0. The games were played in Raleigh. The *New York Age* of May 1, 1913, commented:

It was the first whitewash ever administered to the University lads on their own grounds, and the first clean defeat they have received here in many years.

In 1913 Tuskegee had a 15–2, won-lost record. The two defeats were to Talladega College, 10–8, and Shaw, 5–3. Later Tuskegee beat Talladega, 12–5, and Shaw, 12–2. Tuskegee now had a record of forty-seven wins and four defeats over three seasons.

On Friday, April 24, 1914, Tuskegee defeated Morris Brown College, 8–7, and the next day, Morris Brown won over Tuskegee, 9–8.

On May 7 the *New York Age* wrote:

Both games were largely attended by teachers and students and many of the white citizens of Tuskegee.

On May 1 Livingstone defeated Shaw, 19–4. The next day, Shaw again lost to Livingstone, 12–4.

On May 5 the *New York Age* bannered:

SYKES HELD LINCOLN TO 2 HITS

Melvin "Doc" Sykes and his batterymate, Washeba "Doc" Wiley, played professional baseball for over ten years before turning to the dental profession.

In 1915 Howard again played Lincoln. But this was the Lincoln Stars, a professional baseball team. They played three games, and Howard lost each one. On Thursday, April 22, the Lincoln Stars won, 3–2. In a doubleheader on Saturday, April 24, the Stars won, 13–0 and 6–1. All the games were played in New York's Lenox Oval.

The college men were outclassed by such pros as Spottswood "Spot" Poles, Robert Edward "Jude" Gans, Louis "Top" Santop, Richard "Cannonball" Redding, and John Henry Lloyd, some of the most outstanding players in black baseball history.

In Howard University's second regular season game in 1914, Howard beat the Fredericksburg Giants, 9–0. Howard's captain, Wiley, led the attack with two home runs. Brice allowed three hits.

The 1913 Tuskegee Institute baseball team. (1) Taylor, Coach, (2) Sullins, (3) McNeal, (4) Howard, (5) Harper, (6) Washington, Manager, (7) Demps, (8) Washington, (9) Sloan, (10) Peek, (11) Sampson, (12) Mc-Cullough, and (13) Watson.

In 1913 Atlanta Baptist College was named Morehouse College, after the Reverend Henry L. Morehouse, friend and benefactor of his people, who was corresponding secretary of the American Baptist Home Mission Society.

On Saturday, March 21, 1914, a game between Atlanta University and Morehouse was called at the end of the seventh inning, "because it was almost impossible for one to see the ball on account of the heavy snowflakes." Morehouse was leading, 4–2.

On Saturday, April 4, the Mississippi Industrial Institute beat the University of West Tennessee, 4–3, at Holly Springs.

On Thursday, April 9, Rust College beat Philander Smith College, 6–4. The next day, Rust College beat Philander Smith, 21–3. On the same date, in Raleigh, Shaw University beat the National Religious Training School, 13–6.

On April 17, Harrison, Shaw's pitcher, struck out fifteen batters as he and his teammates beat Livingstone, 14–4.

In 1915 Howard scheduled eight baseball games, the first one starting on Friday, April 16, and the last one on Saturday, May 8.

In the first game of the season, Howard beat the Virginia Normal and Industrial Institute, 3–2. The next day, Virginia Normal beat Howard, 11–5.

In 1915 Morris Brown College won the baseball championship of the Southern Intercollegiate Athletic Conference (SIAC).

In 1916 Howard had a season record of six wins, two losses, and two ties. Morris Brown repeated as SIAC champions that year.

On Wednesday, May 30, 1917, Tuskegee Normal and Industrial Institute awarded 156 students certificates and diplomas at graduation exercises. Robert Russa Moton had fulfilled his first year as successor to the late Booker T. Washington.

Hampton Institute awarded ninety-four degrees. Biddle University graduated thirty-four students from its college division, two from its seminary, and twenty-four from its high school.

The war years curtailed college baseball. But the postwar years—and the attendant boom—gave the sport its final fling, a popularity that reached a crescendo in the early 1920s.

At Hampton, Virginia, on April 6, 1921, the Institute's baseball varsity team went down to defeat Virginia Normal, 4–3.

At Richmond, on April 6, Virginia Union beat Howard, 10–3.

On April 12, in Charlotte, Biddle beat Virginia, 7–5. On April 15, on Biddle's campus, Shaw won, 6–3. The feature of the game was Shaw center fielder Sumner's shoestring catch of a drive off the bat of Biddle's clean-up hitter, Brodie.

On Monday, April 18, Wilberforce lost to Dayton Marcus, 9–2. On Saturday, April 16, Hampton lost to Howard, 2–1.

On Friday morning April 22, Coach John Lander and his Biddle University Golden Bears departed on a southern tour.

On April 23, Virginia Union beat Hampton Institute, 14–6, and at Durham on April 26, Biddle and Shaw played to a 5–5 tie. The game was called after the end of nine innings because of darkness. In a two-game series, Greensboro Agricultural and Technical College and Benedict College split. Greensboro won, 11–6, on April 28, and Benedict won, 12–8, on April 29.

On May 6 Wilberforce University beat the predominantly white college Antioch, 6–5. On May 7 Wilberforce beat West Virginia, 9–5, and 6–2, in Xenia, Ohio.

Biddle University ended its tour in Lynchburg, by beating the Virginia Theological Seminary and College, 7–0. At Petersburg, Hampton lost to Virginia Normal, 8–0, and Virginia Normal claimed

The 1913 Virginia Union baseball team. (1) Bayton, (2) Madison, (3) Hall, (4) Pannell, (5) Ruffin, (6) Gardner, (7) Hayes, (8) Taylor, (9) Daniel, (10) Dawson, (11) Adams, (12) Wilson, (13) Jasper, (14) Nash, (15) Moore, and (16) Perkins.

the 1921 championship of the Colored Intercollegiate Athletic Association, with a record of six wins and no defeats.

Biddle's tour had included Salisbury, Durham, Raleigh, Richmond, Lynchburg, and Bennett College[1] in Greensboro.

The high point in Negro college baseball was the annual Easter Monday game. In 1921 Hampton Institute beat Virginia Union, 7–6. A large crowd looked on at Richmond's Hovey Field.

On March 17, 1922, Howard University reported that over thirty candidates appeared for baseball practice, including Payne, Tollet, Kean, and Johnson, from the 1921 varsity.

Down in Augusta, on March 17, Paine College beat Walker Baptist, 14–8. Two weeks later, Haines Institute beat Paine, 6–2.

In Tennessee, Walden University had the following varsity men returning for the 1922 season: Thomas Young, Edgar Burks, E. C. Woodson, Lawrence Long, Cecil Hinton, Clarence Berry, and Wallace Watson. The schedule called for four games, against Fisk University, Lebanon (Tenn.) High School, Roger Williams College, and Morehouse College.

On April 7 Morehouse beat Clark University, 10–1, and on April 8, Livingstone beat Bennett, 8–7, at Salisbury. Some other 1922 scores follow:

Lane College, 9—Humboldt High School, 4
Wilberforce, 3—West Virginia Institute, 2
West Virginia Institute, 8—Wilberforce, 5
Walden University, 7—Fisk University, 2
Talladega College, 9—Morris Brown, 0
Morris Brown, 6—Talladega College, 5
Talladega College, 9—Tuskegee Institute, 3
Talladega College, 14—Tuskegee Institute, 0
Talladega College, 10—Morris Brown, 4
Livingstone, 6—Virginia Union, 2
Montgomery Grey Sox, 5—Talladega College, 3
Lincoln University, 8—Virginia Theological Seminary and College, 5

---

[1] Bennett College was founded in 1878 as a co-educational institution. In 1926 it was rechartered as a four-year women's college.

Virginia Union, 3—Lincoln University, 2
Morehouse College, 13—Camp Benning, 3
Morehouse College, 12—Camp Benning, 1
Wiley University, 7—Samuel Houston College, 1
Wiley University, 12—Samuel Houston College, 6

On April 28 Lane College won two games by beating Tennessee Mechanical and Industrial College, 12–10, and 8–5, at Jackson, Tennessee. The same date, Wilberforce beat Earlham College of Richmond, Indiana, 13–4, at Wilberforce, Ohio.

At Talladega, Alabama, on Thursday, April 20, Hubert Lockhart pitched a no-hit, no-run game over Morris Brown College. The game was played in one hour and twenty-five minutes.

In a big Easter Monday game in 1922, over seven thousand fans showed up. They saw Livingstone beat the home team, Biddle, at Charlotte's League Park, 9–3.

The Kansas City Monarchs, a Negro professional team, beat Prairie View A & M College, 9–1, on April 13, 1923. The thirty-year-old Wilber "Bullet" Rogan, the Monarchs' ace, limited the college men to three hits.

Coach Harold D. Martins' Virginia Union team won the CIAA baseball title in 1923 with the following players: Adams, shortstop; A. A. Branch, center field; B. C. Gregory, first base; F. D. Johnson, right field; H. Boffman, third base; A. C. Jackson, catcher; E. W. Green, left field; J. J. Wilson, second base; B. Merrit, pitcher; and H. S. Lee, pitcher.

Hampton Institute's 1923 varsity baseball team included George Alexander, David Gunn, Hiawatha Harris, David Burrell, Joseph Jackson, Bertrand Jacobs, Edward Hargrove, Arthur Ruffin, and St. Clair Robinson.

In 1923 Howard's varsity regulars included Charles Doneghy, Thomas Anderson, Ulysses Bagley, Raymond Doakes, Haywood Johnson, Houghton Kelley, Edgar Long, Laddie Melton, Samuel Peyton, Alfred Priestley, Vernon Smith, and George D. Williams.

At five o'clock on March 3, 1924, sixty-five baseball candidates reported to Coach Gideon Smith at Hampton. In 1924 Wiley University's lettermen were Captain Shackleford, third base; Grady Orange, shortstop; "Slim" Ware, first base; and Ben Taylor, second base. (However, Taylor was suspended from school because of a "run-in with the discipline committee.")

Thirty candidates reported to Coach Ulysses S. Young at Lincoln University in 1924. Captain Naylor, Crudrup, Frazier, and Johnson, being returning lettermen.

Wiley University opened its 1924 season with a 12–0 win over Jarvis Institute, at Marshall, Texas. Some other 1924 results follow:

Morehouse College, 13—Lincoln University, 8
Morehouse College, 14—Claflin College, 2
Morehouse College, 16—Claflin College, 1
Morehouse College, 12—South Carolina State College, 2
Morehouse College, 1—Benedict College, 1 (Called because of darkness.)
Walden University, 4—Lincoln University, 2
Walden University, 29—Lebanon High School, 0
Walden University, 18—Roger Williams College, 2
Walden University, 10—Fisk University, 8 (Ten innings.)
Walden University, 3—Fisk University, 0
Wiley University, 4—The Dallas Giants, 2
Wiley University, 3—The Dallas Giants, 2
Morris Brown College, 6—Talladega College, 5
Morris Brown College, 7—Morehouse College, 2
Virginia Normal and Industrial Institute, 14—Hampton Institute, 7
Virginia Theological Seminary and College, 5—Howard University, 3
St. Paul College, 4—Virginia Union University, 3
South Carolina State College, 1—Morehouse College, 0
Hampton Institute, 4—St. Paul College, 3
Talladega College, 3—Morris Brown College, 2
Howard University, 6—Hampton Institute, 2

Andrew "Rube" Foster brought his Chicago American Giants, a black professional team, into Marshall, Texas. The *Chicago Defender* of April 19, 1924, reported:

WILEY GETS 4 IN 9TH OFF FOSTER'S CREW

However the college team's rally fell short, as the Giants held on to win, 6–5.

Historically, one of Negro baseball's all-time great teams, the Chicago American Giants, in 1924 included some of the best in the Negro National League: Floyd "Jelly" Gardner, twenty-nine-year-old speed merchant, Elwood "Bingo" DeMoss, thirty-five-year-old power hitter, and thirty-year-old David Malarcher, outfielder. Three members of the Wiley team would also play in the professional Negro major leagues. Grady Orange, William Ware, and John Shackleford.

On Friday, May 23, 1924, Howard University defeated Virginia Union University, 6–4. It was the first time that Howard had defeated the Virginia Union team in three years on the baseball diamond. It prepared them for the Japanese.

The baseball team of Mejii University of Tokyo was touring the United States in 1924. It had already had victories over Harvard, Yale, and Princeton. But on Howard's campus, on Monday, June 2, the Japanese team was defeated, 4–3, in a thrilling ten-inning game.

In 1925 Virginia Union won the CIAA baseball championship. Alcorn Agricultural and Mechanical College of Lorman, Mississippi, lay claim to the "undisputed championship of South of the Mississippi" baseball title. Wiley University and Prairie View A & M tied for the championship of Texas. The standings follow:

	Games	Won	Lost
Wiley University	10	7	3
Prairie View A & M College	10	7	3
Paul Quinn College	10	5	5
Texas College	10	5	5
Bishop College	10	3	7
Sam Houston College	10	3	7

Baseball in the black colleges as the mid-1920s approached was at its zenith. The *Pittsburgh Courier* of April 18, 1925, had the following report:

DURHAM WINS FROM HARVARD UNIVERSITY '9'

Durham, N.C., Apr. 16—In one of the hardest fought diamond struggles of the season, the Durham State College nine defeated the famed Harvard

University aggregation, 9–8, in an eleven-inning struggle here Monday.

Earl Brown, a black pitcher and himself a 1924 Harvard graduate, was scheduled to pitch his first professional game on July 13, 1924. He was with the Lincoln Giants, and his opponents would be the Bacharach Giants. The Bacharach Giants' pitcher would be Hubert Lockhart, a Talladega College junior.

Many had worried about college athletes playing professional baseball. The *Pittsburgh Courier* of March 27, 1926, commented:

It is an open secret that a large number of college men play summer baseball. For years good college players have been given opportunities to play in the summer on different teams in the Negro National and Eastern Colored Leagues. It is encouraging to know that any boy or young man who shows any ability of a Class "A" player is given a chance to earn money for playing professional ball in either of the above named leagues. Mr. A. Rube Foster, President, Negro National League, and Mr. Ed. Bolden, Chairman, Eastern Colored League, are always on the lookout for college players who show any ability of developing into Class "A" players. The work is more dignified than dish washing, hotel work, dining car and Pullman porter services.

In 1926 the Southeastern Intercollegiate Athletic Conference had overlooked its athletes playing professional baseball as had the Southwestern Athletic Conference.

The Colored Intercollegiate Athletic Association (CIAA) had sent countless athletes into the professional ranks, many playing at the same time that they pursued their studies.

Article VI, Section 5 of the CIAA Constitution provides:

No student shall be allowed to represent any institution in any intercollegiate contest who either before or since entering the institution shall have engaged for money in any athletic competition whether for stake money, prize, or for a share of the entrance fee or admission money . . . Participation of college students in athletic sports as members of professional teams shall render such students ineligible to membership on college teams save that summer teams representing Hotels or Steamboats shall not be affected by this rule.

Talladega College was not a member of the CIAA, but a prominent member of that association was having problems. W. Rollo Wilson, wrote in the *Pittsburgh Courier* of June 2, 1928:

Baseball prospered not at Howard University this Spring. Refusal of CIAA teams to schedule the boys from the Hill put a crimp in diamond plans. The only games they could get were away down South in Dixie and with many miles between. To have attempted these games, would have been disastrous financially.

"Disastrous financially" would reverberate around the nation in over a year, and the resultant crash would signal the Great Depression.

But Howard's immediate problem had begun in the 1924 season, and it was football, not baseball, that started it.

Robert Miller was a 205-pound guard at Virginia Union University in 1923. In February 1924 he left Richmond and enrolled in Dunbar High School in Washington. In September he entered Howard. A tremendous prospect, he made Howard's varsity football team at right guard. At left guard was his brother, G. B. Miller.

Immediate protest went up against Robert Miller's being permitted to play against CIAA teams. The CIAA Constitution stipulated that a varsity athlete who transfers to a college division institution must wait one year before he is eligible to play varsity sports again.

Howard, which in 1924 had neither grade nor preparatory departments, argued that since nearly all CIAA members did, it would be fair to allow entering college athletes to play right away.

Howard attempted to play Robert Miller in the 1924 Thanksgiving Day game against Lincoln. But Lincoln protested so heatedly—even threatening to cancel the game—that Howard was forced to withdraw Miller.

When Howard protested to the CIAA, the CIAA voted against the university. Howard angrily withdrew from the CIAA, and the CIAA ordered a boycott by member schools, all of which complied except Lincoln, keeping in mind the highly lucrative annual Howard-Lincoln Thanksgiving Day football game.

Howard's 1925 schedule contained such non-CIAA schools as Fisk University, Nashville, Tennessee; Wilberforce University, Wilberforce, Ohio; and Livingstone College, Salisbury, North Carolina.

The game in Negro college baseball was the annual Easter Monday game. Livingstone and Biddle University—now Johnson C. Smith—had set the pace in three games in a long and historic series. The *Pittsburgh Courier*, on April 17, 1926, reported on the April 5 encounter:

J. C. SMITHS HALT LIVINGSTONE IN
SOUTHERN DIAMOND CLASSIC

Six thousand fans witnessed the game, won by Johnson C. Smith, 7–3, at Wearn Field, in Charlotte, North Carolina.

Smith's pitcher Hayes struck out thirteen batters and allowed five hits. Livingstone's Yokeley struck out six batters and allowed only three hits. All of Smith's runs were unearned.

Laymon Yokely[2] was born in Winston-Salem, North Carolina, in 1906. Benjamin Church, a playground director, had seen the gangly youngster in a sandlot game and induced him to enroll at Livingstone College. In the 1926 Livingstone-Johnson C. Smith game, Charles Spedden, a white scout for the Baltimore Black Sox, saw him and invited him to try out for that team, which he did successfully.

On Sunday, June 6, 1926, Yokely pitched his first pro game against the Newark Stars and won, 8–6. He allowed six hits, walked five, and struck out five.

Far from Baltimore in 1926 a multitalented athlete was having a field day at his first-base position—and especially at the bat. The *Pittsburgh Courier* of April 26 reported:

WU FANG WARD'S BAT IS DECIDING FACTOR AS WILBERFORCE WINS

At the last half of the eighth inning the score stood 6 to 3 in favor of Defiance. Ward came up with a homer after having two strikes and three balls on him.

---

[2] "Laymon Yokely" is the way the former college and pro star says he spells his name.

The 19-year-old Laymon Yokely in his first season on the 1925 Livingstone College baseball team. (Courtesy John Holway)

Defiance College led by 6–5 as Wilberforce took its last at-bat in the last half of the ninth. There were two outs:

King Callen, Captain of Wilberforce, got a nice little single and stole second. Wu Fang Ward was next up to the bat and with two strikes on him and no balls, he clouted the horsehide to deep right field for three bases. And on an overthrow to third by the Defiance second baseman he went loping home for the winning run.

Harry "Wu Fang" Ward was track, football, basketball, and base-ball star while enrolled at Wilberforce University from 1923 to 1927.

R. S. Darnaby, secretary-treasurer of the Southeastern Intercollegi-ate Athletic Conference, announced on March 18, 1926, an eighty-one-game schedule for Morehouse, Atlanta, Fisk, Morris Brown, Florida A & M, Tennessee A & I, Knoxville, Alabama, Talladega, Tuskegee, and Clark colleges and universities.

The first scheduled games started on March 19 with the final games on May 15.

In 1926 Benedict College was champion of the Georgia-South Carolina Athletic Association. Benedict won ten out of twelve games.

Virginia Normal won the 1926 CIAA championship, led by Wig-gins, Payne, and Scott, who batted .457, .359, and .450 respectively. Virginia Normal won nine out of ten games played.

The *Pittsburgh Courier*, on June 12, took note of the departure of an outstanding college pitcher:

LOCKHART ENDS ENVIABLE ATHLETIC CAREER AT TALLADEGA

The *Courier* said that Lockhart had suffered only one defeat in his four years as a college baseball pitcher at Talladega, and that "he goes from here to the Bacharach Giants."

A harbinger of things to come? In 1927 the Bacharach Giants filed a $30,000 bankruptcy action under the name of the Bacharach Athletic Association of Atlantic City, New Jersey. New management assumed control of the club.

In the big Easter Monday game on April 18, 1927, Livingstone College beat Johnson C. Smith University, 2–1, in Charlotte, before upward of thirty-five hundred fans. Livingstone's Yokeley struck out eight and Johnson C. Smith's Hayes struck out seven.

Claflin College won the Georgia-Carolina Conference championship in 1927. Claflin's season record was 9–2, won-lost.

In 1927 Morris Brown College of Atlanta won twenty-one games and lost seven. Sixteen of the twenty-eight games were played away from its home city. Morris Brown was the first Negro college baseball team in the deep South to travel as far north as Washington, D.C. The twelve-man traveling squad left in two automobiles from Atlanta on Monday, April 28. They beat Howard, 6–4.

Howard's 1927 squad consisted of Douglas Monroe, James Walker, Dowey Lomax, Frederick Slade (manager), Herman Gaskins, Carl Bridges, John Codwell, Harry Payne, Tick Smith, Lester Braden, Roy Hammond, Archeal Roy, Noah Jones, John Hull, Charles Prudhommer, and Issac Gillam.

Some 1927 results follow:

Morris Brown College, 8—South Carolina State Teachers College, 6
Morris Brown College, 9—Virginia Union University, 5
Morris Brown College, 10—Morehouse College, 9
Morris Brown College, 11—South Carolina State Teachers College, 3
Howard University, 9—Livingstone College, 4
Howard University, 12—Morgan College, 4
Howard University, 5—Storer College, 2
Howard University, 1—Morgan College, 0
Virginia State College, 10—St. Paul College, 15

Storer College, 9—Howard University, 6
Morris College, 7—Howard University, 4
Hampton Institute, 13—St. Paul College, 5

Hampton Institute's 1927 baseball lettermen were George Williams, George Byrd, Jesse Murry, James Caster, Longsworth Quinn, Clarence Coles, G. M. C. Butler, Hiawatha Harris, James Adams, Harold Price, John Finch, and Richard Ansley.

The scores of some 1928 games follow:

Wiley University, 7—Paul Quinn College, 0
Haines Institute, 14—Walker Baptist Institute, 0
Haines Institute, 5—Harbison College (Irma, S. C.), 3
Haines Institute, 11—Voorhees Institute, 6
Paine College, 7—Walker Baptist Institute, 4
Paine College, 15—Claflin College, 8
Paine College, 12—Allen, 7
Atlanta University, 5—Clark University, 2
Atlanta University, 13—Morehouse, 3
Morehouse College, 11—Mary Bethune-Cookman College, 2
Morehouse College, 11—Morris Brown, 5
Morehouse College, 3—Clark University, 2
Alabama State Teachers College, 8—Morehouse College, 3 (Southeastern
    Conference champs)
Alabama State Teachers College, 5—Fisk University, 3
Alabama State Teachers College, 12—Fisk University, 6
Alabama State Teachers College, 8—Miles Memorial College, 0
Alabama State Teachers College, 12—Selma University, 5
Alabama State Teachers College, 13—Morehouse College, 4
Livingstone College, 5—St. Paul College, 1
Livingstone College, 17—St. Augustine College, 8
Livingstone College, 18—Brick Junior College, 1
Livingstone College, 8—Paine College, 0 (Yokeley pitched a no-hitter.)
North Carolina College, 20—Shaw University, 1
Greensboro Agricultural and Technical College, 14—Livingstone College,
    10
Harbison College, 3—Allen University, 0
Harbison College, 6—Haines Institute, 2
Harbison College, 11—Allen University, 8
Howard University, 11—Storer College, 9

Howard University, 13—Arnold College (New Haven, Conn.), 6
Howard University, 14—Storer College, 13
Georgia State Teachers College, 6—Allen University, 3
Virginia State College, 18—Hampton Institute, 1 (CIAA 1928 champions).
Johnson C. Smith University, 5—Shaw University, 2

An all-time attendance record of over ten thousand fans witnessed the Easter Monday game between Livingstone and Johnson C. Smith University.

In the Yokeley-Hayes duel, the latter won, 5–3. The game was played in Charlotte's Wearn Field.

The old laissez-faire attitude toward allowing a professional to play in amateur games of college baseball was suddenly no more. The *Pittsburgh Courier* dusted off its boldest captions on May 26, 1928:

TURMOIL THREATENS NORTH CAROLINA IAA

UNFAIR TACTICS OF LIVINGSTONE ARE CENSURED

PROFESSIONALISM INVADES RANKS OF COLLEGIATE BASEBALL

Laymon Yokeley, mound ace of the Livingstone Bears, also performs in a similar role for the Baltimore Black Sox, a professional team. It is said that he divides his services between the Bears and the Sox, journeying to Baltimore to pitch for George Rossiter's ball-hawks and returning to Livingstone to twirl for his Alma Mater.

The Yokeley story was so controversial that the president of the North Carolina Intercollegiate Athletic Association felt compelled to clarify the issues, and said: "There has been no law against bona fide students playing on their school teams, so long as they remained in good standing with their own institutions and so long as they successfully met the scholastic requirements of their colleges."

Clement's response in the *Pittsburgh Courier* of June 2, 1928, asserted that if it were not for Livingstone's 17–4, won-lost record, there would be no furor over Yokeley. He further added:

Yokeley is a bona fide student at Livingstone. Yokeley was discovered while playing at Livingstone, and Livingstone is playing Yokeley within the law of the Conference to which she belongs. Further, the North Carolina Conference is not about to disrupt on account of it.

As if to add an exclamation point to Clement's rebuttal, on the same page was the following headline:

YOKELEY TOPS HAVANA CUBANS, 9–1

Besides pitching an eight-hitter, Yokeley hit a three-run homer in the second inning, and a fourth-inning single.

The *Pittsburgh Courier* reported on a professional baseball team playing a college on April 28, 1928:

HILLDALE SHUTS OUT A & T

Winston-Salem, N. C., April 26—Recruit Twirler Jim Thorpe pitched airtight ball today and the Hilldale Club registered its seventh consecutive victory of its barnstorming trip in the South by blanking the A & T College, 6 to 0. The game was won in the third inning when Charleston and Mackey singled.

The Hilldale Club of Darby, Pennsylvania, was playing independent baseball in 1928. Its lineup included some of the all-time greats of Negro professional baseball, including Frank Warfield, fancy fielding, thirty-three-year-old second baseman; Oscar Charleston, thirty-two-year-old power hitter, and Raleigh "Biz" Mackey, all-time great catcher, then thirty-one years old.

The Hilldale Club was playing independent baseball by necessity. The times were making it hard for the entertainment dollar to be shared, and the baseball competition for it was becoming intense. In the 1929 season, the Depression would reach into the college ranks. The *Washington Tribune* of April 26, 1929, commented:

SUSPENDS SOUTHERN COLLEGE

Prairie View, Texas—At a special meeting of the Southwest Athletic Conference, held at Prairie View College, March 28, Paul Quinn College was suspended for a period of three years and fined $50. This action was the result of Paul Quinn's failure to carry out her conference baseball schedule for 1929. A financial deficit and lack of material or students interested in participating on a baseball team are two of the principal reasons given by President Dean Mohr for Paul Quinn's inability to carry out its schedule.

The big Easter Monday games continued. In 1929 Atlanta University played Morehouse, and, of course, Johnson C. Smith confronted Livingstone.

Morehouse beat Atlanta, 7–5. Second baseman, H. O. Mosley, of Morehouse, led the attack with two triples, a double, and a single.

Johnson C. Smith beat Livingstone, 5–0, before more than five thousand fans, Yokeley and Hayes engaging in another duel.

The postwar boom was at its apex, as was a rollicking, carefree, moneyed class. But there were portents of things to come.

On January 1, 1929, Franklin Delano Roosevelt was sworn in as governor at 12:01 A.M. in Albany, New York. In Hollywood, Daniel Haynes and Nina Mae McKenney completed their starring roles in the first major all-Negro motion picture, *Hallelujah*. The comely Miss McKenney was seventeen years old. Herbert Hoover, fifty-four, took office as the 30th President of the United States on March 4, 1929. Colonel Charles A. Lindbergh married Anne Spencer Morrow, at Englewood, New Jersey, on May 27. On June 17, Mrs. Hoover had as a guest in the White House Mrs. Oscar DePriest, wife of the Negro Representative from Chicago, with about twenty-seven other guests. In 1929 the Kansas City Monarchs were the champions in the Negro National League. The Baltimore Black Sox were the champions in the American Negro League. An average of thirty-eight thousand fans saw the Philadelphia Athletics win four out of five games against the Chicago Cubs in the World Series. Herbert Hoover was at the fifth game on October 14 in Philadelphia. Albert B. Fall, Secretary of the Interior, in 1921-22 under the Harding Administration, was convicted for accepting a $100,000 bribe. The money was paid by Edward L. Doheny, in the leasing of the Elks Hill Naval Oil Reserves, in California, and the oil reserves in Teapot Dome, an area in Wyoming. On November 1, Fall began a one-year jail sentence, and in addition, was fined $100,000, a sum considerably higher than the $5,620.57 that each Philadelphia Athletics player pocketed as his winning World Series share. But with the beginning rumblings on Wall Street, the *Washington Post*, on October 23, 1929, started checking on other shares:

RALLIES IN MARKET OFFSET SALES LOSS
BANKERS VIEW STEADY UPTURN AS FAVORABLE SIGN
IN STREET REACTION

But all was not well—economically. The *Washington Post* of October 24, 1929, reported:

HUGE SELLING WAVE CREATES NEAR-PANIC AS STOCKS COLLAPSE
SUDDEN AVALANCHE WIPES OUT $3,000,000,000 IN PAPER VALUES
CRASH IS QUICKEST IN MODERN HISTORY

The boom had collapsed, and when it was a choice between butter and baseball, the answer was self-evident.

Negro college baseball fought for survival. Schedules were cut, trips canceled, and old rivals replaced.

What at one time had been billed as the South's greatst sports classic, the Easter Monday baseball game, traditionally between Livingstone College and Johnson C. Smith University, was played in 1932 between Johnson C. Smith and Shaw University.

Johnson C. Smith beat Shaw University, 16–3. Norris Pass, pitcher for Johnson C. Smith, hurled a five-hitter. He struck out thirteen, and got three hits.

Virginia State College, under coach Steve Howe, won the CIAA championship in 1931, 1932, and 1933. But games were increasingly fewer. By 1934 baseball in the Negro colleges was almost nonexistent. In Wilberforce University's schedule of eleven baseball games, the university was playing against white colleges and a semipro team.

Wilberforce won its first two games on April 28 and May 1 against Rio Grande College and Otterbein College.

The other results follow:

Wilberforce University, 8—Rio Grande College, 1
Wilberforce University, 13—Defiance College, 3
Wilberforce University, 11—Otterbein College, 2
Wilberforce University, 16—Cedarville College, 10
Wilberforce University, 5—The University of Dayton, 11
Wilberforce University, 10—Defiance College, 3
Wilberforce University, 22—Cedarville College, 4
Wilberforce University, 15—The University of Dayton, 5
Wilberforce University, 10—Cincinnati Excellsiors, 9

The *Washington Tribune* could not report on a Howard baseball team, so it followed a Washington baseball player performing for Wilberforce, Percy "Runt" White.

In the game against Defiance College, on May 9, 1934, Percy White, second baseman, got five hits, including two triples and a double. In the game on May 17 against Otterbein College, the switch-hitting White hit a home run from the left side and a triple from the right side of the plate.

In 1935 the CIAA spring sports calendar listed the following: boxing and wrestling, track and field, and tennis.

At Tuskegee Institute, Washington Field, the site of many thrilling contests, was now the location of Armstrong Hall, Logan Hall, and the Hollis Burke Frissell Library.

James Francis Gregory, a baseball pioneer on both the black and white college campus, decried the loss of baseball when he wrote almost forty years ago:

The high schools do not sufficiently encourage the game, and many of our large universities have eliminated it completely from the athletic program. Perhaps it is largely a matter of sentiment, but I have always regretted the shortsightedness of a great institution like Howard University in dropping the National Sport from its program of physical education.[3]

[3] Edward Bancroft Henderson, *The Negro in Sports* (Washington: The Associated Publishers, Inc., 1949), p. 490.

The pioneers' bats had been long stilled, and their deeds relegated to the box scores of time. The crowd's cheers of yesterday were heard no longer. The Easter Monday classics, and the annual southern tours, were forever gone. Baseball on the Negro college campus was no more.

But the game had had its day in the sun, and at one moment in history it was *the* sport on the Negro campus. Negro baseball on the campus was many things: It was Atlanta Baptist College, Biddle Memorial Institute, and Roger Williams University. It was James Madison Nabrit, Alfred D. Jones, James Francis Gregory, "Bun" Hayes, Hubert Lockhart, Melvin "Doc" Sykes, Harry "Wu Fang" Ward, Grady Orange, and John Shackleford. It was also Laymon Yokeley; tall, 6 feet, 1 inch, 170 pounds, walking atop a mound in 1927 before thousands of Easter Monday fans, and warming up his strong right arm. This was baseball in the Negro colleges.

The sports pages recount no more the sagas of the wins and the losses, but the legacy was indelibly etched. Others would grow from these roots and carry the pioneers' beginnings to olympian heights.

3

The Origins of Basketball and the Emerging Black Stars

The game of basketball[1] was invented by James Naismith on December 21, 1891. Naismith was then a thirty-year-old instructor at the Springfield, Massachusetts, Young Men's Christian Association (YMCA) Training School, later to be known as Springfield College, but then composed of students preparing to become secretaries and physical education directors of YMCAs.

Naismith had a class of eighteen students. Thus his first basketball rules called for a team of nine players on each side.

At the start of the game the nine men would line up underneath their own basket. The referee would toss the ball out into the center of the court, and the nine men on each team would make a mad dash to retrieve it. The ball was advanced by passing only, and the players usually shot whenever they got their hands on it and were in range. If a player scored, the referee had to climb up on a ladder to remove the ball from the basket, which was not open at the bottom.

The first game was played on January 20, 1892.

It is believed that the first two teams to play with five players on each side were the universities of Chicago and Iowa. The game was on Friday, January 16, 1896, in Iowa City, and Chicago won, 15–12.

---

[1] "Basketball" was originally written in two words, "basket ball." "Center" was originally spelled "centre."

Despite basketball's American origins, Naismith was a Canadian. He was born on November 6, 1861, in Almonte, Ontario. He was orphaned at the age of eight and was reared in the home of an uncle. The young Naismith went on to graduate from McGill University in Montreal, in 1887, and studied three years at Presbyterian Theological College, but never entered the ministry.

Before Naismith died at the age of seventy-eight, he was to see his game gain in popularity each year and become a major sport worldwide.

By 1893 *The New York Times* was writing stories about basketball and "its success." By 1894 the game had invaded the YMCAs in New York and nearby surroundings. *The New York Times* noted on May 7, 1894:

. . . Basketball is about the youngest of athletic games, but it has gained great popularity. The game has been played with more enthusiasm than any other sport in the gymnasiums of the different associations in this city during the past Winter.

The first intercollegiate game in the East was played between Haverford and Temple on March 25, 1895. Haverford won, 6–4. In 1901 two leagues were formed. The New England League included Dartmouth, Holy Cross, Williams, Amherst, and Trinity.

It is believed that a black player was in this league because *The Freeman*, a black newspaper, noted on December 24, 1904: "For drawing the color line a basketball team in Massachusetts was fined $100 by the President of the New England League."

The other league was the Eastern Intercollegiate League and was composed of Yale, Princeton, Cornell, Columbia, and Harvard.

It is not known when the first Negroes actually played basketball. Fisk University reports that its students were competing in basketball as early as 1900 at the intramural level. But seven years before Naismith invented the sport a group of black athletes was trying to obtain a gymnasium at Howard University, as indicated by the following letter dated Tuesday, February 18, 1884:

Gentlemen of the Faculty,

Sirs: We, the young men and students of the University in general, believing that regular, methodical exercise is conducive to health, and feeling it a necessity, have organized a club for the purpose of establishing a gymnasium. To this end, we are desirous of obtaining the basement of Clark Hall with your permission.

Done By Order of HUAC Association

J. H. Lawton

Committee[2]

The request was granted, and the first floor of Spaulding Hall was converted into a makeshift gymnasium.

In the summer of 1904, Edwin Bancroft Henderson, an instructor in physical training in the Washington, D.C., high schools attended summer school at Harvard. He learned basketball there and taught this strange new game to the students in Washington's public schools.

In 1906 basketball had invaded the black YMCAs and later the YWCAs. These were teams in the eastern cities of New York, Washington, Jersey City, and Philadelphia. The Smart Set Athletic Club of Brooklyn was the first organized black basketball team in 1906. Later two other teams were formed, St. Christophers and the Marathone Athletic Club. With three clubs now formed, a league was organized and named the Olympian Athletic League.

The Smart Set promptly won the first league championship in the 1907–1908 season. Members of that historic team were Charles Scottron, Chester Moore, Robert Lattimore, Robert Barnard, Harry Brown, Alfred Groves, George Trice, and the manager, George Lattimore.

In the 1908–1909 season, three more teams were formed and joined the Olympian Athletic League: the Alpha Physical Culture Club, St. Cyrian Athletic Club, and the Jersey City YMCA team.

The Jersey City YMCA team beat the Smart Set on December 30, 1908, 14–13, and on February 23, 1909, 8–5, to win the Olympian Athletic League title.

---

[2] *The Bison* (Washington: Howard University, 1925), p. 111.

The 1909-1910 Twelfth Street YMCA basketball team of Washington, D.C. Edward Benjamin Gray (7), Edwin Bancroft Henderson (8), Arthur Leo Curtis (9), J. L. Chestnut (1), Hudson J. Oliver (5), Henry T. Nixon (2), Maurice Clifford (6), Robert Anderson (3), and Lewis S. Johnson (4).

Meanwhile, in 1909, the district government in the nation's capital had hired Edwin Henderson as athletic director in the public school system. Shortly afterward the Washington Interscholastic Athletic Association (WIAA) was formed.

In March 1909 the Crescent Five, champions of the WIAA, issued a challenge to the Smart Set. The Smart Set accepted and walloped the Crescents, 27–11. Later in the month, the Smart Set further demonstrated its superiority by beating Armstrong High School of Washington, 18–4.

In the 1909–1910 basketball season, many of the former Washington, D.C., high school basketball players were members of the Twelfth Street YMCA team. This team consisted of Lewis S. Johnson, Hudson J. Oliver, Arthur Leo Curtis, Henry T. Nixon, J. L. Chestnut, Robert Anderson, Maurice Clifford, Edward Benjamin Gray, and Edwin B. Henderson.

The Washington YMCA won all eleven of its season's games,

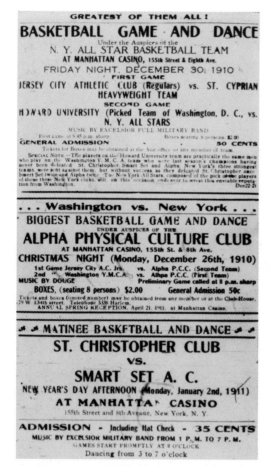

In the early days a basketball game was a sporting event and a social affair. This ad appeared in the New York Age of December 22, 1910.

climaxed by a 44–15 victory over the powerful St. Christophers team of New York. The Twelfth Street YMCA lay claim to the Eastern United States championship. It had defeated the Smart Set twice, the Alpha Physical Culture Club three times, and St. Christophers. They had played before two thousand fans in their win over the Smart Set in Brooklyn.

In the 1910–1911 basketball season, the first strictly varsity team was formed at Howard University. Still without suitable playing space, the team played and practiced on the first floor of Spaulding Hall.

Hampton Institute, which by now was also playing basketball, had the only adequate playing facilities of any of the early black colleges—a 4,000-foot-square court with a seating capacity of two thousand.

Four of the nine players on the 1909–1910 Twelfth Street YMCA team—Curtis, Nixon, Oliver, and Gray—turned up as varsity players on the 1910–1911 Howard University basketball team.

In 1908 Ed Gray had been a freshman at Amherst (Massachusetts) College and was already an athlete of national renown. He had been selected an All-American by Walter Camp, as the third team halfback. Gray entered Howard's medical school in 1909 and graduated in 1913. In 1914 he served his internship in the general hospital in Kansas City, Missouri.

Eligibility standards were not rigid. Students in professional schools were allowed to play as were some prep school athletes.

The 1910–1911 Howard University basketball team. Edward Benjamin Gray (1), Maurice Curtis (2), Arthur Leo Curtis (3), Henry T. Nixon (4), Hudson J. Oliver (5), William Winthrop (6), George Gilmore (7), and J. H. Brown, Manager (8).

In the 1911–1912 basketball season, Howard lost two games, one to Hampton Institute, 19–16. The *New York Age* of February 29, 1912, reported:

HAMPTON HUMBLES HOWARD 19 TO 16

The score of the game, which was played in the Hampton gym on February 22, hardly indicates that the Bisons were humbled. James Gayle was the game's high scorer with nine points.

Howard again met defeat in the next game. The *New York Age* of March 14, 1912, noted:

HOWARD AGAIN MEETS DEFEAT

The Monticello Basketball team of Pittsburgh defeated the champion Howard University team, Friday in Pittsburgh, by the score of 24–19. As this is Howard's third defeat in three years, the colored basketball world will be forced to recognize Monticello as one of the fastest colored quints. The Monticello team is open to meet all comers. It has not met defeat in two years, playing all white teams. . . .

This threat from the West featured a man that many were calling the greatest colored basketball player in the game, Cumberland Willis Posey.

The 1910–1911 Lincoln University (Pa.) basketball team. Felton (1), Bird (2), Giles (3), Jonson, (4), Norris (5), Stewart (6), and Evans, Manager (7).

The 1909–1910 Monticello basketball team of Pittsburgh, Pa. Mahoney, Manager (1), Baker, Coach (2), Dorsey (3), Seward Posey (4), Clark (5), Brown (6), Cumberland Posey (7), Hall (8), and Richmond (9).

In 1913–1914 the Loendi Big Five basketball team in Pittsburgh was formed. Some of the Monticello players—including Cumberland Posey—went to the new team. But this made little difference to Howard, which on January 9, 1914, beat Loendi, 27–14, and later Monticello, 35–12.

Howard returned to its winning ways by blasting Lincoln University of Oxford, Pennsylvania, 51–19, and the New York All-Stars, 39–25.

In the 1912–1913 season, the Alpha Physical Culture Club lay claim to the basketball title of New York by beating the Smart Set, 45–20, and also by beating Monticello, 24–19.

But Howard was still smarting over the loss to Monticello, insisting that the refereeing had not been fair to Pittsburgh. A return game was arranged on a neutral court, and in March 1913, at the Manhattan Casino, Howard got revenge by beating Monticello, 33–17.

In the 1912–1913 season, Hampton's only loss was to Howard,

34–24. But Tuskegee Institute did not play its schedule, as it had to repair its gym. Tuskegee's entire action for the season was limited to intramural games. Lincoln University played one game, a 13–11 loss to St. Peter Claver Club of Philadelphia.

On Saturday, February 2, 1912, a meeting was held at Hampton Institute, out of which was formed a black athletic conference, the Colored Intercollegiate Athletic Association. The charter members were Howard University, Shaw University, Lincoln University, Virginia Union College, and Hampton Institute.

St. Christophers were champions of the land for the 1913–1914 season. They defeated Howard University, 27–17, before three thousand fans in New York's Manhattan Casino.

Hampton Institute had a 15–10 win over the St. Christophers in the 1913–1914 season and was accorded collegiate championship. Hampton had also defeated Howard.

In the 1914–1915 basketball season, the Incorporators were national champions. The runners-up were Hampton Institute, the Alpha Physical Culture Club, Lincoln University, Monticello, St. Christophers, and Howard University.

Howard, one of the first college basketball powers, had fallen on bad days. Long hampered by the lack of a gymnasium, most of its games had to be played on alien courts.

The 1912–1913 Lincoln University basketball team. Hugh Hogans (1), Arthur Taylor (2), William Townsend (3), Walter Anderson (4), Francis Johnson (5), Fred Roseboro (6), John Anderson (7), James Juir, Trainer (8), and Franklin Meyers, Manager (9).

The 1912–1913 Hampton Institute basketball team. George Gurnoe (1), Paul Brown (2), James Gayle (3), Charles H. Williams, Physical Education Director (4), Vernal Brown (5), Harris (6), James Shelton (7), James Johnson (8), and Frank Stony (9).

The club, the YMCA and, of course, the college basketball teams were supposed to be amateur. But professionalism always loomed as a menace to amateur basketball. The Alpha Physical Culture Club and the Incorporators were just two of the teams that had been charged with specific violations of amateur standards.

The *Competitor*, a monthly black magazine, noted:

. . . There is, however, a place for the professional in basketball, but let him promote his own following and not try to feast upon the clientele of the legitimate amateur club. There can be no middle ground between the amateur and the professional, nor can there be any contest of the two standards. The line draws itself, and the duty of each is plain.

Club teams, YMCA teams, and colleges continued to compete against each other. In the 1915–1916 season, Hampton beat the Incorporators, 24–15. In the 1916–1917 basketball season, Hampton again repeated as the nation's outstanding black team. The runners-up were the Incorporators, the St. Christophers, Monticello, the Alpha Physical Culture Club, Lincoln, and Howard.

After the 1919–1920 basketball season, Howard decided to forego varsity play. Meanwhile club and YMCA teams dominated the scene. Some said they were really professional or at least semiprofessional teams. A case study could be the Monticello team.

The Monticello basketball team was organized in 1910. It would also be known as the Monticello-Delaney Rifles. In the 1913–1914 season, some of the Monticello players formed another team, the Loendi Big Five. Led by their great player, "Cum" Posey, they played openly for money from the very beginning.

The Loendi Big Five drew capacity crowds to its home court at Pittsburgh's Labor Temple and started great rivalries against local teams. Loendi even had its own team song:

> Take it slow and easy
> If you want to get along
> with Posey, Young and Betts
> Long Tall Sessoms and all the rest.

James "Stretch" Sessoms, Cumberland Willis Posey, William T. Young, William "Big Greasy" Betts, and James "Pappy" Ricks, formed the nucleus of the Loendi Big Five for many years. William Betts joined them in 1917. In 1973 he looked back over half a century: "We use to get $25 a game when we played little teams. But when we played the big teams, like Coffey and the Original Celtics, we got as high as $75 a game."

Coffey was not only a "big" team, but was difficult to beat. Some years later, when Loendi finally managed to defeat Coffey, the *Pittsburgh Courier* on March 28, 1925, greeted the victory with bold type:

LOENDI BREAKS 2 YEAR JINX AND DEFEATS COFFEY CLUB
BETTS AND HAMPTON BIG GUNS

Loendi won, 25–15. The lineups were:

LOENDI (25)	G	FG	TP	COFFEY (15)	G	FG	TP
Hampton	0	4	4	Levinson	1	4	6
Posey	1	1	3	Sandomire	1	3	5
Williams	1	4	6	Pearlman	0	0	0
Betts	4	1	9	Marks	1	0	2
Young	1	1	3	Levine	1	0	2
Attendance: 600							

William Betts was born on September 29, 1899, in Mt. Pleasant, Ohio. He moved with his family to Pittsburgh in 1911 and started playing in and around the Pittsburgh area in 1916. "In 1927 I joined the Homestead Grays Basketball team. It was owned by the baseball team and some of the baseball players even were on the team. Our coach, Charlie Walker, was also the coach of the baseball team. But we never seemed to be able to beat the Coffey Club. I think we won two games of all we played against them. But we played the Original Celtics eight games and won the first and the last two."

The Original Celtics, of course, were one of the top professional teams of all time. And Betts said they once offered them a proposal: "The Original Celtics wanted us to travel with them one year. They had Haggerty and Joe Lapschick then. I wasn't interested in going to New York or Chicago. Or any of those places. Or even with the Rens. We could stay around Pittsburgh and pick up $75 with the big teams. We were paid for every game played. But when we stopped playing at the Temple, fans stopped coming because it was too far."

It seems apparent that the Loendi Big Five was a semipro basketball team whose members were paid, but not regular salaries as were the Original Celtics and the New York Renaissance Big Five. The *Competitor* of February 1920 reported:

. . . Loendi's team was composed of rugged men, who toss steel ingots and

The Homestead Grays basketball team of Pittsburgh, Pennsylvania. Left to right, seated: Claudie Johnson and Harry "Wu Fang" Ward. Left to right, standing: Douglas Henry, Cumberland Posey, Charles Walker (Manager), W. P. Young, and William Betts. (Courtesy of William Betts)

Robert Douglas, one of the black pioneers in amateur and professional basketball. Shown in 1920 as the Manager of the Spartan Braves of New York. An amateur team, the Braves later became the famed New York Renaissance Big Five, the first black fully-salaried professional basketball team.

mail sacks as a daily toil, and proved a trifle too much for the "marsh-mallow" entry from the Parish House.

The "marshmallow" entry was the St. Christophers, whom Loendi had defeated, 40–27, on December 26, 1919. And, of course, Loendi claimed the national title.

On January 29, 1920, Loendi beat the St. Christophers, 32–13, before five thousand disappointed St. Christophers' fans in New York. The *Competitor* noted that Loendi was so good that "it is hardly possible to pick a basketball team from all the colored players of the country that would have a ghost of a chance to beat the present Pittsburgh five."

In the 1919–1920 basketball season, Hampton Institute was the collegiate king. Meanwhile other black colleges were slowly discovering the game. The CIAA was formed in 1912, and in December 1913 a meeting was held at Morehouse College, Atlanta, Georgia. Out of this meeting came the Southeastern Conference. The charter members were Fisk University, Talladega College, Jackson College, Morris Brown College, Tuskegee Institute, Clark College, Alabama State Normal School (now Alabama State University), Morehouse College,

Florida Agricultural and Mechanical College, and Knoxville College.

In the 1915–1916 basketball season, Hampton Institute lay claim to the national championship, as the result of victories over Howard University, 46–12; the St. Christophers, 24–15; Lincoln University, 44–20; and the Armstrong Manual Training School, 51–14.

The conferences sought to make competition more fair by proposing that colleges whose schedules included high schools and preparatory academies discontinue involving professionals. Howard set the example by ceasing to allow students in the professional schools to become varsity members.

In December 1920 five Negro officials of Texas colleges met and formed the Southwestern Athletic Conference. The charter members were Prairie View A & M College, Bishop College, Paul Quinn College, Wiley College, and Sam Houston College, and Texas College joined in 1922.

Howard resumed varsity basketball play in the 1923–1924 season. Six games were scheduled against Morgan College, Lincoln University, and Hampton Institute. The *Washington Tribune* of January 26, 1924, reported:

HAMPTON OPENS LOCAL SEASON

. . . The Howard Basketball team will open its home season at the Armstrong High Gymnasium on Saturday night, February 2nd, at 8:30 o'clock. . . . This will be the first time a Howard varsity quint has shown before local fans since 1920. With prospects that the new gym for Howard will be completed by next winter, the game was revived this year to arouse interest in the sport. . . .

The teams that then made up the CIAA finished as follows in the 1923–1924 season:

	Played	Won	Lost	Percentage
Hampton	7	6	1	.857
Howard	4	3	1	.750
Virginia Union	6	3	3	.500
Virginia Seminary and College	2	1	1	.500

	Played	Won	Lost	Percentage
Lincoln	4	0	4	.000
Shaw	2	0	2	.000
St. Paul	1	0	1	.000

Virginia Union, like Howard, had no indoor gymnasium, and practiced on an outdoor court. Virginia Seminary and College, and St. Paul, were playing in varsity competition for the first time.

The *Chicago Defender* noted on March 8, 1924, that it was "the first season for the Mid-West team" which finished as follows:

	Won	Lost
Wilberforce	3	1
West Virginia Colored Institute	2	1
Kentucky Normal	0	2
Simmons University	0	2

But Wilberforce played a grand total of seventeen games—losing only to West Virginia Institute in its division—and winning fifteen.

Hampton Institute was once more CIAA champion in 1924–1925.

After years of domination by the YMCA and club teams, the big basketball powers were emerging in the black colleges for the first time. Intersectional rivalries were also forming. In the 1924–1925 season, Morehouse, of the Southeastern Conference, also had a successful team.

Three of Morehouse's four losses were to teams in the Midwest division. In the 1923–1924 season, Morehouse had had a perfect record except for a 38–19 loss to Wilberforce.

In the 1924–1925 season Wilberforce lost only two games—one of them was to the Loendi Big Five, 37–31, a professional team that the *New York Age* would have preferred the black colleges not play:

COLLEGE LAXITY IN REGARD TO PROFESSIONALISM APT TO DO DAMAGE TO STUDENT GAMES

There is a laxity among colored colleges in observing the rules of amateur sportsmanship, which, if continued, will commercialize college sports to such an extent as to cause them to lose their attractiveness. Recently the Howard University basketball team played Loendi Club of Pittsburgh, although the coach and athletes of Howard must have known that Loendi has been playing professional basketball for the past two or three years. . . . The Pittsburgh team has also played white professional teams and should not by any stretch of the imagination be considered as amateurs. . . . The Colored Intercollegiate Athletic Association should have some law to check these violations. . . .[3]

Black colleges had historically played not only pro teams, but semi-pro, club, YMCA, and even high school teams, and they would keep on playing these teams—with or without the approval of the athletic conferences.

Morehouse, however, was champion in its own bailiwick and proved it in the first tournament held in the South, February 8–9, 1925. The competing colleges were Atlanta University, Clark University, Morehouse College, and Morris Brown College.

Atlanta beat Clark on the eighth, 21–19. Morehouse beat Morris Brown, also on the eighth, 48–14. Morris Brown beat Clark for third place, on the last day of the tournament, the ninth, 26–19. Morehouse won the tournament by beating Atlanta, 37–13.

In the 1925–1926 basketball season, Morehouse again won the Southeastern title with a 9–0, won-lost conference record. It was apparent that the three college basketball powers were now Wilberforce, Morehouse—and Morgan College.

Morgan College was a new power to be reckoned with. Volume one of *EM SEE*, the Morgan College yearbook of 1926, noted that if the team played as well as it had been playing, "they will realize the collegiate championship in basketball within two years after the athletic renaissance at Morgan." And all this without a gym.

On March 6, 1926, Thomas W. Young, *Pittsburgh Courier* sportswriter speculated that:

It's not certain whether Wilberforce and Morgan meet on the court this season, and it is not expected that Morehouse will encounter the Baltimore lads. Whether or not Morehouse and Wilberforce play is unknown. But if

[3] *The New York Age*, February 9, 1924, p. 6.

this triumvirate ever engages in a play-off, we harbor a very definite belief that Morgan will be the fittest with Hill and Clark forwards, and Payne and Young, the protectorate, woven around the lone "Lanky." Morgan has a quint almost infallible. If the national championship has to be mythical this year, our unanimous vote is for Morgan College."

The two titans did not clash in the 1925–1926 season. However, Hampton was the CIAA champion. Morehouse, unlike Hampton, did not have a gym and played on an outdoor court and in a small basement. Despite these handicaps the *New York Age* on March 20, 1926, called the readers' attention to the fact that:

MOREHOUSE COLLEGE IS S.E. BASKETBALL CHAMP 10TH SUCCESSIVE YEAR

In the 1926–1927 basketball season, Morehouse's reign ended. Clark won the Southeastern title. The conference standings were:

	Won	*Lost*
Clark University	13	1
Morehouse College	7	3
Morris Brown	6	6
Tennessee	2	8
Tuskegee	1	6
Florida	0	0
Knoxville	0	0

Morgan, meanwhile, was maintaining a power-laden team. The *Pittsburgh Courier* of March 19, 1927, noted:

MORGAN HALTS HAUPTON, 22–10

Fresh from a victory over Wilberforce, Morgan College's great basketball team, admitted the class of big college teams in the floor game, won an easy 22–10 victory over Hampton. . . .

Inevitably, the number one collegiate team was scheduled to meet the number one black professional team. The *Pittsburgh Courier* of March 18, 1927, reported:

The 1926–1927 Morgan College basketball team. Front row, left to right: Payne, Hill, Edward "Lanky" Jones, Wheatly, and Clark. Second row, left to right: McIntyre (Manager), Turpin, Thomas, Shefley, and Charles Drew (Coach).

MORGAN COLLEGE PLAYS CHAMPION RENAISSANCE TEAM

Coach Charlie Drew and his Morgan Bears journey to New York City tonight to do battle with the widely known and highly respected Renaissance Big Five. The Renaissance Casino will be the scene of what should be the biggest, fastest, and most exciting classic of the fast waning basketball season. Lanky Jones and Company versus Pappy Ricks and squad! Oh me! Why couldn't it have been nearer than New York?

The irony of some black papers decrying the playing of colleges and pro teams, while other papers eagerly anticipated these contests, was just one of the paradoxes surrounding sports in the early days.

The *Pittsburgh Courier,* on March 25, 1927, reported that "the Renaissance, colored professional world's champions, defeated Morgan College, collegiate championship five" by a score of 26–22.

In the 1926–1927 basketball season, Hampton won the CIAA title again.

Morgan College's 1927–1928 record follows:

Morgan—30, Howard—27
Morgan—37, Howard—19
Morgan—52, Bluefield—20
Morgan—31, Bluefield—22
Morgan—26, West Virginia Institute—13

Morgan—21, West Virginia Institute—15
Morgan—12, Virginia Seminary and College—20
Morgan—43, Virginia Seminary and College—30
Morgan—26, Wilberforce—25
Morgan—25, Lincoln—20
Morgan—25, Lincoln—17
Morgan—30, Baltimore Elks—31
Morgan—47, Baltimore Elks—17
Morgan—31, Baltimore Elks—27
Morgan—34, Washington Elks—28
Morgan—32, Quaker City Elks—10
Morgan—23, Athenians—10

Morgan had only been defeated by one college team and had avenged that defeat handily. However, Wilberforce laid claim to the national title because of victories over Virginia State, Morehouse, Morris Brown, and two wins over Hampton. Claims and counter-claims to that title were made yearly; and since there were no play-offs to decide the question, its resolution depended upon which sports-writer you wanted to believe. The issue of collegiate and professional competition brought out the editorial ink again. Fay Young of the *Chicago Defender,* on February 18, 1928, wrote:

We are against an attempt down East to promote a Morgan College-Renaissance game. We would be against Hampton, Lincoln or Howard playing Loendi of Pittsburgh and we are against any college playing a pro team. It professionalizes the whole team the minute they play in open competition against professionals even if they are only semiprofessionals.

The black colleges continued to play YMCA, professional, and semiprofessional teams. But the emerging conferences attempted to make sure that only student athletes took part in varsity competition. The Southwestern Athletic Conference met at Waco, Texas, on January 12, 1929, and adopted a one-year residence rule for any athlete who had previously played in college sports at another school.

Members of the conference—all in Texas—were Sam Houston, Paul Quinn, Texas College, Prairie View, and Wiley College.

The previous basketball season, the Southwestern conference had held its first tournament on February 25, 1928. Sam Houston beat Jarvis College, 30–12; Bishop College, 32–21; Wiley College, 21–18, and 16–13. Bishop beat Texas College, 40–23, and 43–29. Wiley beat Jarvis, 33–15. Sam Houston beat Bishop, 30–29. Wiley beat Sam Houston, 22–21. Sam Houston, of course, won the tournament.

Virginia Seminary and College countered Morgan's claim for the national title for 1927–1928 with its own claim, and presented its record:

Virginia Seminary—36, Hampton—19
Virginia Seminary—20, Hampton—16
Virginia Seminary—50, Virginia State—9
Virginia Seminary—45, Virginia State—13
Virginia Seminary—37, Lincoln University—14
Virginia Seminary—52, Virginia Union—16
Virginia Seminary—45, Morris Brown—18
Virginia Seminary—68, Claflin—29
Virginia Seminary—41, Claflin—21
Virginia Seminary—21, Morehouse—20
Virginia Seminary—29, Morehouse—32
Virginia Seminary—37, Bluefield—21
Virginia Seminary—20, Morgan—12
Virginia Seminary—30, Morgan—43

On December 20, 1929, the *Washington Tribune* suddenly blared forth:

MORGAN ENTERS CIAA AND SHAW UNIV. IS DROPPED

Shaw University had fallen from CIAA grace by using an ineligible player during the football season. Shaw was reinstated in February 1930.

On January 21, 1928, a conference was held at Tuskegee Institute, in Alabama, and the name of the Southeastern Intercollegiate Association was changed to the Southeastern Intercollegiate Athletic Conference. Members were Atlanta University, Clark University, Morris Brown University, Tennessee State A & M College, Talladega State College, Alabama State Normal School, Tuskegee Institute, Morehouse College, and Miles Memorial College.

Tennessee A & M, Talladega, and Morehouse were the only colleges in the conference that offered playing facilities and seating arrangements. In some schools the winter sport was still being played on an outdoor court.

Teams were sprouting up all over: Bricker Junior College, Central Mississippi College, Lincoln University (Mo.), Sumner Junior College, and others.

However, any assessment of the "big" colleges would have to include Morgan as one of the best, if not the best, of the collegiate teams.

On March 2, 1929, the *Pittsburgh Courier* ran Virginia Seminary's claim to the national title:

SEMINARY COPS NAT'L TITLE AGAIN

The CIAA Basketball crown has been retained by the Seminary after closing a successful road trip against the strong contenders for the championship. . . . Their next aim is the national collegiate championship. They are joint holders with Morgan College of this title at the present time.

Morgan gave strong indications that it should stand alone atop the national ladder. The *Chicago Defender* of March 22, 1929, reported:

MORGAN COLLEGE RIPS RENAISSANCE

Baltimore, Md., March 20—Morgan College defeated Renaissance of New York, 41 to 40 last night. In the first half Morgan led, 22 to 19. Lanky Jones scored eight baskets and one free throw for a total of 17, while Saunders of Renaissance got seven baskets. Jones outjumped Saunders. Clark and Ricks scored six baskets each and Saitch was held scoreless. . . .

On April 6, 1929, ten thousand fans at New York's 21st Regiment Armory saw the world professional champions, the Original Celtics, defeat the Renaissance by only six baskets more than the number by which Morgan had beaten them. The Celtics beat the Rens, 38–31.

In the 1929–1930 basketball season, Howard won the CIAA title. Claflin College was tops in the Southern Intercollegiate Athletic Association, with a 5–3 won-lost conference record. Knoxville College was tops in the Southern Conference.

Howard had clinched the CIAA title with a 32–26 win over Lincoln University at the Rockland Palace, formerly the Manhattan Casino, in New York before three thousand fans.

Knoxville was Southern Conference champion in 1930–1931. Morris Brown held the Southeastern Conference title in the 1931–1932 season. In the 1932–1933 season, Morris Brown tied with Tuskegee Institute for the honor.

Meanwhile, Wilberforce claimed the national championship and presented the reasons:

Wilberforce—53, Dayton YMCA—35
Wilberforce—45, Cedarville College—22
Wilberforce—41, Lincoln Center—18
Wilberforce—23, Lincoln Center—26
Wilberforce—60, Steiners Furriers—16
Wilberforce—54, Kentucky State University—16
Wilberforce—37, Jamestown Merchants—14
Wilberforce—61, Wheeling West Virginia—35
Wilberforce—26, Loendi Big Five—25
Wilberforce—40, West Virginia State University—36
Wilberforce—46, Jamestown Merchants—30
Wilberforce—57, Cedarville College—12
Wilberforce—20, Detroit Athletic Association—25
Wilberforce—68, Kentucky State University—39
Wilberforce—38, Western Kentucky University—16
Wilberforce—39, Western Kentucky University—22
Wilberforce—28, Lemoyne College—15
Wilberforce—48, Lemoyne College—12
Wilberforce—33, St. Louis All-Stars—24
Wilberforce—42, Kansas City Meteors—26
Wilberforce—54, Western Kentucky University—33

The other perennial basketball power, Morgan, also presented impressive credentials for the 1932–1933 season:

The 1933 Morgan College basketball team: left to right, front row: Howard Wilson, Thomas Conrad, Rufus Hackett, Otis Troupe, and Charles Gibson, with Coach Hurt standing at end of first row. Some of the other stars included Lewis Williams, Hubert Crawford, John Sturgis, Paul Taylor, and Hamilton Jewett.

Morgan—36, St. Paul—14
Morgan—53, Virginia Union—36
Morgan—64, Hampton—23
Morgan—36, Howard—25
Morgan—34, Virginia State—33
Morgan—36, Howard—22
Morgan—45, Lincoln—35
Morgan—49, Athenians—35
Morgan—56, Minor Teachers College—26
Morgan—40, Bluefield—23
Morgan—47, St. Paul—14
Morgan—45, Bluefield—32
Morgan—53, Virginia Seminary—24
Morgan—47, St. Paul—18
Morgan—29, Virginia State—25
Morgan—56, Richmond Athletic Society—29
Morgan—44, Howard—37
Morgan—39, Tribune Big Five—36
Morgan—61, Howard—27

Morgan—41, Lincoln—22
Morgan—49, Virginia State—31
Morgan—45, Hampton—33
Morgan—36, Alphas (N.Y.)—20
Morgan—56, Virginia Union—35
Morgan—37, Hampton—36
Morgan—40, Newark—30
Morgan—25, J. K. Morris Five—28
Morgan—31, Lincoln—19
Morgan—40, Lincoln—28

The leading college teams continued to play the pros. The *Chicago Defender* of January 27, 1934, noted:

SAVOY BEATS WILBERFORCE TEAM

In his column, "Speaking of Sports," the *Chicago Defender*'s Al Monroe allowed that "the newest approach to the Rens right now is the Savoy Big Five."

The Savoy Big Five defeated Wilberforce, 36–27. In the Southwest, Wiley University won the title by winning twenty of the twenty-one games it played.

By now black college basketball was mushrooming. The "national" basketball claimants operated year-in and year-out as if no other basketball was being played.

A monthly magazine for blacks had proclaimed that nowhere were there any colored basketball players who could be rounded up to defeat the mighty Loendi Big Five.

But historically not all "colored" players were members of black teams.

Frank J. Platt, a classmate of Samuel L. Ransom, wrote nearly seventy years later "that from 1904 to 1908, Sam was our outstanding hero in football and basketball" at Beloit College, Beloit, Wisconsin.

Almost from the invention of the game of basketball, a black athlete had occasionally appeared on white college teams. Invariably he would be the only Negro player on his team, and in the conference.

In 1909 Fenwick H. Watkins was captain of the University of

The 1909–1910 University of Nebraska basketball team. Left to right, back row: Amberson, Eager (Manager), Jones, Hiltner, Hewitt (Coach), and Wood. Seated, left to right: Hutchinson, Petrashek, Perry, Ingersoll, and Schmidt.

Vermont's basketball team. Wilbur S. Wood played on the University of Nebraska's team from 1907 to 1910. In the 1907–1908 season, the Cornhusker yearbook noted that the team played twenty games and had a 10–10 won-lost record, and also reported that, "Wood displayed remarkable speed and aggressiveness."

The *Nebraska State Journal* covered the Kansas University-Nebraska game on February 22, 1908. Wood, playing left forward, was outstanding as, "early in the second half the Cornhuskers tied the score on a field goal. Kansas then made another point but Wood soon after threw a field goal and the score stood 17 to 16 in favor of Nebraska." Kansas prevailed and went on to defeat the Cornhuskers, 29–25.

In the 1908–1909 season, the Cornhuskers won eight games and lost fifteen. Wilbur Wood was selected to the second team All-Conference team.

In the 1909–1910 season, the *Nebraska State Journal* of January

29, 1910, covered the game in which Nebraska beat Drake, 36–12. And "Wood at guard . . . played a good game . . . scoring three goals."

The *Nebraska State Journal* covered Wood's play in the February 19, 1910, game as the University of Minnesota trounced Nebraska, 29–9:

Wood for Nebraska played a spectacular game, oftentimes dribbling the ball down the floor and around the Minnesota team. Towards the end of the game the crowd began cheering everytime Wood secured the ball and started dribbling.

In a 40–20 loss to Kansas University as reported by the *Nebraska State Journal*, on February 26, Wood again drew raves in a losing cause:

NEBRASKA WALLOPED AGAIN—WOOD OF CORNHUSKERS STAR
OF BOTH TEAMS

Wood, at right guard, was easily the star of the game. He stuck to Johnson of Kansas with a persistence that kept that Kansan on the run. Johnson could not get away from the colored guard and time and time again his attempts at passing the ball were blocked. Wood was not satisfied with merely taking care of Johnson . . . but fought with other of the Jayhawkers for possession of the ball.

In 1909 Cumberland Willis Posey was a member of the Penn State freshman basketball team. The next season, the college yearbook, *LaVie*, picks up his progress:

Among those who were promoted from the class league or who made good on the squad as freshmen, were Sheldon, Vosburg, Hartz, Posey, Greene, Craig and Young.

In December 1910 Posey was a member of the Penn State varsity. He scored eight points in the opening game against Susquehanna. He started in the game against Albright and scored six points. In February 1911 Posey "left Penn State when permission was refused to make a trip with the varsity floor squad because his studies were not up to the required minimum."[4]

The young Posey would have hardly suffered economically. It was said that even before he was born, June 20, 1891, the elder Posey was the first black man granted a chief engineer's license to run a steamboat on the Mississippi, Ohio, and their tributaries. Later he was the general manager for the Delta and Cyclone Towboat Company in which he owned a five-eighths interest.

The young Posey, a chemistry major, drifted to several other colleges before finally making his mark as the most successful owner ever of a black professional baseball team, the Homestead Grays.

In Dubuque, Iowa, in 1917 was Edward "Sol" Butler, about whom Joseph C. Duke would write over half a century later, that he was "the greatest natural athlete I have ever seen." Butler played baseball, football, track, and basketball.

[4] *The Pittsburgh Courier*, May 5, 1951, p. 32.

The 1915–1916 Duquesne basketball team. Top row, left to right: Leo McIntyre (Scorer), Michael Wolak, Charles Cumbert (Posey), Leo Zitsman, Walter McMath, John McLean, and Matthew Haley. Bottom row, left to right: Michael Obruba, Dr. P. M. Seixas (Student Manager), Rev. C. B. Hannigan (Graduate Manager), and William Morressey. William Alland, Team Mascot, in front. (The 1915–1916 Duquesne team won seven games and lost two. Cumbert [Posey], the team's leading scorer, had 104 points in eight games—in one game there was no listing of points by individual players).

The 1916–1917 Duquesne basketball team. Charles Cumbert (Posey), is shown at top left in back row. The 1916–1917 team won seven games and lost three. Available statistics for five of the games show that Cumbert (Posey) scored 63 points.

Also in 1917, a nineteen-year-old black athlete at Rutgers University was beginning what would be an outstanding collegiate career, both athletically and academically. Paul Leroy Robeson starred for the Scarlet Knights in basketball in 1918 and 1919. *The New York Times* of January 6, 1918, reported:

The 1915–1916 Dubuque basketball team. Back row, left to right: David Rath (Coach), Dodds, Bessemer, Parker, and John Chalmers (Coach). Front row, left to right: Harding, Baker, Abrams, Butler, and Krebs. (Courtesy of the University of Dubuque)

RUTGERS BEAT NYU QUINTET

Rutgers opened its basketball season tonight with an easy 43–25 victory over New York University. The local team led at all stages except during the first few minutes. Kelly and Robeson starred for Rutgers.

Two weeks later, Rutgers beat Pratt Institute, 36–28, and "Robeson was the star for the winners, caging eight field goals."

On February 23, 1919, Robeson's name again splashed across the sports pages of *The New York Times*:

ROBESON LEADS ATTACK—RUTGERS EASILY BEATS
WEST VIRGINIA BY 44 TO 22

The strapping six-foot-four-inch athlete played center, but on occasion he also played forward. On Saturday, March 8, 1919, his college basketball career ended with Rutgers beating Lehigh, 30–20, at New Brunswick. Robeson's two seasons showed a total of eleven victories and six losses.

These were some of the black basketball stars who played on white campuses. They lived in a vastly different world from that of the black athlete at the Negro colleges. They did not have to play on outdoor courts or walk a mile to a streetcar in order to get to a rented dance hall for practice. And they had to be first-class athletes. Few were kept around just to fill out the number as bench warmers. Why, it was thought, should a college that was overwhelmingly white, display a mediocre or ordinary black athlete? If the play was to be less than outstanding, it was just as well that it should be wrapped in white skin.

In the 1918–1919 basketball season, Columbia University had its first black player, John Howard Johnson. There was some anxiety as to whether college sports were to be continued. *The Spaulding Guides* commented that even with America's participation in the war, eastern colleges still played basketball "in spite of the chaos of war conditions."

The nation had entered the First World War on April 6, 1917. On that date a formal declaration was made against Germany by the United States Congress.

The armed forces were to eventually number nearly five million, of which 342,477 were black. America's young men and women—black and white—had answered their country's call in defense of democracy. Before they would return, 48,900 would be killed and another 236,000 wounded.

And as on the playing fields, heroes would emerge.

Americans at home read in their papers strange names in faraway countries. Two hundred thousand black troops served in Italy, Germany, and France. Black infantry landed in France on June 18, 1918, and were brigaded with the French Army. As early as June 1917, a battalion of black stevedores had arrived in France. This regiment would number more than 50,000 before the end of the war and would perform outstandingly at the ports of Brest, St. Nazaire, Bordeaux, Havre, and Marseilles. The French acknowledged the exceptional valor of black soldiers by awarding them the highest medals for bravery. One newspaper commented:

Negro soldiers fought with especial distinction in France in the Forest of Argonne, at Chateau-Thierry, in Belleau Woods, St. Mihiel district, Champagne sector, Metz, Vosges, etc., winning praise from French and American commanders. Colored troops were nearest the Rhine when the Armistice was signed.[5]

The following black regiments were decorated: the 92d, 93d, 369th, 365th, 366th, 371st, 368th, 370th, 372d, and the first battalion of the 367th.

Henry Johnson of Albany, New York; Needham Roberts of Trenton, New Jersey; and William Butler, were awarded one of France's highest medals, the Croix de Guerre, for bravery under fire.

The frontline communiques encapsulated the black soldier's feats:

September 19, [1918]: The 92d Division repulsed an attempted enemy raid in the St. Die sector.

September 20: The 92d Division repulsed two enemy raids in the region of Lesseaux.

---

[5] *The Library of American History* (Cincinnati: The Jones Publishing Company, 1919), p. 224.

November 2: The 92d Division, in spite of machine-gun resistance, pushed forward and advanced the line three kilometers.

November 8: Strong combat patrols were sent out from the lines of the 92d Division. Prisoners were captured and casualties inflicted on the enemy.

November 10: The 92d Division reached Bois Frehaut and captured 710 prisoners.[6]

Finally hostilities ceased at 11 o'clock on the morning of November 11, 1918. On July 1 of the following year the armistice was signed, and the armies of the democracies returned home. The war that had been fought to make the world safe for democracy was ended. A nation looked toward peace.

The hordes of Kaiser Wilhelm II had been vanquished. General John J. Pershing led his victorious armies in a New York parade on September 8, 1919. Confetti streamed from office windows, the moving masses shouted and hugged each other. The war was over. Peace! Tears poured unashamedly down grown men's cheeks as they watched the nation's armed might in full military dress strut by to the cadence of blaring bands. A grateful nation silently murmured "well-done." Nearly twenty months of war was ended. The Treaty of Versailles was signed. Germany's might had been vanquished, hopefully for all time.

It was as though the treaty had been signed in order to get on with the 1919–1920 college basketball season. In 1918–1919, *The Spaulding Guides* had noted that "Johnson of Columbia occasionally showed flashes of form."

On January 18, 1919, Columbia beat St. Johns College, 48–15, and "Farrell and Johnson were the leaders in the Columbia attack." Johnson, who played center in his sophomore year, scored twelve points.

On January 25 Penn State beat Columbia, 31–18, and tempers flared. *The New York Times* of January 26, 1919, reported:

---

[6] *The Library of American History*, pp. 607–608.

The only untoward incident of the otherwise fast and clean game came in the second half, when Johnson, Columbia's Negro center, and Peck, a Quaker guard, lost their heads and exchanged blows under the Columbia basket. Both men were quickly separated by other players and officials, and the incident was closed when the two were banished for the remainder of the game.

The Columbia Lions did not have a good season in 1918–1919, but of coach Fred Dawson's twenty-five athletes, John Howard Johnson was without a doubt one of the best, and had shown more than mere flashes of form. *The New York Times* recorded his exploits on February 2, 1919:

YALE FIVE BEATEN BY COLUMBIA TEAM
JOHNSON WRENCHES GAME FROM FIVE WITH BRACE OF GOALS
IN FINAL MINUTES

Johnson, the center of the victors, was responsible for the victory, throwing the goal which brought Columbia to a tie and then throwing one which won the game, both coming within two minutes of the final whistle.

Columbia eked out a 27–25 win over Yale.

Johnson had a rugged sophomore season. In a game against Princeton University on February 17, *The New York Times* reported:

Johnson, Columbia's Negro player, and Davis, the opposing center, had a bitter tussle all through the game, and in the end held each other to a standoff, each making two baskets.

The Princeton Tigers won the game, 16–11.

The Lions had finished the season with a 3–7, won-lost record. Johnson ranked eighth out of thirty-one players in the individual scoring category, with a total of thirty-one points made in eight games.

In his junior year Johnson was a starter, and played almost every position. In a hard-fought battle on March 3, 1920, Columbia defeated Dartmouth, 28–25. Johnson, playing left forward, scored fourteen points. The season slowly drew to a close. The Lions finished with a

Left: Paul Robeson as a member of the 1918–1919 Rutgers University basketball team. Robeson starred in baseball (catcher), basketball (center), football (tackle-end), and track (shot-put and hammer throw). Right: John H. Johnson, a member of the 1920–1921 Columbia University basketball team (Courtesy of Columbia University)

5–10, won-lost record. In the nine conference games that Johnson played, he scored fifty-one points and ranked tenth of sixty-five players in the individual scoring category.

Columbia University prepared for commencement exercises, and the conferral of an Honorary Doctor of Law degree upon General Pershing. Meanwhile, John Howard Johnson awaited his final season of college basketball in the 1920–1921 season.

In 1920–1921, the Lions had a new coach, John Deering, but Columbia was still destined to have a losing season. Johnson's heroics, however, continued. *The New York Times* of January 8, 1921, noted:

Johnson's foul throwing was the chief factor in Columbia's victory, as he was successful in nine of his fifteen attempts from the fifteen foot mark, and all in all he scored 11 of Columbia's 15 points.

The final score was Columbia, 15; City College of New York, 14.

The Lions played their last game on Saturday, March 13, 1921, a losing one to Dartmouth, 26–21. The final standings follow:

	Games	*Won*	*Lost*
Pennsylvania	8	7	1
Dartmouth	9	7	2
Cornell	10	6	4
Princeton	8	3	5
Columbia	10	3	7

In 1923 nearly half a million Negroes emigrated from thirteen southern states. The postwar economy was booming, and gave birth to the Roaring Twenties and the Golden Age of Sports. A moneyed leisure class could not seem to get its fill of competition, and athletes were idolized.

Jack Dempsey (William Harrison Dempsey) came out of the mining camps of Manassa, Colorado, to captivate the American public as had seldom been done before. At first pug-nosed (he later had his nose straightened) and cowlicked, the youngster was the rage as he captured the heavyweight boxing title in 1919.

And there were others: tennis' Big Bill Tilden; golf's Bobby Jones; and baseball's Babe Ruth (George Herman Ruth), who in 1920 hit the unheard-of number of fifty-four home runs. Ruth and Dempsey symbolized the Roaring Twenties—big, brawling, lusty, and freewheeling.

The boom burst. Perhaps the "Black Sox" scandal was a harbinger. The economic crash descended in 1929. It had been a glorious era, with its apex in 1925. People were dancing to the fox-trot and the charleston. Jazz, with its syncopation, muted trombone, and chuckling saxophone, was the craze. Much of this music was being provided by a twenty-five-year-old black musician up from New Orleans, Louis Armstrong.

Theodore Dreiser's epic, *An American Tragedy,* headed the best-seller list. A tall gangly black youth, De Hart Hubbard, was the lone champion of his race listed by the metropolitan newspapers for the year 1925.

Grantland Rice, dean of America's sportswriters, would write in his book, *The Tumult and The Shouting*, in 1954:

When I began fooling around with sport in 1900, there was a vast discrimination that has since vanished. There were no Negroes in any white competition. Big time sport was almost entirely a white man's playground. . . . The Negro was all but shut out—except in boxing.

The black athlete had competed in nearly all sports—and almost from the beginning. Henry Beckett played on the baseball, football, and hockey teams at Springfield College in 1906. William H. Kindle was captain of Springfield's football team in 1911 and was also a member of the basketball, soccer, and rugby teams.

South Dakota State College produced Ross Owens in 1923. He had earned honorable mention on the All-North Central Intercollegiate Conference teams. Ernie Page starred at Western Illinois State (now Western University) in 1925.

Page played left end on the football team, guard on the basketball team, and relief-pitcher first-baseman on the baseball team. He captained the baseball team in 1927 and the basketball team in the 1926–1927 season.

Still greater black stars would emerge as the 1930s dawned and the 1920s receded as history. One of the greatest black stars, George Gregory, Jr., entered Columbia University in 1927.

Gregory was born on November 22, 1906. He graduated from DeWitt Clinton High School in New York City, in 1927, having dropped out of school for several years. Leonard Palmer, the coach at DeWitt Clinton, had seen Gregory play at a local YMCA and was impressed, and he persuaded Gregory to return to school.

Gregory was a member of the Freshman team at Columbia. In the 1928–1929 basketball season, he played in the Lions' varsity basketball team, the second black to do so. He would go on to score one hundred fifty-five points in seventeen games, and rank fourth in league scoring.

The New York Times picked up one of the games on February 10, 1929:

The 1929–1930 Columbia University basketball team. Left to right, front: Robert McCoy, Lou Bender, George Gregory, David Jones, and Ed Obey. Left to right, standing: Jay Hodupp, Arthur Lautkin, Leonard Hartman, P. H. Blatterman, and Donald McNaughton. (Courtesy of Columbia University)

COLUMBIA DEFEATS NAVY FIVE, 32 TO 31—GREGORY'S TWO FIELD
GOALS IN FINAL MINUTE DECIDE HARD FOUGHT STRUGGLE

Playing right forward, Gregory led all scorers with sixteen points.

In the 1929–1930 basketball season, Gregory finished second in league scoring. In twenty-two games he made one hundred sixty-eight points. *The Times* emblazened the heroics of one of his games on March 12, 1930:

COLUMBIA QUINTET WINS LEAGUE TITLE—10,000 SEE
CONTEST—GREGORY IS STAR OF GAME

COLUMBIA CENTER ACCOUNTS FOR 10 POINTS AND STARTS
VICTORS ON WAY TO TRIUMPH

Columbia won the title by beating Pennsylvania, 29–23.

On March 26, 1930, *The Times* announced:

COLUMBIA SELECTS GREGORY CAPTAIN—ALL EASTERN LEAGUE
CENTER WILL LEAD FIVE—
OUTLOOK FOR NEXT SEASON BRIGHT

The six-foot two-and-a-half inch, one hundred seventy pound Gregory's elevation to the captaincy was not unexpected. He had been the only junior on the previous year's varsity—and he was the team's premier athlete.

In the Lions' 45–28 win over Cornell in Gregory's senior year *The Times* wrote on February 24, 1931:

Gregory scored a sensational basket. He was guarded from behind by Schroeder, so he flipped in the basket from about ten feet out on an overhead toss with his back to the basket.

Gregory scored eleven points in the contest and was runner-up to his teammate, Bender, who scored fourteen points.

On January 7, 1931, before two thousand fans, Columbia beat Colgate University, 33–27. Captain Gregory continued his brilliant plan, and maintained his hold on the headlines as shown by *The Times*'s bold type:

MAROON PLAYER TALLIES 13 POINTS, WITH BENDER AND
GREGORY STARRING FOR VICTORS

Gregory scored nine points, and Sullivan of Colgate led all scorers with thirteen.

The Lions again won the title. *The Times* of March 10, 1931, told the story of their second consecutive title:

LEAGUE TITLE KEPT BY COLUMBIA FIVE—LIONS BEAT DARTMOUTH,
37–31, TO TAKE EASTERN CIRCUIT CROWN SECOND YEAR IN ROW

Gregory climaxed his college basketball career by being selected for the prestigious Helms Foundation Athletic All-American team for 1930–1931. The complete selections follow:

Forward, Richard Linthicum (UCLA)
Forward, Elwood Romney (Brigham Young)
Forward, Carey Spicer (Kentucky)
Forward, Bart Carlton (Ada Teachers College)
Center, George Gregory (Columbia)

Center, Joseph Reiff (Northwestern)
Guard, John Wooden (Purdue)
Guard, Wesley Fesler (Ohio State)
Guard, Ralph Cairney (Washington)
Guard, Louis Berger (Maryland)

In Gregory's last season, he scored 77 points in ten conference games and 186 points in twenty-three games overall. His three year varsity total was 509 points in sixty-two games, an 8.3 average per game—modest by today's standards, but high for the era.

The game, however, was evolving into its present high-scoring form. In 1932 a ten-second rule was adopted to advance the ball from the back court. A three-second limitation was placed on the time the ball could be held in the offensive pivot. And at the end of the 1936–1937 season, the center tap after each goal was removed.

Then on a Saturday night, January 1, 1938, Angelo "Hank" Luisetti of Stanford University startled the basketball world by scoring fifty points against Duquesne University on a neutral court in Cleveland, Ohio.

Departing from the conventional two-handed set shot, Luisetti swished the cords twenty-three times with one-handed jump shots. Eighty-one hundred fans looked on in disbelief as the Stanford star broke the existing record of forty-one points that had been set by Chuck Chukovits of Toledo in 1937. The six-foot two-inch ace played thirty-eight of the forty minutes, and led the Cardinals to a 92–27 rampage over Duquesne University.

In the 1920s the supremacy of the club and YMCA teams was ebbing fast. The black colleges were coming to the fore, and more and more black athletes were to be seen on white college basketball teams: William "Dolly" King at Long Island University; Wilmeth Sidat-Singh at Syracuse; Jim Coward at Brooklyn College; James D. Barnes and his brother, Samuel E. Barnes, at Oberlin; Horace Johnson at Dakota College; Bob Yancey and Ben Franklin at Boston University; Larry Bleach at Detroit; and Frank "Doc" Kelker at Western Reserve.

King had attended Alexander Hamilton High School in Brooklyn where he had starred in baseball (catcher), basketball (center-forward), and football (fullback). He had also been named to the City's All-Scholastic teams in football and basketball in 1934 and 1935.

Dolly King had begun his basketball career at LIU in the 1936–1937 season. The *Brooklyn Eagle* picked up his career as a freshman on January 6, 1937:

LIU CUBS DEFEAT PORT RICHMOND, 36–27

In the 1936–1937 basketball season, LIU's varsity had a 28–3 won-lost record. On March 8, 1937, LIU defeated CCNY, 28–23, and earned the right to represent New York at the National Amateur Athletic Union basketball championship tournament in Denver.

King, now a sophomore, moved up to the varsity at the season's end. On March 18 LIU beat New Mexico Normal College, 43–39, and gained a berth in the quarter finals. Dolly King scored six points.

But LIU lost to the Denver Safe Ways, 49–26. One of the few Negroes in the nation on a major basketball team looked toward the 1937–1938 season. The *Brooklyn Eagle* commented on King's progress in the twentieth game of the season. The date, February 13, 1938:

LIU "5" TRIMS EARLHAM 72–38, AS KING STARS

It was LIU's eleventh straight win. It would go on to have a 23–4 won-lost record.

In the 1938–1939 season, King ran into eligibility problems. He dropped out of school from September until the beginning of the second semester in January 1939.

It was also in 1939 that the student body at LIU voted overwhelmingly to return football to the campus as a varsity sport. It had been eight years since LIU had last had a varsity football team.

Finally in February 1939, Dolly King returned to school—and the LIU basketball lineup. The timing was fortuitous—LIU had agreed to participate in the National Invitation Tournament (NIT), which was in its second year. It was also timely in that two of the leading players, Irv Torgoff and Cy Lobello, were nursing nagging injuries.

But LIU capped its perfect 25–0 season by beating Bradley, 36–32, and Loyola of Chicago, 44–32, to win the NIT.

In the 1939–1940 season, LIU had another good record, 20–4 won lost. But they went down to defeat in the NIT to De Paul University of Chicago, 45–38.

King had had a busy year. The *Brooklyn Eagle* of September 21, 1939, noted:

KING TO START IN WING BERTH

EX-HAMILTON FULLBACK CONVERTED INTO END FOR LIU BY BEE

As it would happen, there was a basketball game and a football game scheduled on the same date. Dolly King played in both. Interest had been building up in anticipation of King's iron-man feat, and the *Washington Star* on November 15, 1939, speculated:

KING OF LIU ON GRID AND COURT SAME DAY

It isn't because he's so confident of winning that coach Clair Bee of Long Island University is considering leaving Dolly King, his star end, at home

The 1939–1940 Long Island University basketball team, plotting before-game strategy. Left to right: Sal Schwartz, Cy Lobello, Ossie Shechtman, Joe Shelley, and Wiliam "Dolly" King.

when the Blackbirds leave to play Toledo (11/18/39). King also is Bee's outstanding basketball player, and he's due for a busy Thanksgiving day when the LIU plays Catholic in the afternoon and the basketball team opens against the Alumni.

The football game at Ebbets Field to be played November 23, 1939, Thanksgiving Day afternoon, was the last game of the season. King was the only member of the team who was also on the basketball team.

King's illustrious career drew to a close before his graduation. On December 18, 1940, the *Brooklyn Eagle* interviewed Coach Clair Bee about Dolly King:

BEE SHUDDERS AT PROSPECTS OF KING-LESS CLUB

It's the same old Long Island University five, that is, point for point, but how will it fall when Bill (Dolly) King, co-captain and spearhead all these years, bows out of the picture come February 17. Unless some one comes along overnight, Clair Bee's Blackbirds are likely to be very blue.

Dolly King, who later received his degree in 1946, turned professional. The *Brooklyn Eagle* of February 6, 1941, reported:

KING MAKES PRO CAGE BOW SUNDAY

Dolly King, Long Island University's outstanding all-around athlete for the past four years, will make his metropolitan professional debut at the Royal Windsor (St. Nick's) Palace Sunday night when he will lead the New York Flashes into action against the King Kullen quintet, composed of former college stars. The second game of the twin bill brings together the Philadelphia Sphas and the Jewels in an important American Basketball League contest. . . .

Wilmeth Sidat-Singh was with Syracuse during the same period that Dolly King was with LIU. But Coach Lew Andreas elected to use him in basketball games rather sparingly.

Wilmeth Sidat-Singh was born in Washington, D.C., in 1918. He

The 1938–1939 Syracuse University basketball team. From top, left to right: Wilmeth Sidat-Singh, Mark Haller, and Bob Stewart. Bottom, left to right: Billy Thompson and Johnny Schroeder.

was the son of Elias and Pauline Webb. His father died when he was five years old, and the boy was subsequently adopted by his stepfather, Dr. Samuel Sidat-Singh.

Raised in New York, Sidat followed a long line of great scholastic athletes that had starred at DeWitt Clinton High School. In 1936 he enrolled at Syracuse, where he was to star on the gridiron and the hardwood whenever given a chance. *The New York Times* picked up his basketball career in his senior year on January 1, 1939:

SYRACUSE IN FRONT, 43–23

SUBDUES PENN STATE AS SIDAT-SINGH CAGES 18 POINTS

The game was played on December 31, 1938, before sixteen hundred fans.

Then Syracuse beat Pennsylvania, 49–38, as covered by *The New York Times* on February 23. Sidat-Singh played right forward before four thousand fans at the Palestra and scored twenty points to equal the season's record at that arena that had been set by Cadet Walter Brinker of Army. Sidat-Singh had eight field goals and four foul goals.

Frank (Doc) Kelker after his graduation at age twenty-four from Western Reserve University (now Case Western Reserve University) in 1938. One of the greatest all-around athletes in Cleveland collegiate sports history, he starred in football, basektball, and track. After graduation, Kelker took a job as a coaching assistant at Cleveland's Central High School. After two years, he moved on to the Cedar YMCA as an executive director. (Courtesy of Case Western Reserve Archives)

On March 5 *The New York Times* noted that Sidat-Singh was playing his last college basketball game. Syracuse beat Colgate, 51–32. Sidat-Singh got eight points. Syracuse finished with a record of fourteen wins and four losses.

Another outstanding black star appeared on a white team in the late 1930s. Frank "Doc" Kelker, before being nominated as an All-American end for Western Reserve in 1937 also starred on the hardwood.

The *Cleveland Plain Dealer* noted on January 3, 1937, that "Andrews, Kelker and Bate, with nine, eight and seven points, respectively, were Reserve's big scorers." All that talent was in vain as Western Reserve was overwhelmed by Stanford, 67–27. The night belonged to Stanford's Hank Luisetti when he scored twenty-six points on thirteen field goals. And he only played for half of the game!

Three nights later John Carroll University beat Western Reserve, 29–22, but it was reported that "Doc Kelker registered the first three points for Reserve on a free throw and a field goal." Kelker finished as the team's high scorer with nine points.

On January 10 Kelker again grabbed the headlines in the *Cleveland Plain Dealer*:

KELKER CAGES 17 POINTS TO LEAD AMAZING CATS

Western Reserve beat CCNY, 38–34, in overtime before thirty-two hundred fans. And "Frank 'Doc' Kelker sent the battle into overtime when he potted one from under the hoop with only seconds to tie the score at 32–all."

On January 16 Kelker's heroics continued:

KELKER'S SHOT WITH MINUTE AND HALF TO GO
CLINCHES RED CAT VICTORY

Western Reserve beat Baldwin Wallace, 39–38. Kelker scored nineteen points to finish as the game's high scorer.

On January 16 Western Reserve lost to Syracuse, 35–21. There were few plaudits for Reserve because "only the fine all-around performance of Frank 'Doc' Kelker kept the Red Cats in the game." Kelker led his team in scoring with twelve points.

Western Reserve finished the 1936–1937 basketball season with a record of eleven wins and nine losses. Then the six-foot one-inch, one hundred ninety-five-pound Kelker turned to football.

The next basketball season, Kelker took up where he had left off. Western Reserve had a twelve-win three-loss season for the 1937–1938 campaign. Playing right guard on January 5, 1938, Kelker pumped in seventeen points as he led his teammates to a 66–32 victory over Fenn College. Two nights later, playing left guard, Kelker scored fourteen points to lead all players as Reserve beat Baldwin-Wallace, 40–32.

On January 14, 1938, Kelker again made the headlines of the *Cleveland Plain Dealer*:

RESERVE WHALES CINCINNATI, 35–18—KELKER
SINKS 16 POINTS TO PACE TRIUMPH

Bullseye shooting of Doc Kelker, ace Western Reserve guard, put the game on ice. He led all scoring. . . .

In a game the next night, the *Cleveland Plain Dealer* headlined:

KELKER'S 13 HELP CONQUER DAYTON

Reserve had defeated the University of Dayton, 42–33.

On February 5, 1938, Western Reserve beat Wesleyan, 67–36. Blair, for Western Reserve, scored eleven goals for twenty points. But "the Reserve followers cheered loudly when it became known that Frank 'Doc' Kelker, who scored twelve points, had established a new record for the University."

The old mark of 435 points set by George Berwald in three seasons was erased by Kelker in two seasons; his total was 443 points.

On February 22, Western Reserve beat Baldwin-Wallace, 50–39. Kelker had eleven points—and an incentive. He had been elected team captain on February 21.

Finally, sportswriter Alex Zien of the *Cleveland Plain Dealer*, on March 5 paid Kelker a tribute for his fine play in the last game of the season—and Kelker's last basketball game as a collegian:

RESERVE DEFEATS CASE CAGE TEAM—TRIUMPHS, 44 TO 36, TO RUIN RIDER'S BID FOR SECOND TITLE; KELKER TALLIES 19 POINTS

One of the greatest all-around athletes in Cleveland collegiate history, Frank "Doc" Kelker, climaxed his brilliant career before 4,500 spectators at the Arena last night. Kelker, celebrating his election to Phi Beta Kappa, national honorary scholarship society, peppered the hoop for nineteen points and played a stellar floor game to give the Red Cats a 44 to 36 victory over Case and at least a tie for the Big Four championship.

Later in the season, the scholar-athlete was selected to the All-Ohio basketball team by the Associated Press.

There had been many great athletes who had performed on white college teams, and most of them were true talents who participated in more than a single sport. Then came the most versatile black athlete (or athlete of any color for that matter) of them all—surely the greatest since the incomparable Indian Jim Thorpe—John Roosevelt "Jackie" Robinson.

Jackie Robinson's baseball career has been well chronicled. Base-

Jackie Robinson shown on the 1939–1940 UCLA basketball team. He won Pacific Southern Division scoring title with a 12.3 average. In twelve conference games he scored 148 points. He repeated in the 1940–1941 season as scoring leader with 133 points in conference games, an 11.1 per game conference scoring average, low by today's standards, but high for the era.

ball, however, was just one of the sports he played. The grandson of a Georgia slave, Robinson was the youngest of three boys and a girl in a fatherless Cario, Georgia, home. His mother, Mallie Robinson, somehow kept the family together after Jackie's father deserted the family when Jackie was six months old. By the time Jackie was one year old, Matthew, Edgar, Willie Mae, and Frank, along with Jackie, had been bundled up and moved to Pasadena, California.

It was in California that the country heard about the ebony-skinned youth starring in baseball, basketball, football, and track at Pasadena Junior College. Robinson would later try tennis, golf, and any other sports that were open to him.

In 1939 Robinson went to UCLA on a scholarship and played varsity basketball. That season the Bruins finished last in the ten-team Southern Division of the Pacific Coast Conference. Overall their season's record was eight wins and seventeen losses. On January 6, 1940, in UCLA's 40–36 loss to Loyola, Jackie had ten points to tie his teammate, Shumes, for scoring honors.

On January 12 the *Los Angeles Times* spotlighted his performance:

ROBINSON SCORES 25 POINTS BUT STANFORD WINS, 53–38

It was UCLA's 28th consecutive conference loss, a streak that was to continue. The *Los Angeles Times* of February 2 reported:

BRUINS UPSET STANFORD FIVE—WESTWOOD TRIUMPHS IN
OVERTIME FRAY AS ROBINSON LEADS

The Bruins upset Stanford, 42–37, as Robinson led all scorers with fourteen points.

On February 24 the Bruins won their third Southern Division Conference game for their coach, Wilbur Johns. They defeated California, 35–33. The *Los Angeles Times* was there:

UCLA's triumph was achieved chiefly through the brilliance of its ace forward, Jackie Robinson, who walked off with scoring honors by pelting the netting with 18 points. And it was Jackie's final field goal that put the Bruins ahead to stay, 34–33.

In the last game of the season on March 2, Robinson won the Southern Division's scoring title by getting seven points in his team's 47–35 loss to USC. His rival for the title was the opposing forward, Ralph Vaughn, who had four points and finished with 138 points in twelve conference games, an 11.5 average. Robinson finished with 148 points in twelve conference games, a 12.3 average.

Ralph Vaughn was a first team all-conference selection, and first team All-American. Robinson was a second team all-conference selection. But sportswriter Dick Hyland on March 2, in the *Los Angeles Times*, gave an expert's opinion of Jackie's talent:

. . . Nibs Price, who is more on the smart side than most when it comes to things basketball, comes out wham-bang with the statement that Jackie Robinson is the best basketball player in the United States. I don't know whether that is so, but I do know that he is the best I've seen perform. On performance around here Jackie Robinson has looked the best. He has a natural, instinctive quickness, straight-away speed, body control and judgement of distance that is so outstanding it is difficult to describe. He is in a class by himself.

The 1940–1941 season rolled around. A sound Robinson reported having escaped unscathed from the football wars. The Bruins were as hapless as ever. Jackie's play continued to be outstanding. He again won the Southern Division scoring title with 133 points and an 11.1 per conference game average. The Bruins overall season's record was six wins and twenty defeats. They had a two-win, ten-loss conference record.

Again Robinson was involved in a close race for the scoring title. This time Stanford's Don Burness was close on Jackie's heels. The *Los Angeles Times* on March 2, 1941, covered Jackie's last game. The Bruins were beaten by the USC Trojans, 52–37:

TROJANS BEAT BRUINS AGAIN; ROBINSON SNARES SCORING TITLE—
JACKIE TOTALS 133 FOR YEAR

The main interest of the occasion was whether or not the Westwood forward, Jackie Robinson, would be able to capture the individual scoring title of the Southern Division of the conference for the second straight year. He did it. The game at the Shrine Auditorium was Robinson's last for the Bruins and he played the second half with a sprained ankle.

Sprained ankle and all, Jackie Robinson had eleven points to tie for game scoring honors. His 133 points were based on conference games.

Don Burness finished the season with 123 points in conference games.

John Roosevelt "Jackie" Robinson symbolized the complete emergence of the black basketball player. As the 1940s approached and unfurled, the black basketball player became less of a novelty on white college teams. He was no longer the lone black on a white team. His number grew as the years passed, until the complete revolution— five black starters on a white college basketball team and finally five black basketball players picked for the All-American basketball teams.

The black basketball player, however, was in a netherworld that was seldom visited by sports fans. The most revered names of black college basketball heroes were virtually unknown to the public. Lanky Jones, George Gilmore, Ed Gray, and Harry "Wu Fang" Ward were names that would draw only a puzzled look from many.

But these black athletes and their black teams were the roots from which today's superstars would spring.

4

Outstanding Black Basketball Players on College Teams

On a Saturday night, December 29, 1934, Edward "Ned" Simmons Irish, dubbed the "boy promoter," introduced the college basketball doubleheader to Madison Square Garden. He was twenty-three.

A crowd of 16,138 (3,000 were turned away) saw the matching of St. Johns and Westminster, and NYU and Notre Dame. They were the first on a schedule that would include six more doubleheaders.

At 8:15 P.M., an unbeaten St. Johns faced Westminster, the Tri-State Conference champions of 1933–1934. Westminster won, 37–33.

In the second part of the doubleheader, undefeated NYU, with nineteen straight wins over a two-year span, faced a perennial Middle West power, Notre Dame. NYU won, 25–18.

In the first four years, Ned Irish, who had been a New York sportswriter, drew 564,000 fans to see his college doubleheaders at the Garden. He was so successful that Mike Jacobs, Madison Square Garden's rival at the Hippodrome, also started promoting college basketball games.

Did this sudden prosperity also extend to black college basketball? Generally it did not, at least not while the playing facilities at many black colleges were still substandard. A decade earlier there had been intense rivalries between such black colleges as Loendi, Monticello, the Alphas, St. Christophers, the Incorporators, and others, but now most of the YMCA and club teams had fallen from power. Few, if any, of the black colleges could draw three or five thousand, as the bitterly contested series between Howard University and the Loendi Big Five had once been able to do. Pittsburgh's Labor Temple and New York's Manhattan Casino had been two arenas that swayed with the overflowing crowds in that era which was fondly being recalled as the "good old days."

On occasion a black athlete could be seen on a white basketball team, but all-white teams constituted what was known as big-time college basketball. Some of the white conferences, and not just those in the South, had barred Negro basketball players. The *Afro-American* of January 27, 1934, reported:

U. OF MICHIGAN LIFTS BIG TEN BASKETBALL BAR

An alleged "agreement" between Big Ten coaches to keep colored players off basketball teams in the conference was broken this week when Coach F. C. Cappon of the University of Michigan was forced to place Franklin Lett, star athlete, back on the Freshman squad. Lett was removed from the team some two weeks ago and told that a "gentleman's agreement" between coaches automatically barred him from practice.

Lett had been an all-state center on his Battle Creek, Michigan, high school team and an all-state end on the football team.

Coach Cappon of Michigan told the *Pittsburgh Courier* on January 13, 1934:

There has never been a colored boy to play basketball in the Big Ten. It has been a mutual agreement between the coaches not to use a colored boy in basketball. There is no rule in the Big Ten in writing that says a boy cannot play basketball because of his color, but just this unwritten agreement of the coaches, to keep them out. No other Big Ten school has used a colored boy, and I do not want to break the ice. That would put me on the spot so to speak.

Another black high school "phenom," John Watts had starred for

Beloit High School in Wisconsin. He had led his team to two state basketball titles and had been chosen as an all-state forward.

In February 1933 Dr. Walter E. Meanwell, coach of the University of Wisconsin's basketball team, saw Watts play in one of his high school games. Meanwell was very impressed; he called Watts the "finest prospect the State has ever turned out."

In ten games the high school junior had set an all-time scoring record for the Big Eight Conference. He scored ninety-seven points on thirty-eight field goals and twenty-one foul goals. The old record was broken by four points, which had been set in twelve games.

The *Chicago Defender*'s Dave White asked the youngster if he was going to attend the University of Wisconsin. Watts said it would be useless even to apply as everyone knew that the Big Ten did not play colored basketball players. However, it was now thought that since Meanwell's public statements regarding Watts's prospects were so favorable, a breakthrough might be near.

Walter Meanwell had arrived at Wisconsin in 1912. He promptly led the Badgers to their first Big Ten title. The University of Missouri sought out Meanwell's services. In 1917 he went to the University of Missouri and won the Missouri Valley Conference title twice for the Tigers. After the First World War, where he served in the medical corps as a doctor with the rank of captain, Meanwell returned to Wisconsin.

When reporters sought out Meanwell, he said: "So far as I know there is no unwritten rule and you can say for me that Watts will be given every consideration if he comes here. There is no reason why a colored boy should not play basketball. They compete in football, and track and basketball is no different. Any boy will get a fair chance to make my team, regardless of color. Watts is a fine prospect and I'd like to see him enter Wisconsin."

The National Association for the Advancement of Colored People had by now filled the air with angry protests over Cappon's remarks. The young assistant secretary of the NAACP, Roy Wilkins, wrote a letter to Coach Cappon. He said in part that the coach's remarks were an "insult to young Lett personally and to the race of which he happens to be a member."

Receiving no response, the NAACP official demanded a statement from the president of the University of Michigan, Alexander Ruthven. None was forthcoming. Ruthven was on an expedition in Egypt.

Meanwhile, Watts did not enter the University of Wisconsin.

The Big Ten's gate receipts were not affected. Basketball was growing in popularity each year. The Western Conference (the Big Ten) drew nearly a million fans during the 1936–1937 season. Notre Dame drew one hundred forty-five thousand fans who paid between $1 and $3.30 to see them play in twenty-three games in the 1936–1937 basketball season.

James Meelix was an all-state forward for his Columbus, Ohio, high school basketball team. But Macea Hill did not hold out any hope for him in the state's colleges and said so in the *Pittsburgh Courier* of January 25, 1934: "Ever since there has been an Ohio State University there has never been a Negro to get further on the freshman squad than the door."

Increasingly, it was not only the black newspapers and periodicals that noticed that big-time basketball was nearly all white. Curt Riess, in an article in *Esquire* magazine in September 1941 called national attention to the situation:

A sport in which the Negro undeniably excels is basketball. Although the sport is continued mainly in high schools and colleges, he rarely has a chance to play except in the colored colleges. The courts of the Big Ten are closed to him, in spite of the fact that there have been such great colored basketball stars as Sidat-Singh, George Gregory and William King.

The popular press, of course, did not follow the basketball doings of the "colored colleges." The only black basketball players worthy of mention—as far as Riess's thesis went—were the ones who had performed on white college teams. But there were many outstanding black college basketball teams, and some outstanding black athletes · on these squads. This in itself was remarkable in that many of the black colleges lacked a gymnasium, and teams very often had to go miles to find a place to practice.

Morgan College of Baltimore was one of the truly outstanding basketball teams during a ten-year dynasty from about 1923 until 1933.

Morgan reached its peak in the 1932–1933 basketball season, when it repeated as champion of the CIAA.

In February 1933 Morgan ran roughshod over Howard, 61–27.

In January 1933, Paul Quinn College beat Wiley College, 29–23, which was the first defeat suffered by the Texas champions in two years. But Morgan College had consistently vied for national honors. And in the days of low-scoring games, a ten-point night was a hot shooting spree. The *Chicago Defender* of February 24, 1934, reported:

TROUPE ON WILD SCORING SPREE: GETS 12 POINTS

Morgan beat Lincoln, 29–23.

In January 1934 Howard defeated Morgan, 26–24. It was the first time since the 1931–1932 season that Morgan had been beaten by a CIAA team. In that season Morgan had lost to Howard, 34–29, and to Virginia State College, 28–25.

Morgan's defeat by Howard in 1934 was its first home loss to a

The 1933–1934 Championship Howard University basketball team. Left to right, seated: William Wynne, Joseph Ware, Frank Pinn, James Mc-Carther, and Thomas Reid. Middle row, left to right: James Bayton, Laynard Hollomon, Lee Bridges, Emerson Parker, Charles Wesley, Thomas Walker, Chappelle Cochrane, and Thomas Bland. Left to right, back row: Granville Warner (Manager), "Happy" Johnson (Trainer), John Burr (Head Coach), and Sallie Hall (Assistant Coach).

college team in seven years. Later, in February, Hampton Institute defeated Morgan, 29–15. This was Morgan's first loss to Hampton since the series began in 1925.

In the 1933–1934 season, Howard University won the CIAA title and repeated the next year. Runners-up in the 1933–1934 season were Morgan; Greensboro Agricultural and Technical College (N.C.); Bluefield State College; Lincoln University (Mo.); Johnson C. Smith; Hampton Institute; Virginia Union College; Virginia State College; St. Paul's College; Shaw University; and St. Augustine's College.

A harbinger that Morgan's glory days were past perhaps arrived during a game on Friday, March 23, 1934, against former Morgan stars who were playing on a team called the Druid Hill Avenue Y. The lineups follow:

DRUID HILL AVENUE Y (41)	G	F	TP	MORGAN COLLEGE (27)	G	F	TP
Wyatt, RF	7	2	16	Gibson, RF	2	0	4
Allor, RF	1	0	2	Conrad, LF	4	1	9
Clark, LF	2	0	4	Simpson, LF	0	0	0
Tucker, LF	1	0	2	Mosby, C	0	1	1
Wood, C	0	0	0	Wilson, LG	1	0	2
E. Jones, C	5	1	11	Troupe, RG	3	5	11
B. Jones, LG	1	3	5				
Brown, RG	1	1	1				

The Druid Hill bunch included some of Morgan College's great players. There were Edward "Lanky" Jones, who practically invented the pivot play in the 1920s, Pinky Clarke, Cutie Brown, Babe Jones, and the rest—immortals all. They had reached back in time and fashioned a tremendous game, and they gave the present quintet a glimpse of how it had been at the old Morgan.

But the likes of Otis Troupe, Skippy Gibson, Tom "Big Tank" Conrad, and Howard "Brutus" Wilson also were stars that had reached to the sky many a night for Morgan and grabbed a handful of nuggets. The brilliant past was present when they beat Morgan College, 41–27.

Black colleges were striving to even up competition, and varsity eligibility standards were announced. On January 19, 1933, the South Atlantic Conference had met in Columbia, South Carolina, and instituted code changes that required all students competing in varsity sports to have at least fifteen units of high school work and to be in regular enrollment in a course leading to a bachelor's degree.

On March 8, 1934, the Southeastern Intercollegiate Athletic Conference was formed. Charter members were Allen University, Benedict College, Georgia State College, Morris College, and Paine College.

But it was the 1930s, and a black family had priorities other than the price of a basketball ticket. The *Chicago Defender* of January 14, 1933, reported:

BASKETBALL RETURNS TO THE FRONT LINE TRENCHES;
MANY EMPTY SEATS GREET SPORT

Competition continued nevertheless. Wiley College was a Texas power. Morris Brown College compiled a thirty-three-game winning streak by late January 1933, when it defeated Clark College, 34–18, and had not lost a game to a college team since January 1931. The black colleges were still regularly playing pro, semipro, and other noncollegiate teams.

In March 1934 the Savoy Big Five of Chicago defeated Morris College, 46–38.

Why would a pro team play a college team? Expediency. There were no black professional basketball leagues, and the schedule was made up with any team available and able to draw a decent gate.

In the 1934–1935 season twelve black colleges played in a tournament in which Alabama State Teachers College emerged as the winner, thereby winning the Southern Intercollegiate Athletic Conference title. The complete results of the two-day tournament follow:

Fisk University, 47—Florida Agricultural and Mechanical College, 31
Talladega College, 45—South Carolina State College, 28

Morehouse College, 36—Knoxville College, 34
Lemoyne College, 46—Tuskegee Institute, 37
Xavier University, 44—Morris Brown College, 37
Alabama State Teachers College, 44—Clark College, 24
Morehouse College, 22—Talladega College, 19
Lemoyne College, 38—Fisk University, 21
Lemoyne College, 31—Xavier University, 29
Alabama State Teachers College, 36—Morehouse College, 25
Xavier University, 35—Morehouse College, 15 (consolation game)
Alabama State Teachers College, 35—Lemoyne College, 28 (finals)

Coach John Burr's Howard University Bisons were at their peak in the strong CIAA conference with lettermen William E. "Willie" Wynne, James A. Bayton, Arthur M. Carter, James M. McCarther, Frank S. Pinn (captain), Thomas E. Reid, Joseph L. Ware, Thomas Walker, and Granville W. Warner (team manager).

Morgan College, which had been at the heights that Howard looked down from, was suspended by the CIAA in December 1935.

An anonymous charge was filed with the CIAA eligibility committee that William "Wildman" Simpson, star halfback and forward on the basketball team, had withdrawn from college and returned in the fall for varsity competition.

Morgan College was reinstated in February 1936 and thought that the suspension was unjustified. The college officials declared that Simpson was "technically academically eligible" because he had made up the school work that he had missed, and the professors so testified. But any championship hopes that Morgan might have had were dashed because it had missed too many CIAA games.

Meanwhile Hampton Institute had formed a strong team. On Saturday night, February 15, 1936, Hampton beat Howard, 59–46. It was the first time in two years that Howard had been beaten on its own court.

After two seasons as titleholders, Howard was dethroned in its third bid for the CIAA crown by Hampton Institute in the 1935–1936 basketball season.

In the 1936–1937 season, Greensboro A & T College defeated

Morgan College, 37–26, and won its first CIAA title. A & T was led by its captain, Bill McClain with James Neely, Edison Conway, James Riddick, Sanford Roan, James Mitchell, Allen Lynch, Maceo Glenn, Doromus Snuggs, Samuel Hodges, Arthur Coles, Ralph Wooden, and Coach Harry K. Parker.

In the 1936–1937 basketball season, Wiley College won the southeastern tournament and thereby the SIAC title. The results follow:

Langston University, 42—Bishop College, 31
Arkansas Baptist College, 46—South Carolina State College, 31
Wiley College, 48—Prairie View A & M College, 21
Langston University, 39—Texas College, 23
Southern University, 34—Prairie View A & M College, 31
Arkansas Baptist College, 31—Wiley College, 22
Bishop College, 53—Texas College, 28
Wiley College, 44—Southern University, 30
Langston University, 30—Arkansas Baptist College, 25
Wiley College, 33—Bishop College, 19
Wiley College, 33—Arkansas Baptist College, 25
Wiley College, 44—Langston University, 31

Wiley won five of six games to win the crown, and Oklahoma's Langston University won three of four games to finish in the runner-up position.

Wiley was led by its captain, "Stretch" Byrd, with "Crab" Neely, John Aikens, Bill Spiller, Chuck Johnson, Fess Widemon, and Coach F. T. Long.

In the 1937–1938 season, Coach Henry Huckles of Virginia Union College rounded up some top-flight athletes: "Pickles" Frazier, Wylie "Soupy" Campbell, Obie Knighton, Kavanzo Hyde, Wendell Williams, Artie Storres, Alvin Storres, Norman Hines, Howard Jones, Lewis White, Floyd Atkins, Vincent Tinsley, and Mel Glover.

In the 1937–1938 season, Morgan College and Virginia State College finished in a deadlock for the CIAA title. They won the same number of games, but despite being in the same conference, did not play each other during the season.

Howard University won fourteen and lost seven. Willie Wynne, their star player, led the team with 214 points on ninety field goals and thirty-four foul goals.

In the 1938–1939 season, Virginia Union College captured its first CIAA title, and led by its great player, Wylie "Soupy" Campbell, it was also victorious in the 1939–1940 season.

Sportswriters were now calling the Virginia Union Panthers the "dream team," and ranking them with the all-time great teams of the past.

Their foremost player and captain, Soupy Campbell, had been signed by chance. The black trainer for Duquesne University had traveled with his team to Richmond where the white team was going to play another white college. Since he could not stay with his athletes, the trainer stayed with a black family, that of Coach Huckles. During his visit with Huckles, the trainer continually raved about a sensational all-state selection from Rankin, Pennsylvania. Huckles was impressed, and Campbell turned up at Virginia on a scholarship in 1937. Now the drums started beating for a "dream game" involving the dream team and the best all-star players in the CIAA.

Finally, after the 1939–1940 season, the game was arranged. The *Afro-American* of March 16, 1940, reported:

UNION TOPS ALL-CIAA IN FIRST ANNUAL GAME

A college team winning against the best players of the other teams in the conference was an amazing feat. Union was truly a dream team as it beat the All-CIAA team, 54–51. The lineups follow:

ALL-CIAA (51)

	G	F	TP
Percy (Eagle-Eye) Smith, F—Virginia State	7	0	14
Billy Giles, F—Howard University	0	0	0
Deuce Gibson, F—Morgan College	2	0	4
Shrimp Johnson, F—J.C. Smith University	0	1	1
Jim Parker, C—Howard University	5	2	12
Ernie Young, C—Lincoln University	3	1	7

	G	F	TP
Perry Honey, Lincoln University	2	0	4
Al Waters, St. Paul College	0	0	0
Willie Hurst, Virginia State	4	1	9
Sanford Roan, Greenboro, A & T College	0	0	0

VIRGINIA UNION (54)

	G	F	TP
Campbell, F	5	1	11
Hyde, F	3	1	11
Atkins, F	0	0	0
Knighton, F	3	0	6
Daughtry, C	1	0	2
Glover, G	3	3	9
Kennedy, G	0	0	0
Frazier, G	8	6	19
Burton, G	0	0	0
Hayes, G	0	0	0

Meanwhile, elsewhere in black basketball during the 1939–1940 season, Clark College was champion of the Southern Intercollegiate Athletic Conference; Alcorn College was champion of the South-Central Athletic Conference; Bordentown was champion of the Middle Atlantic Association of Junior Colleges and Normal Schools (MAAA); West Virginia was champion of the Mid-Western Athletic Association; and Miners Teachers College won the Eastern Intercollegiate Athletic Conference title.

But the major activity in black colleges still centered around the CIAA.

After Virginia Union's victory against the all-stars, sportswriters started to agitate for a match involving Union and a white college basketball team. Finally a game was scheduled against Brooklyn College. On December 27, 1940, the sports banners of the *Afro-American* trumpeted:

UNION FIVE CONQUERS BROOKLYN COLLEGE CAGERS
PANTHERS TRIUMPH BEFORE 3,500 FANS
GLOVER AND CAMPBELL LEAD CIAA CHAMPIONS

The Virginia Union team had maintained its magic and the dream team won rather easily, 54–38. The lineups follow:

VIRGINIA UNION (54)	G	F	TP	BROOKLYN COLLEGE (38)	G	F	TP
Campbell, F	8	0	16	Harwitz, F	2	0	4
Knighton, F	1	2	4	Kasner, F	6	2	14
Atkins, F	0	0	0	Kapust, F	0	1	1
Davis, C	2	0	4	Gussolff, F	1	0	2
Blair, C	2	2	6	Pauker, C	2	0	4
Glover, G	4	5	13	Hirsch, C	1	0	2
Daughtry, G	3	2	8	Accardi, G	0	0	0
Hyde, G	0	0	0	Landesman, G	0	0	0
Culberson, G	1	1	3	Lubin, G	3	0	6
Burton, G	0	0	0	Firkser, G	2	1	5

The Brooklyn College coach, Artie Musicant, said, "They moved like lightning and acted like they knew what was going on at all times. They were in wonderful shape and played like champions."

Back in conference play the next season, the champions were dethroned after a two-year reign. The *Afro-American* of March 8, 1941, noted:

N.C. STATE WINS CIAA TITLE WITH UNDEFEATED RECORD

The North Carolina State Eagles from Durham finished with a 14–0, won-lost record. Virginia Union had a single loss to Virginia State.

The Eagles lost to Southern University of Scotland, Louisiana, on March 22, 1941, 48–42, in a postseason tournament. The First Annual National Invitational Intercollegiate Basketball tournament was held in Cincinnati, Ohio. Arranged and staged by private promoters, it was a financial flop, albeit an artistic success. Six teams were entered: Southern University, West Virginia State, Clark College, North Carolina State, Kentucky State, and Greensboro A & T College. The tournament fell far short of the black college's answer to the white-run National Invitational Tournament, held annually since the 1937–1938 season in Madison Square Garden.

The success was only on the playing floor. North Carolina State's six-foot six-inch Harold Colbert and six-foot eleven-inch Norbert Downing were impressive. Southern University's Everett Taylor was the tournament's outstanding player and its highest scorer. In the four games Southern played, he totaled eighty-one points.

Many sportswriters voted the mythical national title to Southern for the 1940–1941 season. Among other titleholders that season were: North Carolina State (CIAA); Xavier University, in New Orleans (SIAC); Bishop College in Marshall, Texas (SWAC); Tougaloo College (SCAC); and West Virginia State (Mid-Western).

Brooklyn College, which had played the 1939–1940 CIAA champions, now scheduled a game with the 1940–1941 CIAA winner.

The Eagles were not as strong as in 1941. Coach John McLendon had lost Colbert to the armed service, and Downing had graduated. But they were strong enough. The *Afro-American* of February 7, 1942, reported:

N.C. STATE BEATS BROOKLYN 37–34—EAGLES LEAD WHITE
FIVE ALL THE WAY

Convinced that the stronger black college basketball teams could hold their own with the white college teams, sportswriters on many of the black newspapers campaigned to get an NIT invitation for one of the colored teams.

They wrote reams, but all their ink fell on blind eyes. Ned Irish's invitations to the 1941–1942 NIT went to LIU, with a 25–4 won-lost record; Rhode Island State, 18–4 record; Toledo University, 23–5 record; West Kentucky State, 29–5 record; West Texas State, 28–3 record; West Virginia, 19–4 record; and Creighton University, 19–5 record.

Big-time basketball had another virtually lily-white tournament. Toledo had two black players, Dave Minor and Emlen Tunnell.

On March 26, 1942, *The New York Times* gave the result:

WEST VIRGINIA HALTS WESTERN KENTUCKY IN NATIONAL
INVITATION BASKETBALL FINAL

The crowd was 18,251, the score 47–45. Creighton won the consolation game by beating Toledo, 48–46.

It was no secret that the writers were itching for Virginia Union to be invited to the NIT. Under Coach Henry C. Huckles, who had been at Virginia Union since 1926 and had formed another outstanding team, the Panthers had a record as good as, or better than, any of the teams invited to the NIT, with a 21–2 won-lost record, losing to North Carolina State and Kentucky State. They had avenged both these losses by beating North Carolina once and Kentucky three out of four times.

Virginia Union used Richmond's recreation center to practice, amassing its amazing record without a college gymnasium.

In the 1941–1942 season Langston University won the Southwestern basketball championship with the following players: Tom Smith, Lawrence Cudjoe, John Smith (captain), Lance Cudjoe, Roger Pierce, Clyde Terrill, Thomas Edwards, Elliot Reed, Frank Luster, Lester Lolliss, and Coach C. F ."Zip" Gayles. The conference standing was:

	Won	Lost
Langston University	10	2
Bishop College	9	3
Wiley College	8	4
Southern University	8	4

In the 1942–1943 season Southern University won the Southwestern basketball title. The players were Thaddeus Gordon, Arthur Wilson, Benjamin Bluett, Albert Ford, Mac Charles Byrom (captain), William Yancey, Roscoe Moore, Kenneth Watkins, Alvin Owens, Marshall Keys, and A. W. Mumford (coach).

Kentucky State College finished first in the Mid-Western Athletic Conference with a 4–0 won-lost record. Runners-up were Lincoln University (Mo.); Wilberforce; Tennessee State; and Philander Smith College.

Coach A. S. "Jake" Gaither had returned a winner at Florida A & M College in the 1941–1942 season. The *Journal & Guide* of March 7, 1942, noted:

FLORIDA SHADES TUSKEGEE TO WIN SIAC TITLE

Florida beat Tuskegee, 53–52, and South Carolina State College beat Knoxville College for third place. The tournament to decide the SIAC championship was held at Tuskegee.

In 1942–1943 the Virginia Union College Panthers won another CIAA title. Or had they? In conference play Union's record was 8–3 won-lost, for a .727 percentage. North Carolina State College had a 9–3 won-lost conference record, for a .750 percentage.

The CIAA used a complex standard for picking and deciding champions, the Dickinson Rating System. It took into account the caliber of the teams that wins were scored over, as well as the number of wins and losses. Teams were separated into "first" and "second" divisions. Thus victories over first division teams gained more percentage points than wins over second division teams.

The final standings released by the CIAA follow:

	Won	Lost	Dickinson Scoring
Virginia Union College	8	3	22.73
North Carolina State College	9	3	22.22
Johnson C. Smith University	7	4	20.00
Hampton Institute	6	3	19.44
Greensboro A & T College	11	6	19.33
Morgan College	5	3	17.50

The second division colleges were Virginia State College, Howard University, Saint Augustine College, Shaw University, Lincoln University, West Virginia College, and Bluefield State College.

The Panthers were a throwback to the strong Morgan College teams of the 1920s. Virginia Union had won four of the last five CIAA championships.

But it was the war years, and lineups were no longer stable. Young men who had played on the hardwood were now familiarizing themselves with guns and army packs. A new cohesiveness gripped the nation. In the 1940s it was not so much "separate but equal," as "united for victory."

Sonny Jameson, City College of New York. He was one of the first Black co-captains of a major college basketball team. Shown above in the 1940's.

In Los Angeles in the early 1940s a young man was honing the skills that in 1946 would revolutionize baseball and, later, all of sport.

A decade earlier, it was alleged that the Big Ten had a "gentleman's agreement" against playing black basketball players. By the mid 1940s, the barriers were beginning to become invisible. Ed Younger played with LIU. UCLA's six-foot five-and-one-half-inch Don Barksdale was outstanding. Tom Wood and seventeen-year-old Norman Skinner played with Columbia University, Jay Swift with Yale, Sonny Jameson with CCNY. Arthur Wilson became the first black basketball player in Princeton University's history—and the honorary captain of his team. Dick Culberson transferred from Virginia Union College to the University of Iowa. A black basketball player was finally in the Big Ten.

Also in the 1942–1943 season Wayne University had not one but two Negro varsity players: Joe Franklin Holloway, twenty-four years old, and Clifton P. Mobley, twenty-one-year-old transfer student from West Virginia State College.

Military demands were increasing. Four games before the last game of the 1942–1943 season, Morgan College lost six of its players to the army: Oscar Givens (captain), Joe Eggleston, Aubrey Woods, Reginald Ballard, Leon Bressant, and Robert Duncan. Bob Smith was Coach Edward P. Hurt's lone varsity player for the last game of the season, and Johnson C. Smith University defeated a draft-riddled Morgan squad, 41–33.

J. C. Smith too had problems. The Golden Bulls lost Nat Jenkins, Kenny Powell, Laurence Byrd, Ollie Cox, and Eddie Jackson, all of whom graduated.

In the 1942–1943 season South Carolina State College in Orange-burg won its first SIAA title with Ezra Moore, Charles Penn, William "Ducky" Copeland, Luther "Pepsi-Cola" Bligen, Curtis Torrey, Walter "Dynamite" Palmer, Curtis Moreland, Morris Esmond, Henry "Mice" Holden, and Coach Ollie Dawson.

Henry "Mice" Holden, six-foot two-inch junior at the South Carolina college, was one of the great ones. Holden scored the awesome total of fifty points in the 1941–1942 season in a game against Delaware State College and scored a total of 458 points in twenty-five games, both SIAC records.

He broke the record of 336 points in eighteen games set by Horace "Itty" Dalton of Clark College in 1927. He also erased the six-foot three-inch Frank "Blotto" Crozier's 1939 mark of 343 points for Xavier.

Later in the season, Frank "Brooms" Abramovic of Salem University scored fifty-three points to erase Holden's mark. There had been other single-game high scorers.

Howard's Marshall Hill made thirty-five points in 1942. Fisk's William Ridley scored thirty-four points in 1942, and did it twice. The Eagles' Norbert "Slim" Downing earned thirty-four points in 1941 and the Eagles' Harold "Slam" Colbert made thirty-four points in 1940.

On February 20, 1943, Rudolph "Rocky" Roberson outdid them all. He set a new national single-game scoring mark of fifty-eight points against Shaw University. Roberson scored twenty-five field goals and eight free throws. He passed George Glamach's set at the University of North Carolina's forty-seven-point mark and Hank Luisett's fifty-two-point record made at Stanford. He ended the season with 404 points in nineteen games for a 21.79 percentage average per game.

Coach John McLendon, a native Kansan, had known the high-scoring junior when he was a standout at Lincoln High School in Atchison, Kansas. The six-foot one-inch, 189-pounder had competition, however, as the best player in Negro basketball from an SIAC conference player, Xavier's six-foot six-inch Nathaniel "Sweetwater" Clifton, who had a high of 42 points and an average of 21.5 points a game.

North Carolina State, of course, won the game against Shaw University. The score was 92–43.

Some colleges considered curtailing their athletic programs as the war intensified, creating manpower shortages. But CIAA officials reasoned that it would be in the nation's interest to keep sports programs going in order to provide "strong, able-bodied, patriotic, healthy, and intelligent manhood for the service of our country." As the country tightened its belt and girded for war, ten of the fourteen CIAA colleges voted to continue their varsity athletic programs. The athlete that left college for war was in general physically larger than his counterpart in the First World War.

Edward "Lanky" Jones made all-state as an Orange, New Jersey, high school boy in the 1924–1925 season. A freshman at Morgan College in the 1925–1926 season, he was a sensation—and looked down on his teammates from his six-foot two-inch height.

Whether because of nutritional or medical advances, many athletes were getting bigger, faster, stronger—and taller. And they would get even bigger with the postwar baby boom yet to come.

In the 1943–1944 basketball season Coach Edward H. Adams led his Tuskegee Institute team to the Southern Conference championship by winning twenty-one of twenty-two regular season games, with Calvin Jones, William Dennison, Pernell Miller, William Bethel, Andrew McBride, John T. Parker, Alvin Taber, Wilbur George, Charles Perry, Charles Smith, Albert Crawford, and Thomas Hornburger, who was the Southern Conference's leading scorer.

In the 1944–1945 basketball season, Bishop College won the Prairie View Invitational Tournament early in the season. With two losses eliminating a team, Bishop College swept four games. Southern and Wiley were runners-up.

But later in the season, the *Chicago Defender* announced:

LANGSTON WINS SOUTHWESTERN CAGE TOURNEY FOR
SECOND STRAIGHT YEAR

Langston University in Oklahoma beat Southern University 39–20 in the finals. The complete tournament results follow:

Langston University, 66—Arkansas State College, 31
Langston University, 70—Prairie View College, 50
Langston University, 55—Southern University, 27
Southern University, 38—Wiley College, 37
Wiley College, 62—Texas College, 36
Bishop College, 56—Wiley College, 53
Southern University, 55—Samuel Houston College, 21
Prairie View College, 41—Texas College, 37
Wiley College, 53—Samuel Houston College, 45
Texas College, 44—Arkansas State College, 29
Southern University, 62—Bishop College, 54
Texas College, 61—Bishop College, 45
Wiley College, 39—Texas College, 30

During the tournament, Langston had a forty-six-game consecutive winning streak. The four tournament victories pushed the total to fifty straight. In the 1943–1944 season, Lincoln University rebounded from a bad season to finish undefeated—and win the CIAA title. Coach Manuel Rivera had the following players: John Armstead, W. Smith, William Hall, W. Hoffler, Leon Hainey, Hugh Johnson, Raymond Gray, Charles Chamberlain, Clarence Hawkins, C. Johnson, Cornelius Jenkins, Rudd Johnson, and Herman White. The team was led by Captain Rudy Johnson, forward, from Baltimore's Douglas High School, and Leon Hainey, from West Philadelphia. The last game was played at New York's Manhattan Casino before about three thousand excited fans.

However, such trips were not frequent in these war-weary years because of travel restrictions. For the first time in memory, the major-league baseball teams would not be going to Florida, Arizona, and other warm climes to train.

The Brooklyn Dodgers were training at Bear Mountain, New York, in April 1945. And it was by this fortuitous circumstance that an encounter with the rigid patterns of southern customs could be avoided. A decision was made to test a plan of action.

Joe Bostic, sports editor on the *People's Voice,* barged into the Dodgers training camp unannounced. He had David "Showboat" Thomas, a thirty-four-year-old Negro first baseman for the New York Cubans, and Terrace McDuffle, a thirty-two-year-old left-handed pitcher for the Newark Eagles, in tow. The small group was accompanied by a photographer to record the historic event. Bostic demanded that the two players be given a workout and possible contracts to play in the white major leagues.

The sports revolution began at Bear Mountain that April day in 1945. Later in the month, shortstop Jackie Robinson, pitcher Marvin Williams, and outfielder Sam Jethroe, also worked out before the Boston Red Sox hierarchy.

Bostic of course knew that on March 5, 1945, the New York State Senate had given final approval of the Ives-Quinn Bill by a 49–6 vote and the Assembly had concurred by a vote of 109–32. All that remained was Governor Thomas Dewey's signature before it would be effective on July 1, 1945. The Fair Employment Practice Commission was the outgrowth of the Ives-Quinn Bill.

The Negro amateur athlete had already come a long way, and now the path was being laboriously paved for him to earn a living as a professional—if he possessed the ability—and this would include all sports, be it baseball, basketball, boxing, or football.

That white and black athletes could play together was little doubted. In the 1942–1943 basketball season, the Chicago Studebaker Aviation plant entered a team, drawn from its own ranks, in the professional league. The ten-man squad was fully integrated and included the following black players: Hillery Brown, Agis Bray, Wyatt "Sonny" Boswell, Bernie Price, Rossy Hudson, Tony Peyton, and Duke Cumberland.

Most of the players were former New York Rens and Globetrotter stars.

On May 8, 1945, the German Army surrendered; Japan surrendered on August 14. The colleges and universities were soon clogged with the returning veterans, as were the sports arenas.

Basketball was now a different game, played by a different athlete than had played before and during the war. The black basketball pioneers had been worthy adversaries in their own right. In 1945 it was just another game and another era. It is doubtful whether the present athlete could have been as skillful at lightning-swift passes, ball control, two-hand set shots, and other aspects of low-scoring as his predecessor, just as it is unlikely that his forerunners could excel in today's run and shoot game. Each athlete's talent seems suited to his particular time. In a center-jump after every basket, the tempo of the games would certainly be different than in a less constrained game.

The saga that has made for the history of the game is comprised of many elements: five-foot nine-inch, one hundred forty pound Cumberland Willis Posey, lightning fast, controlling the ball and the tempo of a game, and being regarded as the "best colored player in America."

An Edward "Sol" Butler, the shortest player on the court, and always the tallest in jumping and getting the ball with a tremendous spring in his legs.

And a John Roosevelt "Jackie" Robinson, pigeon-toed, and quickly mincing-stepping, before making a startling acceleration of speed; two hundred pounds of ebony-streaked controlled agility, perhaps the greatest athlete ever to play in sports.

We have seen a mere glimpse of the black pioneers on the court, but such was their awesome talent and versatility that we will meet them time and time again in other uniforms.

That the Negro athletes played on white college basketball teams, at least as far back as 1904, is recorded fact, but their legacy and roots are bound to the Negro college.

They played in halls, basements, lofts, and also under leaden skies.

They played in far-away gymnasiums, casinos, arenas, and town recreation centers.

They scheduled high schools, semipros, Ys, elks, alumni, and even on occasion, white colleges.

Their schools had nicknames of a bountiful menagerie of golden tigers, golden bulls, rattlers, panthers, bisons, jaguars, bears, wolverines, and lions.

They were named Edwin Bancroft Henderson, Hudson "Huddy" Oliver, Edward Benjamin Gray, Thomas "Big Tank" Conrad, Edward "Lanky" Jones, Harry "Wu Fang" Ward, Wylie "Soupy" Campbell, Henry "Mice" Holden, and Rudolph "Rocky" Roberson.

They rode in streetcars, carriages, trains, buses, and cars. And they passed the mantle to today's William Felton Russell, Wilton Norman Chamberlain, Elgin Baylor, and Kareem Abdul-Jabbar.

They were proud members of a colored college basketball team.

5

Black Stars on White College Football Teams

The first intercollegiate football game was between Princeton University and Rutgers University on November 6, 1869, at New Brunswick, New Jersey. Rutgers won, 6–4. The game was played under soccer rules and had twenty-five men to a side.

It is not known who was the first Negro to play in an intercollegiate game. Among the first, however, were W. T. S. Jackson and William Henry Lewis at Amherst College in 1889, three years before the first Negro intercollegiate football game was played. In 1889 Amherst was a member of the New England Intercollegiate Athletic Association, consisting of Brown, Bowdoin, Dartmouth, and the Massachusetts Institute of Technology.

On Wednesday, October 2, 1889, Amherst dedicated its new twenty-acre Pratt Field and it was decided that the college would organize a football team, joining the company of Dartmouth, Williams, Stevens, and M. I. T. Amherst's new uniforms were described as white sweaters with a large "A" in front, white caps edged with blue, white canvas jackets, and knickerbockers with brown stockings. The athletic association passed a resolution restricting the use of the "A" on jerseys to members of the athletic teams, the idea being that only Amherst's athletes should receive the honor that the letter would connote.

With William Lewis playing "center rush" nearly every game, and

The Amherst College football team of 1889. Left to right, front row (3): G. S. Holden, H. C. Crocker, and W. H. Lewis. Second row, left to right (6): G. S. Raley, W. T. S. Jackson, C. L. Upton, W. H. Smith, G. A. Morse, and F. W. Allen. Back row, left to right (2): M. H. Houghton, and W. M. Weldon.

Jackson playing halfback, Amherst played ten games, finishing with three wins, five losses, and two ties.

In the 1890 season, Lewis played in every game but Jackson saw very little action after the first one. In this game, played on October 4, Amherst defeated Williston, 48–6.

During this season, Amherst played twelve games and won five, lost six, and tied one. This was the year that President Merrill Edwards Gates of Rutgers University announced his resignation on August 29 and accepted the presidency of Amherst College, effective October 1. Dr. Gates, Ph.D., LL.D., L.H.D., who was born in Warsaw, New York, on April 6, 1848, the son of Seth M. Gates, an early antislavery member of Congress, would preside over a college of three hundred fifty students and thirty professors.

Among his students, William Lewis, having played outstandingly in 1889 and 1890, was rewarded for his prowess. *The New York Times of December* 21, 1890, reported:

The election of Lewis, "92," a colored man, to the football captaincy for

George Jewett, half-back, and member of the 1890 University of Michigan football team. (Courtesy of the University of Michigan)

next year does not cause much comment, owing to the democratic spirit of Amherst. Lewis is undoubtedly the best man for the place, having played a very strong game as centre rush the last two years.

Meanwhile another black collegian on a white team, George Jewett, was enjoying a measure of success at the University of Michigan.

On October 18, 1890, before a small crowd reduced by a driving rain, Michigan beat the Detroit Athletic Club, 38–0. The *Detroit Free Press*'s sportswriter dusted off his most sparkling polysyllabic prose for his story:

Eleven altitudinous, broad gauge, enthusiastic gentlemen came from Ann Arbor to Detroit yesterday and demonstrated the value of a collegiate course in the development of football genius.

Jewett was one of the stars as a running back. He was also the punter, and field-goal kicker. This was at a time when a touchdown counted for four points, and a field goal, for two points.

On October 25, the University of Michigan beat Albion College, 16–0. The *Detroit Free Press* noted:

In the second half U. of M's, had the ball. It was passed to Jewett, who ran almost to the twenty-five yard line. Then the U. of M. took it inside.

Sherman was ruled out for slugging.

Mallery advanced to five yards.

Sutherland ruled out for slugging.

Jewett got the ball and ran to the twenty-five yard line. Anderson got the ball by a pass and kicked it outside. Jewett ran well and carried it over the Albion line.

Jewett then kicked a field goal.

This was football in the early days. The "slugging" and rough play in general would have serious effects on the game as the years unfurled and deaths and serious injuries began to mount.

The Indianapolis *Freeman,* a black newspaper, also reported on the feats of George Jewett on November 8, 1890:

George Jewett, the Afro-American "phenomenon" of the University of Michigan football team, played a remarkable game last Saturday week in Detroit, and was very favorably spoken of by the daily press. He is an Ann Arbor boy and won applause by his wonderful runs and tackles.

At MIT W. A. Johnson, a freshman, was winning honors as the first Negro on the college's football team in 1890. Johnson, like Jewett, was in the backfield, at halfback.

Meanwhile, the *Detroit Free Press* reported an injury to Jewett in his next game:

Ann Arbor, November 1—The University football eleven today defeated the eleven of Purdue College by a score of 36 to 6. The game was hotly contested. James E. Duffy, the famous half-back of the team of 88 and 89, played in this game relieving Jewett, who was injured.

Jewett returned to the lineup on November 15, in a loss to Cornell, 10–0. But Jewett had his moments. He got the ball and by clever running crossed the Cornell goal line. The score was disallowed, however, because of an infraction by Michigan. The game, which was played at Detroit's recreation park, was sparked all afternoon by displeasure at the officials' decisions. Finally, tempers that had been smoldering, exploded. The *Detroit Free Press* reported:

Jewett, the colored youth who plays with the U. of M., landed a right handed soaker on the jaw of a Cornell man and was ruled off.

Jewett's season and his collegiate football career ended. The University of Michigan had had a good season, winning four and losing one.

In the 1889 football season, Amherst made 173 points to its opponents' 194, and won three, lost five, and tied two. In 1890 Amherst earned 182 points to its opponents' 209, and won five, lost six, and tied one. The 1891 season was Lewis's and Jackson's last at Amherst. The team scored 318 points against the opponents' 154, with Jackson making nine touchdowns.

In September 1891 twenty-five candidates under the captaincy of William H. Lewis began football practice. The eventual squad that Lewis and Coach Dudley Dean agreed upon were Upton, Raley, Jackson, Griswold, Alexander, Baldwin, Nourse, Talcott, Gould, Hess Hawes, Penney, H. L. Pratt, and, of course, Lewis.

On October 10, 1891, Amherst and Harvard engaged in a contest at Harvard's Jarvis Field, in Cambridge, Massachusetts. Harvard won, 18–0. *The New York Times* of October 11, 1891, reported:

Jackson, a young colored fellow played half-back for Amherst and was by all odds the best man on the field. His tackling was clean and sure; he made some phenomenal runs, and was well guarded by the rest of the team. Lewis, the colored center, also played a phenomenal game.

On October 24, on a bleak and cold afternoon at Jarvis Field, Amherst again went down to defeat before Harvard, this time, 39–0. The *Boston Globe* noted:

Amherst had four halfbacks in the game. Jackson played throughout and always gained until he was sent around the end three times in succession. . . .

On October 31, 1891, before more than six hundred spectators, Amherst got on the winning track, beating MIT 24–14. Amherst's two black players drew plaudits:

Jackson who was substituted for Ewing in the first half . . . played a good game. In the line, Lewis and Baldwin played the best game.

On November 7 Amherst and Dartmouth played to a 14–14 tie. In Dartmouth's lineup was the first of what would turn out to be a long line of fleet-footed Pollards, both black and white.

John W. H. Pollard shared the halfback duties for Dartmouth with Ide, and his brother, Charles W. Pollard, was also on the 1891 Dartmouth team.

Leslie Lawrence Pollard and Frederick Douglass Pollard were black and brothers.

There was no indication that John Pollard balked at playing against Lewis or Jackson in 1891, but in 1907, when he was coach of the University of Alabama's baseball team, he went along with the custom and wishes of his team members.

In Nebraska another black football player surfaced, George A. Flippin. The *Nebraska State Journal* of October 8, 1893, reported:

The game of football is only in its infancy in Nebraska, yet a great deal of interest is manifested in the approaching fall games. So far as the colleges are concerned the state university is probably foremost in football, but she has never shown the skills that Doane has shown. Flippin is said by those who have witnessed his playing to be half of the university team. . . .

On October 21, 1893, the University of Nebraska played Doane College and won, 28–0. Flippin was outstanding:

Nebraska started from the five-yard line and never stopped till they raced to the far end of the field, and Flippin made another touchdown.

On October 28 Nebraska and Baker University battled to a 10–10 tie. Flippin scored a touchdown.

On November 5 the University of Nebraska played the Denver Athletic Club in Denver, Colorado. The ugly specter of vicious slugging reappeared. The *Nebraska State Journal* noted:

NEARLY HAD A RIOT
MORE SLUGGING THAN FOOTBALL IN THE DENVER GAME
THE GAME AWARDED TO NEBRASKA

Ten minutes before the end of the game, with darkness approaching, the Denver Athletic Club walked off the field in protest over an official's ruling. At the time the score stood at 4–4. The game was officially awarded to the University of Nebraska. Twenty-five hundred frenzied fans watched the action, as the DAC, who "have the reputation all over the country as being sluggers," seemed to màintain their reputation:

Flippin went through the center like a cannonball and Denver had a special pick at him. He was kicked, slugged, and jumped on, but never knocked out, and gave as good as he received.

In 1893 the University of Nebraska played six games and won two, lost two, and tied two. In 1892, Flippin's varsity debut, the University of Nebraska had only played two games, losing one and tying one.

Amherst, in 1891, won six, lost four, and tied three. After graduation, W. T. S. Jackson entered the field of education.

The five-foot seven-inch, 180-pound William Henry Lewis headed for the Harvard Law School and a continuation of his football career. The son of Reverend Ashley H. Lewis and Josephine Lewis, he was born in Berkley, Virginia, on November 28, 1868. He attended preparatory school at Virginia Normal and Industrial School, at Petersburg, Virginia. On Saturday, October 1, 1892, he became the first Negro to play in a game on a Harvard varsity football team. Harvard soundly thrashed Dartmouth, 48–0, at Harvard's home grounds, Jarvis Field. Lewis was under intense scrutiny by spectator and media. The *Boston Globe* observed: "Lewis . . . put the ball in play fairly well."

On October 8, before over fifteen hundred spectators, Harvard beat Amherst, 26–0, and on October 15, swept aside Williams College, 55–0.

Then in the Crimson's 45–0 win over the Boston Athletic Association, on October 22, Lewis, who had played regularly, was substituted for by "Brice."

The 1892 Harvard University football team. William Henry Lewis is third from right, with large "H" on sweater.

Amherst returned to Jarvis Field on October 29, and again went down to defeat, 32–10. Harvard's twenty-three-year-old black center was again a regular: "After Amherst made the second touchdown, Macke was taken off the Harvard line and Lewis put in his place." Lewis never saw service on Harvard's bench thereafter.

On November 5, against Cornell, in a game played at Springfield, Massachusetts, Harvard won, 20–14. The first half lasted forty-five minutes, and the second half, twenty minutes.

The big game was next, to be played on November 19 against Harvard's arch rival, Yale. Before some twenty thousand fans at Springfield, Yale defeated Harvard 6–0. The *Boston Globe* devoted nine full columns and a side-bar to this major New England annual event. Mr. Football himself, Walter Camp, was in attendance. Lewis —and Harvard—had a successful season, with an overall record of ten won and one lost. In 1892 William Henry Lewis was selected for Walter Camp's All-American team at "center rush."

Camp had been a great star at Yale in the 1870s. He later coached at Yale in 1878–1879. He then coached at Stanford, 1892–1895, and returned to Yale as advisory coach until 1910. He has been acknowledged as the father of American football.

Camp described the responsibilities of the center rush:

As soon as the ball is fairly held, that is, both player and ball brought to a standstill, the referee blows his whistle and the runner has the ball "down," and someone upon his side, usually the man called the snap-back or centre-rush, must place the ball on the ground at that spot for a "scrimmage," as it is termed. The ball is then put in play again (while the men of each team keep on their own side of the ball, under the penalty of a foul for off-side play) by the snap-back's kicking the ball or snapping it back, either with his foot, or more commonly with his hand, to a player of his own side just behind him, who is called the quarter-back.

A center rush with experience was very valuable, and it was the policy to "keep the centre rush in his place, so long as his legs are good, rather than to replace him by a substitute with whom the quarter-back is not familiar."

Camp was instrumental in devising many of the early plays and formations. He was captain of the Yale teams of 1878–1879. Later, in 1889, when he selected his All-American team, he was considered *the* authority on the game of American football.

In 1893 Harvard opened its varsity season against Dartmouth College. Over two thousand fans looked on at Jarvis Field as Harvard won, 16–0. The *Boston Globe* noted:

In the other rushers Harvard was invincible. Macke and Lewis both played a strong dashing game and broke through their lineman opposite them with ease.

The 1893 Harvard University football team. Lewis is third from left in back row.

Camp usually acted in an advisory capacity at Yale, but he or his associates personally saw all of the Big Three games played by Harvard, Princeton, and Yale. Harvard's winning streak continued:

> Harvard, 32—Amherst, 0
> Harvard, 52—Williams, 0
> Harvard, 36—Dartmouth, 0
> Harvard, 68—Brown, 0

And on November 4, 1893, Harvard defeated Cornell, 34–0. The game was played on New York's Manhattan Field and was beset with a steady hard rain that reduced the crowd to about twelve hundred hardy souls, who braved the cold north wind that swept through the stadium. There were also a few women in attendance, clutching parasols, and clad in rubber boots. The game was described as follows:

Brewer, Lewis, and Newell were the bright particular stars of Harvard's game. . . . Lewis was everywhere and followed the ball beautifully.

Again the big game awaited against Yale on November 25, 1893, at Springfield, and again Yale won, 6–0. The Harvard followers, and of course the players, were heartsick. Lewis had played his heart out in this next to last game of his football career. He had recklessly flung his 180-pound frame into the wedge and the *V* formations and performed as a man possessed. When Yale finally scored late in the game, Lewis was, literally, spent.

The *Boston Globe* observed:

Lewis the Harvard centre rush was left silent and motionless on the sod like a dead log thrown shoreward in a storm.

But earlier in the game, before he was spent, he was:

Tackling like a Fiji Islander, and the Yale center found it always impossible to stop him.

The 1896 Harvard University football team. Howard Joseph Lee is shown at left.

Lewis was again selected to Walter Camp's All-American first team in 1893.

Howard Lee was a freshman at Harvard in 1896, and on October 31, he played in his first game, a 4–0 win over the Carlisle Indian School. Lee was born in Weston, Massachusetts, on June 27, 1878. He graduated from Newton High School and received an A.B. from Harvard in 1900. Later he went to Mexico to work in the mine and plantation businesses.

On November 7, 1896, Lee played the entire game at right tackle, because of a rash of injuries that struck his Harvard team. Princeton won, 12–0, and Howard Lee never appeared in a game thereafter.

On October 2, 1897, George M. Chadwell played left end for Williams College in the season's opener against Harvard before more than two thousand fans. Harvard won, 20–0. Among the interested spectators was William Henry Lewis, then a practicing Boston lawyer and member of the firm of Lewis, Fox & Andrews.

On October 9, 1897, Yale beat Williams, 32–0, in New Haven. The 1897 Williams team won one game and lost seven, but even in a losing season Chadwell was a standout, and had his moments. The *Boston Globe* reported:

Chadwell, the colored end rush of the Williams line played a fairly strong game and got considerable applause.

As the nineteenth century drew to a close, William Washington played for Oberlin in 1897, 1898, and 1899.

At the turn of the century, Matthew Washington Bullock played left end on the Dartmouth College football team. Bullock was born on September 11, 1881, in Dabney, North Carolina, and entered Dartmouth in September 1900. In the 1901 season, he was a substitute. Dartmouth's record that year was nine wins, and a single defeat by Harvard.

In the 1902 season, Bullock was a regular at end. On October 4, in the season's opener against the University of Vermont, he "ran the ball up 25 yards" on the kickoff, as Dartmouth won, 11–0. Twenty players were in and out of the Dartmouth lineup, but Bullock played the entire game at his left-end post.

In the 1902 season, Dartmouth won six games, lost one, and tied one.

In the 1903 season, after Bullock played in six games, a player named "Lillard" replaced him at left end, and Bullock did not appear in any more games. In the 1903 season, Dartmouth won nine games, and lost one to Princeton.

In the next decade there would be more outstanding black football players on white college teams: George Collins, Cedar Rapids, Iowa, halfback; Samuel Ransom, Beloit College, Wisconsin, quarterback; W. N. Johnson, left end; Robert Taylor, right guard, both from the University of Nebraska; and Beloit's 5-foot 3¾-inch, 132-pound Theodore Lucius Strothers, right end.

And then there were superstars such as Leslie Lawrence Pollard, Fred "Duke" Slater, Edward Benjamin Gray, Frederick Douglass "Fritz" Pollard, Paul Leroy Robeson, and Robert W. "Bobby" Marshall.

Robert Marshall was born on March 12, 1880. He graduated from Minnesota's Central High School in 1902 and entered the university that fall.

In 1905 Marshall became the second Negro to be selected as an

All-American. He was a second team selection in both 1905 and 1906. Walter Camp wrote in 1905:

Very few gains have been made around his end this year. He is quick in discerning a play, powerful and sure as a tackler and in carrying the ball has made consistent gains.

But in 1903 Marshall was a substitute player. The *Minnesota Journal* of October 10 reported:

Substitute material in the line is not of so good quality. For the ends Marshall and Luce are the best men. Marshall has the experience, but is easily drawn in on trick plays. He is strong in advancing the ball and a good punter. As a defensive end, however, he is hardly up to standard, and defensive play is the important quality in an end.

Each year Minnesota played local high schools and preparatory schools before starting the regular season against college opposition.

On Saturday, October 24, 1903, Marshall played in his first regular season game against Beloit in a substitute role at left end. Minnesota won, 46–0. It was its seventh game—and its seventh victory.

In 1903 Beloit won three games and lost six, but did have some outstanding stars. The *Minnesota Journal* on October 26, 1903, called the attention of its readers to one of them:

The 1904 Harvard University football team. William Clarence Matthews is shown at left in first row.

This was particularly true of Strothers, the little colored lad at right end. . . . Strothers weighs but 132 pounds, but on defensive play is a marvel. It was him who laid the redoubtable Heston low and caused his retirement from the Michigan-Beloit game.

All-American William Heston was one of the mainstays of the University of Michigan's great team in 1903. Coach Fielding H. Yost had assembled a team that would finish with 565 points scored, against its opponents' 6.

In the Michigan-Beloit game on October 12, 1903, Heston had touchdown runs of eighty-five, eighty-five, sixty-five, forty-five, and thirty-five yards, but little Strothers cut him down. Michigan won, 79–0.

The Wolverines were next on the Gophers' schedule. On Saturday, October 31, 1903, before more than ten thousand fans at Minnesota's Northrop Field, a "vicious and clean" contest was staged before two evenly matched football giants. The final score was Minnesota, 6, Michigan, 6.

The University of Michigan had scored 437 points going into the game with Minnesota, while holding Minnesota scoreless.

The University of Minnesota had scored 412 points, going into the Michigan game, and had held Michigan scoreless.

Marshall, the substitute, was pressed into service in the big game because of an injury to Burdick, the regular right end. The *Minnesota Journal* reported:

Another surprise was the defensive work of Marshall. The colored end, playing in Burdick's place, did not let a single play around him. He smashed the interference well and invariably turned the runner in if he could not tackle him.

Burdick returned to the lineup in the next game, on November 7, against Lawrence University, and Marshall went back to the bench for the remainder of the season during which the Minnesota dreadnought swept on undefeated, winning its last four games.

The University of Michigan and the University of Minnesota ended deadlocked for the Western Conference title.

Robert W. "Bobby" Marshall was the regular end in the 1904 football season, and Minnesota continued its winning streak. On Saturday, October 1, Minnesota rolled to its third win over Carleton College, 65–0.

The *Minnesota Journal*, on October 3, described Marshall as "one of the most slippery men to ever don football armor."

In the first half, Marshall received the kickoff by Carleton's Cundy and ran it back eighteen yards. When the ball was nestled a little beyond midfield, according to the *Journal*:

Bobby Marshall wormed his way around the end for a forty-five yard run and a touchdown.

In the second half, Marshall received another Cundy kickoff on the ten-yard line and returned it back to the thirty-yard line. After several attempts into the line, as the *Journal* reported:

Marshall then jumped back and went around left and seventy yards for a touchdown.

Four thousand fans at Northrop Field were jerked out of their seats to watch this run and applauded it wildly.

Minnesota—and Marshall—rolled on. On October 15, 1904, at

The 1904 University of Minnesota football team. First row: Burgan, Brush, Ricker, Strathern, Thorpe, Case, and Marshall. Second row: Harris, Kremer, Current, and Davies.

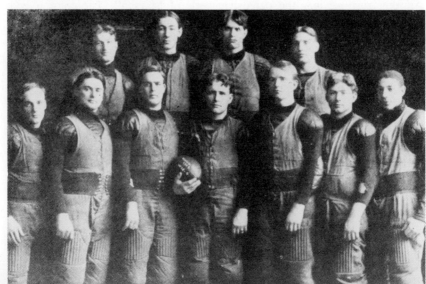

Northrop Field, before five thousand fans, Minnesota defeated Iowa State, 32–0.

In the second half, Jones of Iowa punted out to his own thirty-five-yard line. Hunter got five yards for Minnesota on a smash through the line. And then:

Marshall then got away for the most sensational run of the day, by good judgement, quick dodging and jumping over opposing players, he ran the ball thirty yards for a touchdown.

On Saturday, October 22, the University of Minnesota ran up its all-time point total against Grinnell College, 146–0! In 1904, a field goal counted for four points, and an extra point counted for one point. A touchdown counted for five points. Marshall's totals alone were seventy-two points. He scored four touchdowns, and kicked thirteen field goals.

Marshall did not play in the next game against Lawrence University on November 5:

Marshall was out of the game, and while the brilliant lad can hold his own anywhere in the West, the followers of the Minnesota team become apprehensive when considering the substitute material.

Minnesota's mighty football machine continued by overwhelming Lawrence, 69–0.

On November 19, at Chicago's Marshall Field, Bobby Marshall returned to the lineup against Northwestern University. However, the injury to his leg that had kept him out of the Lawrence game acted up again. Burgan was substituted for him, and Minnesota won, 17–0.

On Thanksgiving Day, November 24, Minnesota was again without its brilliant end. He was benched during a game against the University of Iowa, and Burgan replaced him once more. Minnesota defeated Iowa, 11–0. It was the final game of the season.

In the 1904 football season, Minnesota and Michigan again tied for the championship of the Western Conference.

Michigan scored 567 points against its opponents' 22 points, while Minnesota scored 618 points against its opponents' 12 points. Both colleges finished undefeated.

The University of Minnesota started preparations for the 1905 season early. A "conditioning sojourn" was begun on September 1 at New York's Coney Island with preseason games against the local high schools and preparatory schools. These were usually high-scoring victories for Minnesota.

The 1905 season was a continuation of the 1904 season: St. Thomas College, 0, Minnesota, 42; North Dakota College, 0, Minnesota 45; Iowa State, 0, Minnesota 42; The University of Iowa, 0, Minnesota, 39; Lawrence College, 0, Minnesota, 46.

In the Lawrence game, on October 28, Bobby Marshall kicked six out of seven field goals.

Then came the big game against the University of Wisconsin. Before the largest number of fans that had ever seen a football game in Minneapolis the Badgers defeated the Gophers, 16–12.

Over twenty-eight thousand fans groaned in agony at the first defeat Minnesota had suffered in thirty-three games. We go to the *Minnesota Journal* to appraise Marshall's performance in the first loss of his college football career:

Marshall was a whirlwind on defense at left end. . . . He was persistent in breaking thru and spoiling attempts at his end of the line, but was not called on for a great deal of ball carrying.

On November 11, Minnesota beat South Dakota State, of Brookings, South Dakota, 81–0. On November 18, Marshall, left end, faced

The 1905 University of Minnesota football team. Robert W. "Bobby" Marshall is shown at right in second row.

Nebraska, which also had a Negro left end, W. N. Johnson. Robert Taylor, right guard, was another Negro on the Nebraska squad, but did not see action. Minnesota won, 35–0. The *Minnesota Journal* noted:

Marshall at left end played another brilliant game. On the defense he seemed everywhere. He did more ball carrying than he did in the Wisconsin game and netted good gains.

Marshall also kicked three field goals against the Cornhuskers. On November 25, the Gophers ended their season with a 72–6 win over Northwestern University.

The *Minnesota Journal* summed up Marshall's outstanding season:

Marshall played another great game, another clinch in the title of All-Western end, which must be given him by all fair-minded critics. He was everywhere and played like a demon despite his injury.

The article was prophetic. The *Minnesota Journal* of December 1, 1905, reported:

PUTS MARSHALL ON ALL-WESTERN

CHICAGO TRIBUNE ANNOUNCES ITS SELECTION—MARSHALL ONLY
GOPHER PLAYER HONORED

Marshall, the Gopher outpost, has been death to all end runners as a rule, and is remarkably fast in getting down the field under punts, tackling with certainty in the open.

The University of Chicago had four selections. The University of Michigan had four. The University of Wisconsin had two—and Minnesota one. The won-lost records of the Big Four follow:

	Won	*Lost*	*Points*	*Opponents*
The University of Chicago	9	0	212	5
The University of Michigan	12	1	495	2
The University of Wisconsin	9	1	226	28
The University of Minnesota	8	1	414	22

Finally, there came Marshall's last season, 1906. On October 27, Minnesota beat Iowa State, 22–4. Marshall contributed a fifty-two-yard kickoff return, a field goal, and three points after touchdowns.

In Beloit, Wisconsin, on this same Saturday, Samual L. Ransom was at quarterback for Beloit against Lawrence in a 10–5 loss.

Marshall kicked two field goals in Minnesota's 13–0 win over the University of Nebraska on November 7 at Northrop Field.

The next game would be the big one against the defending Western Conference champions, the University of Chicago, at Marshall Field in the Windy City, on November 11. The *Minnesota Journal* blared the results on page one:

MINNESOTA ROOTERS OWN ALL OF CHICAGO
THEY CELEBRATE THE CAPTURE OF WESTERN CHAMPIONSHIP BY
THE GOPHERS—GAME PLAYED IN THE MUD

In a hard-fought defensive battle, Minnesota won, 4–2. The Minnesota score came late in the first half:

Minnesota, with the pigskin on Chicago's thirty-nine-yard line resolved to have a stab at the goal. Marshall dropped back, Larkin poised the ball for him and the player's feet sent the ball true between the posts.

The Minnesota rooters in the crowd of over twenty thousand fans went wild. And almost at the same time, about five thousand fans who had gathered in front of the *Journal*'s Building, on Fourth Street, also became delirious with joy when the news was flashed to the big board at the *Journal*.

The 1906 University of Minnesota football team. First row: Marshall, Case, Smith, Safford, Vita, Wiest, and Ittner. Second row: Schuknecht, Larkin, Current, and Doane.

The next day the fans had the story to savor in their hands:

BOBBY MARSHALL BOOTS WET BALL OVER FROM 39-YARD LINE—
CHICAGO SCORES ON SAFETY

The great colored football player kicked his way high upon the roll of honor in Minnesota's athletic history this afternoon when he dropped back to Chicago's 40-yard line and booted the soggy football over the sacred goal of the Maroons.

On November 17 the Carlisle Indians deflated the Gophers' egos by a 17–0 victory in an intersectional contest.

In the last game of the 1906 season, Minnesota eked out an 8–6 win on the toe of Marshall, beating Indiana. Marshall booted two field goals, one from twenty-five yards out.

The University of Minnesota and the University of Wisconsin were co-champions of the Western Conference for the 1906 football season. Each had four conference wins, against no defeats in the conference.

Marshall was again named to Camp's All-American team.

After leaving college, Marshall played semipro football, and also in a new league just starting, the National Football League. He later was employed by the State of Minnesota, in Minneapolis, and reputedly owned and managed a café there. In the 1950s he was honored for his long state service and for his past athletic achievements at a civic dinner, attended by the governor and other civic leaders. Robert W. "Bobby" Marshall was elected to the Hall of Fame—posthumously.

The game of college football was gaining in popularity yearly. But news of the sluggings and other forms of often brutal play spread, even to the White House.

The New York Times front-paged on October 10, 1905:

ROOSEVELT CAMPAIGN FOR FOOTBALL REFORM—HE SUMMONS
UNIVERSITY ADVISERS AND ASKS THEM TO AGITATE
THEY ARE TOLD THAT BRUTALITY SHOULD BE ELIMINATED
AND FAIR PLAY BE ASSURED

On October 9, 1906, President Theodore Roosevelt met with D. H. Nicholas and W. T. Reid of Harvard, Arthur T. Hillebrand and John B. Fine of Princeton, John Owsloy and Walter Camp of Yale.

Camp later released a statement:

At a meeting with the President of the United States it was agreed that we consider an honorable obligation exists to carry out in letter and in spirit the rules of the game of football relating to roughness, holding, and foul play, and the active coaches of our universities being present with us, pledged themselves to so regard it and to do their utmost to carry out that obligation.

Glenn S. Warner, Cornell's head coach, stated that "a very simple way to fix things would be to allow off-side on all punts, to let the ball be free after kicks, and to increase the distance to be gained in three downs from five to ten yards."

According to the *Chicago Tribune,* in 1905 football deaths hit a high of eighteen, and there were 159 serious injuries. The only reason that a public outcry did not demand that the game be abolished was perhaps because most casualties occurred at the grade- and high-school levels with few in the games attended by the great mass of spectators, or in the big schools.

The new rules prohibited mass formations, flying wedges, piling-on, hurdling, and roughing the kicker. They also introduced the forward pass and divided the game into two halves of thirty minutes each. Coach Warner's suggestion of ten yards for a first down was instituted, and the number of downs required was changed from three to four.

With the new changes, the game became faster and cleaner, and relied upon more than brute force, physical condition, and endurance.

But the rules did not bar discrimination. *The New York Times* of November 22, 1903, noted:

COLOR LINE IN FOOTBALL

GEN. LEW WALLACE LECTURES COLLEGE PLAYERS

AND GAME IS PLAYED

In a game scheduled between DePauw University and Wabash

College, in Crawfordsville, Indiana, the DePauw manager and players headed for their hotel after discovering upon leaving the gymnasium that their opponents on the squad had a Negro guard, Samuel Simon Gordon from West Virginia. General Lew Wallace, the Reverends Edwin A. Scheir and Cornick, all prevailed upon the DePauw players finally to abide by good Christian principles and play the game. The outcome is not known, but apparently Wabash won, as the article enigmatically states: "The team went into the game, and as it turned out, Wabash had no need of Gordon's services."

Gordon left Wabash after one year.

Meanwhile, in Boston in 1903, William Henry Lewis was appointed United States Assistant District Attorney for the Boston District by the District Attorney, Henry P. Moulton, at the suggestion of President Theodore Roosevelt.

That same year, Joe Walcott, the world welterweight boxing champion, purchased a house on Belmont Street in Malden, Massachusetts. Walcott's next-door neighbors were Colonel Harry S. Converse, millionaire rubber-goods manufacturer, and E. S. Converse, the richest man in the city. Walcott moved in with his mulatto wife, white mother-in-law, and four young children. A twelve-year-old sister of Walcott's also moved in with the family. The house cost $5,000 and the champion spent $1,000 more on improvements.

The treatment of the Negro, of course, was not uniform throughout the nation. It depended not only upon who he was, but also upon where he was, geographically.

The United States Census of 1910 showed a Negro population of 1,621 in the state of Vermont. From 1840 to the end of 1909 there were four Negro college graduates from Middlebury College, in Middlebury, and there were three Negro college graduates from the University of Vermont, in Burlington. In the ten years between 1900 and 1910 the Negro population in Vermont increased 96.2 percent, from 826 in 1900 to 1,621 in 1910.

In 1900 there were 454 male and 372 female Negroes. But when the population jumped in the next ten years, there were 1,173 black males, and 448 black females in the state. The 1910 census showed that 27 percent of the total black population was born in the state, and 52.9 percent was born "in other states" besides the East or West, suggesting that southern migration took place in significant percentages.

Vermont has historically been a state that yearly lost population by departures of its residents. The ratio of 261.8 black males to every 100 black females decreased the total Negro population in the next ten years to 572 (1920).

What had attracted blacks to the Green Mountains' northern farmland of apples and maple syrup? The Vermont Constitution outlawed slavery as early as 1777, one of the first states to do so. The transportation of fugitive slaves from its state was prohibited in 1843.

The Judge of the Supreme Court of Judicature in Vermont from 1783 to his death in 1813, Theophilus Harrington, had ruled against the Fugitive Slave Law even earlier, as described in the following account:

A Claimant to a run-a-way slave demanded that his slave be returned.
"Well, put in your title," the Judge said.
The Claimant produced a bill of sale and affidavits on his run-a-way.
Examining the papers, the Judge asked: "Is that all?"
The Claimant produced a bill of sale from the mother of the run-a-way.
The Judge asked again: "Is that all?"
"Why, yes"; the Claimant stammered.
"I have gone back to the ownership of the mother."
"Yes," said the Judge, evenly. "But you have not gone back to the original proprietor. A bill of sale from God Almighty is necessary to make title to a man in Vermont."

The former slave went free.

As we come to the 1907 football season, we find a black graduate of the University of Vermont, one of the first three who had always been a freeman.

Fenwich Watkins, also a member of the University of Vermont's baseball and basketball teams, was at left halfback in 1907. The *Burlington Free Press* of October 28, 1907, reported:

VERMONT BEAT HOLY CROSS
LONG RUN BY CAPT. WATKINS
CARRIED BALL 70 YARDS

In the last five minutes of play in the game, Watkins set up the game's only score with a seventy-yard run from scrimmage. He also kicked the point after touchdown for a final score of the University of Vermont, 6, Holy Cross, 0.

On November 2, 1907, Williams College defeated Vermont, 17–5. On November 9, Vermont beat New Hampshire State College, 34–0.

Watkins, the 164-pound Negro halfback, again led the assault "with numerous 10- and 20-yd., eel-like squirmings and spectacular 60 and 90 yd.-runs to his credit. . . ." Watkins scored two touchdowns and kicked four field goals.

Vermont lost its last game of the 1907 season to Brown University, 34–0, at Providence, Rhode Island, on November 16, for a final record of four victories, two losses, and one tie.

On September 30, 1908, Vermont opened the season at Hanover, New Hampshire, with a 10–0 loss to Dartmouth College. On October 3 Vermont again lost, 5–0, to Holy Cross, and on October 10 the team fought to a 0–0 scoreless tie with Amherst College, at Amherst, Massachusetts.

On October 17 Vermont defeated Norwich University, 11–5.

Vermont's first score came in the first half. According to the newspaper account:

Watkins got the ball on a fumble. Cassidy went through the Norwich line for 12 yards. Watkins followed around right end for 5 yards. After two short gains through the line, Watkins got away on an end run for 35 yards.

Keislick, Vermont's fullback, crashed over for the score seconds later, and Watkins kicked the extra point, making the score, 6–0.

The second score was described as follows: "Watkins then made 12 yards through left tackle and followed it with a forward pass for a touchdown. Thus the score was 11–0 with five minutes to play. Watkins failed to kick the goal."

Vermont's season record was three wins, three losses, and three ties.

In 1908, Fenwich Henri Watkins was one of the first black athletes to captain a white college football team. That year there were several other black football players on white college teams. John Pinkett, described as the finest center since William Henry Lewis, was at Amherst, as was Edward Benjamin Gray, end-back field standout, while Leslie Lawrence Pollard was halfback at Dartmouth College.

Cornell College defeated Amherst on November 7 by a score of 6–0. The *Boston Globe* of November 8 reported: "Gray, a colored boy at right halfback for Amherst, played a whirlwind game and bored through the line time after time and picking holes on every side. . . ."

Walter Camp was at the game and was impressed by the future doctor's performance.

In Amherst's first three games, Edward Gray played left end. Meanwhile, Leslie Pollard was playing outstandingly at Dartmouth. On October 24, at Worcester, Massachusetts, Dartmouth beat Holy Cross, 18–5. The *Boston Herald* reported:

Pollard the colored halfback, who took the place of Ingersoll, looked to be playing sensational football, as he made several long end runs. Most of his runs were made by running straight across the field without interference and getting by a slow defense.

Amherst and Dartmouth played on October 31. Dartmouth won, 17–0. For Dartmouth, Pollard saw little action, but Pinkett and Gray

Henry Freeman Coleman, seventh from left in back row, as a member of the Cornell College (Iowa) football team of 1908. (Courtesy of Cornell College)

played nearly the entire game for Amherst. And Gray "was called upon time and time again, and from tackle formation repeatedly smashed through the Dartmouth line for gains averaging six yards each," according to a contemporary report.

Ingersoll was injured again in Dartmouth's 6–0 loss to Harvard on November 14, and Pollard's running back of punts was described as "the most spectacular feature of the game. He bounded like a black ball and showed amazing speed."

This was nearly the same tribute that would be accorded his brother some eight years later.

At Columbus, Ohio, the next week, trouble loomed involving a Negro player, Nathaniel P. Brown.

The *Ohio State Journal* of November 22 reported:

Fullback Gibson was thrown out of play for roughing Brown, the Oberlin colored halfback. . . . Umpire Durfee charged Gibson with uppercutting Oberlin's Negro who played a strong game for the first half. . . .

Oberlin lost to the Ohio State University team, 14–12, and finished with a season record of three wins and four losses. Nathaniel Brown saw part-time action in two games in the 1908 season.

The Negro newspapers were properly impressed with the anomaly of a black football player, on a white college team, starring against a major white college eleven. The *New York Age* of November 19 reported:

NEGRO IN FOOTBALL GAME
POLLARD ONE OF THE STARS OF HARVARD-DARTMOUTH MATCH—GREAT
LEFT HALF-BACK—THE PAPERS CALL HIM 'THE BLACK WHIRLWIND'

The Harvard game was witnessed by thirty-eight thousand fans in Harvard Stadium.

Leslie Lawrence Pollard was born in Chicago in 1888. He left Dartmouth after his freshman year in 1908–1909. The Big Green football team won six, lost one, and tied one, in 1908.

Edward Gray also left Amherst after his freshman year in 1908–

1909. He headed for Howard University. Pollard went on to coach the Lincoln University football team, before meeting an untimely death in New York City on April 22, 1915, having been accidentally asphyxiated on April 19.

Walter Camp, writing in *Collier*'s magazine of December 19, 1908, hailed Gray's athletic prowess on the gridiron:

Gray of Amherst, a colored star, showed good quality, and the whirlwind way in which he repeatedly went through the Cornell line when Amherst held them to a single score was worth noting.

Amherst won three games, lost three, and tied two in the 1908 season. Pollard was awarded his letter despite the fact that he was a substitute player. The *New York Age*, on December 3 explained why:

Among the players to receive a letter "D" at a meeting of the Dartmouth Athletic Council Monday afternoon was . . . Pollard, the crack colored half back who distinguished himself in the Harvard-Dartmouth game. The requirements for the "D" this season was that a man shall have played in at least one-half of either the Harvard or Princeton game. Pollard also received with several other players a gold football watch charm engraved with the Princeton score.

As 1915 dawned, more black stars would appear on the horizon. In 1915 and 1916 Joseph Edward Trigg, a graduate of Washington's M Street High School, played tackle for Syracuse University. A substitute player in 1915, Trigg played in his team's 82–0 slaughter of Rochester on October 16 in Syracuse. As a substitute for Schlachter, on November 13, Trigg and Syracuse defeated Colgate, 38–0. Syracuse won nine games in 1915, lost two, and tied one.

In 1916 Trigg was a starter. He played right tackle in Syracuse's 73–0 win in the opener on October 7 against Ohio University. On October 21, at Syracuse's Archbold Stadium, Pittsburgh won over Syracuse, 30–0. For Trigg and the Scarlet Knights, the loss was particularly embarrassing because Walter Camp was in attendance.

Syracuse's season record in 1916 was five wins and four losses.

In 1915, in the East, another Negro was preparing to enter a large white university. Paul Leroy Robeson was born on April 9, 1898, in Princeton, New Jersey. He entered Rutgers University in September 1915 on an academic scholarship, having scored on the college qualifying test the highest of any high school student in the state of New Jersey.

His activities at Rutgers were many: debating team, glee club, track, basketball, baseball, and football teams.

In 1915, the seventeen-year-old freshman saw substitute action in the third game of the season, when Robeson, a tackle, briefly replaced Austin at end. This game was played on New Brunswick's Neilson Field against Rensselaer Polytechnical Institute. Rutgers won, 96–0.

Robeson next appeared against Springfield YMCA College, on October 30, at Federal League grounds, in Harrison, New Jersey. Rutgers beat Springfield, 44–13.

The *Newark Evening News* noted in commenting about Robeson's next game:

Robeson, the colored tackle who played a good game in Nash's position in the last quarter of the Springfield game was tried out again and pleased the coaches.

In the latter contest Rutgers emerged victorious, 39–3, over the Stevens Institute of Technology.

Rutgers finished the 1915 season with seven wins and one loss, scoring 351 points to its opponents' 33 points.

In the 1916 season forty candidates took part in the first practice on September 6. All-American Nash had graduated and Robeson had earned the first string position at tackle. Rutgers won the opener against Villanova, 14–0.

The next scheduled game was set for October 14, at Neilson Field, capacity, thirty-five hundred fans. The opposition, Washington and Lee University, was thought to have reservations about competing against a Negro, but Robeson solved the problem. He was injured, and the two teams battled to a 13–13 tie. The *Newark Evening News* of October 18 stated:

A decided improvement was shown in the Rutgers line yesterday afternoon with Robeson back at his old place at tackle. The whole line seemed to stiffen as soon as he got back.

In the 1916 football season, Rutgers' record was three won, two lost, two tied.

In the 1917 football season, Coach George Foster Sanford moved Robeson to end. The *Newark Evening News* of September 26 declared:

Robeson, the biggest man on the squad, and nearly as fast as the swiftest backfield candidate. The big colored fellow, weighing 225 pounds in his suit, six feet three inches in height, is there with the team, but Sanford has chosen to put him in at end.

Rutgers beat Ursinus College in the opener, 25–0. Sanford's decision was examined:

The big colored fellow, Robeson, an offensive end, had been placed behind the line on defense, and unlike most tall, heavy men, seemed well adapted to this secondary work. He gives the team a double line.

In the next game, Rutgers beat Fort Wadsworth, 90–0. The *Newark Evening News* wrote:

The attack is further strengthened by the presence of Robeson at end. Robeson is tall, with exceptionally long arms, and is one of the surest catchers of forward passes on the gridiron today. Rutgers would not depend upon this play, but with it to fall back on to use as a threat the team is strengthened considerably.

Rutgers went on to win seven games, losing one, and tying one. It ended the season on Saturday, November 24, 1917, at Ebbets Field in Brooklyn, New York, beating the Newport Naval Reserve football team, 14–0, with the following news report: "Robeson, the end, was active in clearing the way, charging forward and cleaning up with his broad shoulders."

Walter Camp did not select a college All-American team in 1917. Instead, because of "war conditions," he selected All-Americans from the service teams.

Rutgers opened the 1918 season by overwhelming Ursinus, 66–0. Next the Pelham Naval Reserves fell, 7–0.

An influenza epidemic forced the next game, originally scheduled for Lehigh's home site in Bethlehem, Pennsylvania, to be moved to Rutger's Neilson Field, but it did not change the results as Rutgers won, 39–0.

The Rutgers players had all been vaccinated three days before the game, but Robeson showed no side effects from the serum, as he scored two touchdowns. The press reported:

In the second period, the colored giant, received a forward from Kelly and ran 45 yards for a touchdown. Four of the Lehigh team each took a turn at trying to bring him to earth, but with no avail.

Robeson's next tally was in the third quarter, the first score being in the first quarter:

Robeson intercepted a forward from Wysacka and crossed the line after a 30-yard run.

In the next game, Rutgers beat Hoboken's Naval Transport eleven, 40–0. The coach opened up his offense, described as follows:

Sanford showed a brand-new play yesterday in the form of a double pass. He sent in the regular quarterback, Baker, for this one play, just to try it out. Baker fell far back of the line to take a long direct pass from the center. In the meantime, Paul Robeson, the giant end, raced over behind Baker and received a backward pass from Baker. Standing deep in the back field, with no one near him, Robeson hurled the ball on a 40-yard forward pass through the air to Captain Feitner, who was down in Transport territory waiting for it. The play is spectacular and worked perfectly.

In June, Robeson received his college degree. On February 22, 1919, he had been initiated to membership in Phi Beta Kappa. He led his senior class academically and athletically.

In December 1918 Walter Camp selected Paul Robeson for his first team as an All-American end.

Quarterback Cliff Baker said of Robeson, " 'Robey,' recognized by close critics as the greatest and most versatile player of all time, possessed what is known as 'football instinct' and was able to fathom the attack of every opponent with lightning-like quickness."

Walter Camp called Robeson the finest end that ever trod upon a gridiron. In Robeson's last season, Rutgers won five and lost two games.

Robeson earned a law degree from Columbia, played pro ball briefly, and finally found great success upon the stage and in concerts as the possessor of a magnificent baritone voice.

Frederick Douglass "Fritz" Pollard entered Brown University in 1915.

After the 1915 football season, Pollard was selected to the Providence Journal's *All-Eastern second team, at half-back. The 1915 Brown team is shown. From left to right: Weeks, right end; Farnum, right tackle; Wade, right guard; Sprague, center; Staff, left guard; Ward, left tackle; Butner, left end. Back row, left to right: Purdy, quarterback; Andrews, right half-back; Saxton, fullback; Pollard, left half-back.*

In the opening football game in 1915, Brown beat Rhode Island State College, 18–0. Then in the next game, on October 2, Brown and Trinity College fought to a 0–0 tie. The halfbacks these first two games were Andrews, Hillhouse, Devine, and Purdy.

On Thursday, October 7, Pollard in one of the daily scrimmages scored two touchdowns via long runs on Andrews Field, and Coach Edward North Robinson sent him into the game against Amherst on October 9. Amherst won, 7–0. Pollard, who did not start, but substituted for Hillhouse, ran a punt back for sixty yards to his own twenty-two-yard line, in his brief appearance.

In the next game, on October 16, Pollard started against Williams College. Brown defeated Williams, 33–0. Pollard scored three touchdowns (one touchdown from a fifty-five-yard run was called back because of penalty). Pollard also set up another score with a seventy-yard run.

Against the University of Vermont, Brown won, 46–0. Pollard set up two touchdowns with forty- and thirty-two-yard runs.

Then in the big game on November 6, before more than twelve thousand fans in New Haven's Yale Bowl, Brown won, 3–0. It was Brown's first victory over Yale since the 1910 season.

Pollard was apparently under instructions to signal for fair catches on punts in the close, hand-fought contest. His usual style was to play way back on punts and when the ball was in the air come dashing up and take the ball on the dead run. Of course this daring maneuver would sometimes result in a fumble, but more often it led to a long gain or a touchdown.

In the Yale game, Pollard still had runs of thirty-two and twenty-three yards from scrimmage. The three points were scored on a twenty-two-yard field goal by Andrews, the captain.

The next game was also a big one. On November 13 Brown played Harvard before over twenty-five thousand fans. Harvard won, 16–7.

Pollard, besides gaining five, six, and seven yards at a clip, in which he would burst through the line as if shot from a cannon, also had runs of twenty-two, twenty, eighteen, nineteen, and seventeen yards.

The last game was on Thanksgiving Day, November 25, against the Carlisle Indians. Brown won, 39–3. The *Providence Journal* reported:

Pollard, maker of three touchdowns, thrilled the thousands time and time again with his sensational thrusts through the line, one of which carried him 18 yards through a swarm of tacklers to a touchdown. His next best effort was a dash around the flank that gave him 19 yards . . . he ripped the Carlisle forwards to tatters in his vicious plungers. And was good for a gain on nearly every plunge.

Brown University ended the regular season with a record of five wins, three losses, and one tie. Mostly on the basis of its victory over Yale, Brown was selected to appear in the Rose Bowl on January 1, 1916.[1]

The Coliseum at Pasadena, California, was a quagmire from the rain and bad weather conditions. Pollard's running was curtailed as Washington State beat Brown, 14–0.

Brown started the 1916 football season off at a fast clip. In the first game, on September 30, Brown defeated Rhode Island State College, 18–0, at Andrews Field. Pollard had a thirty-yard runback of a punt in his brief appearance, as reported:

Pollard played only one quarter, trainer Huggins not wishing to take any chances on having him injured when his presence was not needed.

In the next game, on October 7, Pollard also saw limited action as Brown defeated Trinity, 42–0.

The *Providence Journal* noted:

Pollard got into the game only a short time. Trainer Huggins not deeming it advisable to take a chance on his leg becoming worse when his presence was not needed. The short time that he was in, however, he showed all his old-time form, making several long gains through Trinity's line for first downs and then carrying the ball over for the last touchdown of the day.

---

[1] Football made its first appearance as part of the Tournament of Roses festivities on January 1, 1902. Its revival was not until the January 1, 1916, game.

Amherst fell before Brown, 69–0; Williams, 20–0. Pollard ran for a forty-seven-yard touchdown in the Williams game, and made three touchdowns in the Amherst game on sprints of fifteen, twenty-five, and thirty yards. He also played a strong game on defense, as one newspaper reported:

In desperation Amherst essayed to score via the aerial route, but the ever vigilant Pollard batted it to the ground and the golden opportunity to escape a white-wash vanished in thin air.

On October 28 Pollard faced his friend Robeson and the Rutgers team. He scored two touchdowns, one on a forty-eight-yard run, and in the last period on a delayed pass, he eluded the entire Rutgers eleven and ran forty-four yards for a touchdown. Brown University won, 21–3.

The lineups with the two Negro future All-Americans follow:

BROWN (21)		RUTGERS (3)
Marshall	LE	Wittpenn
Devitalls	LT	Randall
Spagna	LG	Garrett
Sprague	C	Mason
Zeicer	C	
Wade—Brace	RG	Bursch
Farnum—Robertson	RT	Robeson
Donovan—Williams	RT	
Ormsby	RT	
Weeks	RE	Elliott—Hausel
Purdy—Conroy	QB	Scarr
Murphy—Jemail	QB	
Brooks	QB	
Pollard—Annan	LHB	Bracker
Conroy	RHB	Geiger—Wallace
	RHB	Kelly—Sturkek
Hillhouse	FB	Hazel—Lawes

In the next game against the University of Vermont, on November 4, 1916, Brown won, 42–0, Pollard scoring two touchdowns.

In the big game on November 11, before more than twenty-five thousand fans, Brown beat Yale, 21–6, at New Haven.

Frederick Douglass "Fritz" Pollard, with about one quarter of frenzied activity, stepped onto the stage of football history—and immortality. He scored two of the three touchdowns, and set up the third one. The *Boston Globe* noted:

Pollard, the colored right halfback of the Brown team, was the leader of the day, and his work in the last half of the game staged him as one of the best backs of the year. Pollard was not unknown when he appeared this afternoon, for last year his sensational runs proved the feature of the game in which Yale was shut-out, 3–0.

Pollard scored one touchdown when he caught a punt on his own forty-yard line and returned it sixty yards for the score. He had another sixty-yard run in which, as one reporter noted, he "trickled through the entire Yale team, worming out of the grasp," of would-be tacklers before finally being brought down. His next score was on a sixteen-yard run. Besides these runs, Pollard's other contributions were a twenty-yard run in which he circled right end in the first quarter for Brown's first first down and a thirty-four yard run to Yale's four-yard line.

On the eve of the next game with Harvard, the *Boston Globe* in bold caps exclaimed:

BROWN PINS ITS FAITH IN POLLARD

The Harvard-Brown series dated back to 1893, and the only thing Brown had to show for engaging in the past twenty-one games was a tie in 1914. Then, suddenly, on November 19, 1916, the *Boston Globe* front-paged:

POLLARD, BROWN'S WIZARD, BEATS HARVARD ALMOST ALONE

Brown beat Harvard, 21–0, before some twenty thousand fans. Pollard scored two touchdowns and set up a third one. His offensive

On November 18, 1916, a darting, crouching, Frederick Douglas "Fritz" Pollard (see arrow), on a 34-yard rocket-like burst against Harvard. Final score: Brown University 21—Harvard, 0.

contributions were indeed remarkable and included the following: a fifty-yard run with a pass reception at his own forty-seven-yard to the three-yard line; he later scored from the two-yard line; a forty-seven-yard touchdown run from scrimmage; a thirty-five-yard run, circling right end and literally outrunning the secondary; a thirty-four-yard run on a rocketlike burst straight up the middle.

On defense he was also a stalwart. The *Providence Journal* reported:

As they neared him the interference launched themselves through the air to ward him off. But in the same instance, Pollard sidestepped and then hurled himself full tilt at Bond's legs. Like a steel trap his arm closed and runner and tackler went down.

Pollard bounced to his feet. Bond had to be helped off by teammates.

Frederick Douglass "Fritz" Pollard was hailed nationally, receiving accolades from the nation's press including the *New York Telegraph, The New York Times,* the *New York World,* and, of course, the Negro weeklies. Mighty Harvard, historically one of the powers in college football year in and year out, had been vanquished.

But Harvard attempted to belittle Brown's hour of triumph. Harvard claimed to have circulated a letter before the game, stating that only a few "regulars" would play in the game against Brown. The reasoning was that most of the regulars were being "saved" to guard against injury and having to miss the all-important Harvard-Yale game the following week. If a loss were to be sustained, it would be better against Brown, than the arch-rival Yale.

Harvard suffered a double loss. Yale won, 6–3.

After selecting Pollard for his number-one team as an All-American, Walter Camp wrote in *Collier*'s magazine of December 30, 1916:

The Yale-Brown score was due to two hard-line plungers by Yale in the early periods, followed by a couple of brilliant runs by Pollard. . . . Pollard of Brown was the most elusive back of the year, or of any year. He is a good sprinter and once loose is a veritable will-o'-the-wisp that no one can lay hands on. He was never down and is hard and resilient as an india rubber ball; but so often his offensive work, on account of its very brilliancy, obscured his really sterling defense. . . .

Brown's Colgate game on Thanksgiving Day, November 30, was won by the Red Raiders, 28–0. Colgate had lost only one game in 1916, to Yale, 7–3, and had won eight. Brown's record was also eight wins, and a single loss.

The Colgate game was Pollard's last college football contest. On October 30, 1954, Frederick Douglass "Fritz" Pollard was inducted into football's Hall of Fame.

Fred "Duke" Slater was a nineteen-yard-old freshman in 1918 at the University of Iowa, and under wartime regulations the freshman rule against varsity competition was waived. His first game, playing right tackle, was on September 28 against the Great Lakes Naval team. Iowa lost, 10–0.

In the next game on October 5, Iowa beat the University of Nebraska, 12–0, at Lincoln, and on October 12 beat Coe College, 27–0, at Iowa City. On the same day, at Grinnell, Iowa, Edward "Sol" Butler led the Dubuque Seminary College to victory over Grinnell College, 13–0, Butler making both touchdowns.

When the Hawkeyes beat the University of Minnesota, 6–0, on November 9, Duke Slater had played every minute in every game in this, their sixth contest. The *Des Moines Register* commented after the game against the Gophers:

The championship 1915 Dubuque football team. From top, left to right (14): Bruns, Knopp, E. Niebruegge, Kor, Reemtsma, A. Niebruegge, Chalmers (Coach), Buchholz, Knapp (Assistant Coach), Dirks, Albrecht, Apel, Marks, and Abben. Middle row, left to right (11): Wettstein, Luth, F. Baker, DeBerg, Parker, Hook, Bessemer, Lay, Arends, S. Butler, and Schneck. Bottom row, left to right (8): Smith, Trimble, Brown, B. Butler (Trainer), E. Baker, Dodds, Bregman, and Abrams.

Trainer Jack Watson's magic was again working today. He had the Hawkeyes in such good physical trim that they played through the game without making a substitution.

On November 16 Iowa beat Iowa State College, 21–0. The *Des Moines Register* commented on the six-foot two-inch, 210-pound right tackler's performance: "Slater the big Negro tackle and Captain Reed were also big factors in the Cyclone's defeat." After six games, Walters replaced Slater at right tackle, and Slater went to the bench amidst a standing ovation.

The next week, Iowa beat Northwestern University, 23–7. The game was played in Iowa City.

Meanwhile in Cedar Rapids, Iowa, on the same day, George Collins of Coe College grabbed the ball on a fumble and ran twenty-five yards for a touchdown. Coe College, led by its Negro halfback, defeated Iowa State Teachers College, 52–3.

The first Negro athlete at Coe had been Henry Thomas, who, in 1904, was an all-around player, competing in football, basketball, and track.

In 1913 Eugene Collins was on the freshman football team at Coe. He also competed in track, running and winning the two-hundred-twenty-yard dash in twenty-four seconds. He was slated to be the regular left halfback in Coe's football plans for 1914; however, he contracted typhoid fever.

George Collins, Eugene's brother, entered Coe College in 1918. He dropped out of school in 1919 and returned to varsity competition, including baseball, in 1920. He was on the Coe varsity in 1921, 1922, and 1923. The *Acorn*, the college yearbook, states, "Collins was a hitter ranking with Makeever in effectiveness, while both Rapaport and Pence were able men with the bat."

On November 30, 1918, Brigadier General B. T. Simmons, Commander of Camp Dodge, north of Des Moines, threw out the football before a game against Iowa. In the last game of the 1918 football season, the Hawkeyes and the soldiers battled to a 0–0 tie. The University of Iowa's season record was six wins, two losses, and one tie.

At season's end, talents were appraised by the *Des Moines Register* of December 15:

ALL-STATE ELEVEN

TWO NEGROES EARN PLACES

The outstanding feature of this year's All-state selections is the fact that two Negroes, Slater of Iowa and Collins of Coe, are named on the first selection and that Butler of Dubuque College and Seminary, another Negro, is placed on the second eleven.

In the 1918 football season, Coe College won four games, lost one, and tied one. George Collins dropped out of school in 1919.

Iowa opened the 1919 season at home against the University of Nebraska on October 4, 1919. Iowa won, 18–0.

On the same day, Charles Howard made a touchdown as Drake University beat Penn College, of Oskaloosa, Iowa, 33–0.

On October 18, 1919, Iowa squeezed by the University of Minnesota, 9–6. Meanwhile, at Drake Stadium, in Cedar Rapids, Simpson College met defeat, 12–10. Howard scored a touchdown on a pass reception of thirty yards. He started as a fullback, but was switched to end.

Having played all of the first three games, Slater was relieved briefly by Van Osterhaut in the South Dakota State game, which Iowa won, 26–13.

Slater played in all of the last three games with the following record: Iowa, 14; Northwestern, 7, before more than ten thousand fans in Evanston, Illinois. Iowa, 6; the University of Chicago, 9, before some eighteen thousand fans at Chicago's Stagg Field. And Iowa, 10; Iowa State College, 0, before more than ten thousand fans in Iowa City.

At season's end, three Hawkeyes were selected to the all-state team, Lohman, Belding, and Slater.

There were grumblings among Iowa sportswriters when Walter Camp selected Slater on his third team All-American squad. Many thought that Slater's consistent performances should have earned him a first-place nomination. However, neither Lohman nor Belding made any of Camp's teams.

In the 1919 football season, Iowa won five games and lost two. Drake University won four games and lost three.

Iowa opened the 1920 football season at Jordan Field in Bloomington, Indiana, before more than seven thousand fans, beating the University of Indiana, 14–7.

Back home on October 9, Iowa romped over Cornell College of Mount Vernon, Iowa, 63–0. White substituted for Slater in the runaway game.

On the same Saturday, at Cedar Rapids, all-stater George Collins was back at Coe. He scored three touchdowns and kicked four extra points. Coe drubbed Monmouth College, 34–0. One of Collins's tallies was on a twenty-five-yard run. And the *Des Moines Register* reported on another:

Collins broke loose and raced thirty-five yards for Coe's final marker. Wood kicked goal. Collins, Coe's dusky halfback, proved to be the star, making several long runs.

On October 16 Iowa went down before the University of Illinois, at Champaign, 20–3. More than fifteen thousand fans looked on.

On the same day, at Dubuque, Iowa, Coe College and Dubuque College and Seminary played to a 7–7 tie. The *Des Moines Register* of October 17 reported:

Dubuque had Johnny Armstrong, versatile, lightning-like quarterback, and Coe had Collins, a Negro, at left half, who tore through time and again for long gains. He did all the passing and punting the ball three-quarters of the length of the field.

Iowa's season rolled on: Iowa, 0; the University of Chicago, 10. Iowa, 20; Northwestern University, 0. Iowa, 28; the University of Minnesota, 7.

Duke Slater, seemingly impervious to injury, was playing full time

Left: George Collins, all-time great Coe College half-back, in 1920. Right: "Duke" Slater after having been selected to Walter Camp's All-American second team, at tackle in 1921.

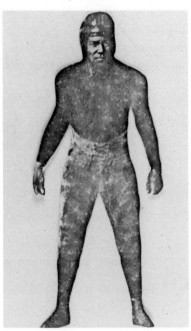 

Fred "Duke" Slater. All-time great University of Iowa tackle from 1918–1921.

in all the games against stiff opposition. The *Des Moines Register* commented after the Minnesota game:

Slater, the giant Negro played a good game but had little chance to star as he was a marked man and had two and three Gophers playing against him all the time.

Slater again made all-state, as did Collins. Collins's coach, Moray Eby, proclaimed his halfback with these words: "Collins is one of the best football players ever developed in the State of Iowa and I consider him on my all-time college eleven."

The *Des Moines Register*'s reporter was awed by one of Slater's idiosyncrasies: "The big Negro refuses to wear headgear, being the only man of the twenty-two to play bare-headed through the Iowa-Illinois game."

On October 22, 1921, Iowa was idle, after having won the first three games, but Coe—and Collins—were drubbing Dubuque at Cedar Rapids, 28–7. Collins scored two touchdowns, one on a thirty-yard pass reception, and one on a twenty-five-yard dash from scrimmage.

Iowa returned to action on October 29 at Lafayette, Indiana. In a mud-slogged contest, Iowa defeated Purdue, 13–6.

Three more wins resulted in a perfect season:

November 5: Iowa, 41. Minnesota, 7.
November 12: Iowa, 41. Indiana, 0.
November 13: Iowa, 14. Northwestern, 0.

Seven straight wins!

While Iowa was winning the Big Ten Championship in Evanston, the first conference championship since 1900, Coe College was defeating Cornell College, 28–7. George Collins scored three touchdowns, as Coe finished with a record of five wins, two losses.

Slater wound up his collegiate career on Saturday, November 19, 1921, against Northwestern in Evanston, his thirtieth game. He had played virtually every minute of each one.

The plaudits rolled in for Iowa—and Slater. He was selected for the fourth time for the all-state team, and Walter Camp named him as tackle on a second 1921 All-American team. Others disagreed with Camp, calling Slater the finest tackle ever, and placed him on their All-American first teams. He landed on the first All-American eleven of International News Service, Newspaper Enterprise Associations, Walter Eckersall's All-American team, and Walter Trumbull's All-American selections for the *New York Herald*.

Eckersall said, "Slater is so powerful that one man cannot handle him and opposing elevens have found it necessary to send two men against him every time a play was sent off his side of the line."

Herbert Crisler, a third-string left end on Walter Camp's 1921 All-American team, who became a prominent coach at the University of Michigan, played two games against Slater in 1919 and 1920, when he was at the University of Chicago. Crisler said: "Duke Slater was the best tackle I ever played against. I tried to block him throughout my college career but never once did I impede his progress to the carrier."

After leaving college upon graduation, Slater played professional football with the Rock Island Independents and the Chicago Cardinals. He later earned a law degree and then became a judge in Chi-

The 1919 Dartmouth College football team. Left to right, first row: Merritt, Crisp, Holbrook, Cannell, Sonnenberg, Streng, and Gordon. Second row, left to right: Cogswell, Myers, Murphy, Grundman, Cunningham, Healey, Youngstrom, and Spears (Coach). Third row, left to right: Southwick (Mgr.), Dorney, Robertson, Shelburne, Shepherd, Threshie, Jordon, and Freeman (Assistant Manager).

cago. Six hundred sportswriters in 1946 chose Slater as a member of their all-time All-American elevens. In December 1951 he was named to the National Football Hall of Fame.

On September 22, 1918, Dartmouth announced that it was suspending intercollegiate athletic competition in all branches of sport for the duration of the war. John W. Shelburne did not see much action as a fullback when play was resumed at Dartmouth in 1919, but he received his "D" along with twenty others, for "having played one whole period in the Pennsylvania, Cornell, or the Brown game."

On October 23, 1920, Shelburne started his first game at fullback against Syracuse, which won, 10–0. In the Cornell game on November 6, Dartmouth won, 14–6. Shelburne scored his first touchdown in the last quarter when Carey's punt was blocked by Sonnenberg, and Shelburne recovered on the three-yard line and ran it in for the score.

On November 20, 1920, Dartmouth beat Brown, 14–6. *The New York Times* gave two reasons: "The Brown team was without its star end, 'Ink' Williams and its regular tackle Johnstone. They were sorely missed."

Both Shelburne and Williams departed for the pros after graduation, Williams in 1921 and Shelburne in 1922.

These were the pioneers on white college football teams in the late nineteenth and the early twentieth centuries. They were the Negroes who played at Amherst, Beloit, Brown, Coe, Dartmouth, Drake, Dubuque, Harvard, Iowa, Michigan, Wabash, MIT, Nebraska, Oberlin, Springfield, and Williams, and while there were over nine million Negroes in the U.S. between 1890 and 1910, around two million were in the states of the above colleges. They may have studied, played, and attempted to socialize in an isolated world; yet they were the surrogates of the hopes, desires, and aspirations of thousands of Negroes.

They were William Tecumseh Jackson and William Henry Lewis, being introduced to Senator George Hoar of Massachusetts by John Langston, president of Virginia Normal and Collegiate Institute, and the Senator urging them to attend Amherst.

They were George Jewett, W. A. Johnson, William Washington, George M. Chadwell, Howard Lee, and William Clarence Matthews, starring in football in 1904—at end.

They were also Matthew Washington Bullock, Samuel Simon Gordon, Theodore Lucius Strothers, Samuel Ransom, George Collins, Robert Taylor, W. N. Johnson, Fenwich Henri Watkins, Robert W. "Bobby" Marshall, Leslie Lawrence Pollard, Edward Benjamin Gray, Fred "Duke" Slater, Paul Leroy Robeson, and Edward "Sol" Butler. Butler might have been acclaimed as the best of them all (had he not been tucked away from the teeming metropolises) for electrifying a crowd on Friday, November 16, 1917, as Dubuque overran Buena Vista College, of Storm Lake, Iowa, 125–0. Butler's performance included averaging twenty-five yards per carry with a one-hundred-yard punt return, a forty-five-yard run, a fifty-yard run, and a day's total of five touchdowns.

There was the incomparable Frederick Douglass "Fritz" Pollard, John Shelburne at Dartmouth College playing fullback as the 1920s neared, Jay Mayo "Inky" Williams at Brown, playing spectacularly at his end post following Pollard's departure.

Then in 1923 came Amherst's Charles Richard Drew, who later

Left: The twenty-one-year-old Charles Richard Drew, half-back-end, as a member of the 1925 Amherst College football team. Later famed as a surgeon, Dr. Drew spearheaded research for blood preservation and started the first blood bank in 1941, a revolutionary idea of a central depository for blood. Head of Surgery at Howard University Medical School in the 1930's, Dr. Drew was killed in an automobile accident on April 1, 1950, along with Drs. John Ford, Samuel Bullock, and Walter Johnson. Besides football, Drew was the holder of the 120-yard high hurdles record at Amherst and captain of the 1925–1926 track team. Right: David Myers, right guard-right end, as a member of the 1927 New York University football team. Myers played tackle and end in 1927–1928. In 1929 he was moved to quarterback and half-back.

received his medical degree from McGill in Montreal, and became the first director of the American Red Cross Blood Bank, supplying plasma to United States forces in 1941.

Another future doctor was the five-foot ten-inch, 170-pound backfield star, Charles West, at Washington and Jefferson in 1920, who had been born in Washington, Pennsylvania, on January 25, 1899. In 1921, Washington and Jefferson finished with a 10–0 won-lost record and accepted a Rose Bowl invitation to play the University of California in January 1922. The Golden Bears sneered at Washington and Jefferson. It was thought that California's 9–0–1 record, with 312 points scored against its opponents' 33, had been gained against superior opposition to that which had confronted tiny Washington and Jefferson, a school with an enrollment of less than three hundred students.

The word came out of California, with its more than twenty thousand students, that Washington and Jefferson were two Presidents—both of whom were dead. To complicate matters, on the eve of the game, Washington and Jefferson's quarterback, Ray McLaughlin, became ill.

Charles "Prunes" West, Number 9 and perhaps the team's best athlete, replaced McLaughlin. After traveling some three thousand miles, the first Negro to quarterback a Rose Bowl team led them to a moral victory. As underdogs, they held California to a scoreless tie. Neither team used any substitutes in the clean hard-fought contest.

West's college football career was not without the inevitable and ubiquitous specter of racial discrimination. On Saturday, October 6, 1923, a game was scheduled against Washington and Lee College of Lexington, Virginia. But when Washington and Lee's coach, James DeHart, discovered that West was scheduled to play, he attempted to persuade Washington and Jefferson's graduate manager, R. M. Murphy, to bench West. Failing to line up an ally in Murphy, DeHart then went to Washington and Jefferson's coach, John Henderson, protesting against West. Finally in desperation, DeHart informed Washington and Jefferson's president that the game would have to be canceled if his coach insisted upon playing Charles West.

President S. S. Baker was also firm. He stated: "I am sorry that unfortunate condition arose. I respect the tradition which Washington and Lee followed in refusing to play the game, but Washington and Jefferson is a northern school with traditions, too. It has never made any distinctions against color or creed in enrolling its students."

As the 1920s drew to a close, David Myers enrolled at NYU, and Raymond Kemp at Duquesne University. On October 5, 1929, Duquesne played West Virginia University at Morgantown. The score was 7–7. On the same day, NYU played West Virginia Wesleyan of Buckhannon in New York's Polo Grounds before thirty thousand fans, and NYU won, 26–0. Neither black athlete was permitted to play against the West Virginia teams.

In 1929 Kemp was a substitute for the regular tackle Kirby, until on October 19, Kemp started in his first game against Loyola. Duquesne won, 7–6.

When David Myers, a 175-pound Negro, had come off the 1926 freshman squad, NYU's head football coach, John F. "Chick" Meehan, looked forward to a good 1927 season. He played Myers equally at right guard and right end during both the 1927 and 1928 seasons.

On October 20, 1929, we find *The New York Times* reporting:

30,000 SEE MYERS STAR
WATCH PLAYER MAKING DEBUT IN BACK FIELD—CRASH ENEMY
DEFENSE AND REPEL ATTACKS

NYU defeated Penn State, 7–0.

On October 26 Myers played quarterback, as NYU defeated Butler University, 13–6. The game was played before twenty-five thousand fans at Indianapolis.

On November 9 NYU defeated the University of Georgia, 27–19. The quarterbacks from whom Myers had won the position, O'Herin and Gaudet, returned to run the team. Myers did not play, because of NYU's acknowledgment of Georgia's demands that he be benched, He returned to action against Rutgers on November 23. NYU won, 20–7. *The New York Times* noted:

MYERS RACES 50 YARDS FOR THE SECOND VIOLET
TOUCHDOWN AFTER SCORE IS TIED AT 7–7

Before over twenty thousand fans at New York's Yankee Stadium, Myers also had a thirty-five-yard run from his halfback position.

David Myers and Raymond Kemp both had brief pro careers.

Columbia University disbanded its football team from 1905 to

1915. In 1931 Manuel Rivero, a Negro Cuban, was starring on the diamond and the gridiron for the Lions.

On September 26, 1931, Columbia beat Middlebury College, 61–0. Rivero, from his left halfback position, scored one touchdown and caught a twenty-seven-yard pass from quarterback, Ralph Hewitt.

The Lions rolled over Wesleyan, 37–0, at Middletown, Connecticut; Dartmouth, 19–6, at New York's Baker Field before over twenty-three thousand fans; Williams College, 19–0, at Baker Field before over fifteen thousand.

In the 1931 season Columbia won seven and lost one. They also had one tie.

The Lions opened their 1932 season on September 24 and soundly whipped Middlebury College of Vermont, 51–0, with Rivero making a run of forty-eight yards. Columbia's season record was again 7–1–1.

The black athlete on white college football teams was making significant contributions, while the doors were now bolted tight against his entry into major professional teams after the 1933 season.

The black college stars were many. A panorama of the 1930s would portray the beauty of the runners: Bernard Jefferson at Northwestern, running to touchdowns of eighty-five yards against Iowa and thirty-four yards against Purdue in 1937; Ozzie Simmons at Iowa, with touchdowns of forty-seven yards against Northwestern, eighty-five yards against Ohio State, fifty-one yards against South Dakota State, seventy-one yards against Illinois, and a fifty-nine-yard run against Colgate; Fritz Pollard, Jr., at North Dakota, running to touchdowns of seventy-two yards against DePaul in 1936, sixty-nine yards against Luther College in 1937, fifty-six yards against North Dakota State, and forty-one yards against South Dakota in 1937.

These runs should have brought the scouts panting.

The panorama would also have to show a razor-sharp Wilmeth Sidat-Singh on Saturday, October 15, 1938, completing seven of eight passes as Syracuse upset Cornell, 19–17.

Also, in 1937, when Syracuse went to play the University of Maryland, the triple-threat star was not allowed to play. This too has to be part of the panoramic setting of the 1930s.

On October 15, 1938, Wilmeth Sidat-Singh's bullet passes totaled nearly 200 yards and three touchdowns as Syracuse beat a strong Cornell University team, 19–17. He is shown in 1938.

They played. And they were many. They were: William H. Craighead at Amherst's Massachusetts State University, Oberlin's Samuel Morrell, Illinois's Roy M. Young, and William H. Williams, A. A. Alexander, Charles Elliot Roberts, Gerald N. Lew, Benjamin Hubert, Edward Niles, Joseph Washington, Charles Ray, David Ray, Gideon Smith, William Kindle, Leonard Gibson, Arthur Wheeler, Joseph Bolden, Mack Greene, Arthur Neilson, Louis Watson, Robert Hamlin, Chester Jackson, Ray Vaughn, D. B. Crosby, B. T. Harvey, Leon Taylor, T. D. Hansbary, S. Jamison, James D. Barnes, Carlos Berry, Major Cleveland Abbott, Samuel Barnes, and Henry Thompson

To these names were added, in the 1930s and even into the 1940s, the likes of Joe Lillard, George Calloway, Jim Holland, Ernie Parks, Richard Jackson, Robert Reynolds, Homer Harris, Dennis Hoggard Ed Williams, Robert Lee, Frank Kelker, Harvey Grimsley, Robert Mike, Jimmy Johnson, Don Simmons, Willis Ward, Hayle Parker, Walter Gordon, Ted Morrison, William King, Ed Trigg, Archie Harris,

William Bell, Johnny Reagon, Julius Franks, Jerome Holland, Fritz Pollard, Jr., Jackie Robinson, Ray Bartlett, Woodrow Wilson Strode, and Kenneth Stanley Washington.

Strode and Washington would fuse past with present in major pro football. Joe Lillard had been the past. We now pick up his college career in the *Los Angeles Times* of October 4, 1931:

LILLARD LEADS WEBFOOTER ATTACK TO CONQUER IDAHO BY 9-TO-0 SCORE

At Multnomah Stadium in Portland, Oregon, before about ten thousand fans: "Big Joe Lillard, the Negro star of the Oregon backfield, was the chap who brought the spectators to their feet in the last period with a thrilling touchdown after he had fumbled a few minutes before just one foot from the Idaho goal line."

The University of Oregon had the ball on Idaho's seven-yard line after a sustained drive, when: "Lillard again took it. He hit left end, scattered the opposition and with three men running interference, crossed the goal line standing up."

Then suddenly the *Los Angeles Times* announced on October 9, 1931:

JOE LILLARD WILL PLAY TOMORROW—OREGON NEGRO STAR
CLEARED OF PRO CHARGES BY FACULTY;
FACES HUSKIES

Jonathan Butler, commissioner of the Pacific Coast Conference, met with H. C. Howe, chairman of the Oregon Faculty Athletic Committee, and Lillard, and also with Dr. Clarence W. Spears, Oregon's football coach.

Chairman Howe was investigating charges that Lillard had played semipro baseball with the Gilkerson Union Colored Giants of Chicago the past summer. Lillard admitted that he had played in a few games, but claimed that he had received money not as a player but as the team's chauffeur. He said he only filled in when an emergency arose. Chairman Howe indicated that the investigation was continuing.

On October 11, 1931, Oregon beat the University of Washington,

13–0, at Seattle before over thirty thousand fans. One touchdown came on a pass interception by Bremman, and Lillard scored from the one-yard line. Joe Lillard also played a stellar game defensively: "Shufflin Joe Lillard, the midnight express, twice intercepted their forlorn hope passes."

The next game was scheduled against the University of Southern California, for Saturday, October 17. The Oregon team detrained at Glendale, California, at 8:45 A.M., on Friday, October 16, and went by bus to the Miramar Hotel.

Meanwhile in Portland, Oregon, at the Multnomal Hotel, Commissioner Butler had submitted his resignation to the ten representatives of the Pacific Coast Conference, meeting in special sessions. The commissioner was perturbed that his efforts to have Joe Lillard declared ineligible had been stymied by H. C. Howe, Oregon's faculty representative. Butler's resignation was rejected.

Then suddenly, on October 17, 1931, the following newspaper headline appeared:

LILLARD OUT AS OREGON BATTLES TROJANS

Joe Lillard had been declared ineligible to complete in varsity athletics because of playing semipro baseball for remuneration in the past baseball season. Coach "Doc" Spears said that Lillard was fifty percent of his offense and could see no reason for his suspension.

The University of Southern California overwhelmed Oregon, 53–0. Lillard joined the Chicago Cardinals of the National Football League in 1932.

The first black athlete to sign to play major pro football was also from the Pacific Coast conference. We pick up his career via the front page of the *Los Angeles Times* in September 1937:

WASHINGTON HERO OF BRUIN WIN—NEGRO STAR THRILLS THRONG
OF 40,000 AT COLISEUM OPENER

UCLA beat the University of Oregon, 26–13, on September 25, 1937. Kenny Washington had a fifty-eight-yard touchdown run in the first quarter, and his pass to Bob Nash in the third quarter was also a touchdown heave. He also scored a touchdown on a five-yard run.

An end on UCLA's team with the number 27 was also black—Woody Strode.

The *Los Angeles Times* announced Coach Spaulding's plans on October 29, 1937:

WASHINGTON TO CALL SIGNALS FOR BRUINS AGAINST CALIFORNIA

Washington, UCLA's best all-around player, called signals for the strong Bruin Frosh team last year and before that was used in the same capacity when he led Lincoln High to a City championship in 1935.

UCLA lost, 27–14. But Washington had his moments:

WASHINGTON PROVES STAR—UCLA'S HALFBACK STEALS THUNDER
BEFORE 65,000 FANS

Washington completed one of the longest touchdown passes in college football history to Hirshon—sixty-two yards on the fly. He also completed another one for forty-eight yards to Hirshon, and one for thirty-three yards to Strode.

But for all of Kenny Washington's heroics, the Bruins finished the 1937 season with a record of two wins, six losses, and one tie.

In 1938 the Bruins improved their record to seven wins, four losses, and one tie. In 1939 their record was six wins, no losses, and four ties, the best record in UCLA's history, or since they played their first intercollegiate football game in 1920.

In 1939 the two Negro stars, Strode and Washington, were joined by Ray Bartlett and Jackie Robinson.

Kenny Washington's statistics follow for the 1939 season:

Passes		*Rushes*	
Games played	10	Games played	10
Passes attempted	91	Number of rushes	168
Completions	37	Yards gained rushing	811
Yards gained	559	Yards gained rushing and passing	1,370

And in 1939 Jackie Robinson had an average per carry every time he touched the football of 12.2 yards, the nation's highest made on twelve rushing plays.

A glimpse of how they rolled up these statistics for 1939: On October 7, UCLA 14; the University of Washington, 7. Jackie Robinson made a long run of sixty-four yards after he fielded a punt on his own thirty-one-yard line and ran it to the five-yard line.

On October 14, UCLA, 14; Stanford, 14. Jackie Robinson intercepted a pass on his own thirty-yard line and returned it forty-nine yards to Stanford's twenty-one-yard line.

On October 21, UCLA, 20; the University of Montana, 6. Robinson, used as a decoy, did not carry the ball from scrimmage once all day. He did have a thirty-three-yard punt return however. Kenny Washington scored three touchdowns. He also had a run from his own sixteen-yard line for a sixty-eight-yard gain to the Grizzlies' sixteen-yard line, and touchdown runs of twenty-four and twelve yards.

From the beginning to 1924, when he died on March 14, Walter Camp had selected six Negroes for his All-American teams. Thereafter, universal acclaim was not extended the Negro football player as an All-American until 1937 when Jerome "Brud" Holland was selected to Grantland Rice's prestigious All-American first team at end. Rice had succeeded Camp as the rater whose picks were carried in *Collier's* magazine.

In 1939 *Liberty* magazine also selected their All-American eleven. The magazine called the selections "the real All-American Football Team." *Liberty* covered one hundred ten major football colleges in the nation and twenty-two hundred judges, who were the players themselves.

At the end of the season, *Liberty* sent the twenty lettermen of each team an all-player form. Each judging player would select only eleven men. Of the 110 schools, 106 played in one or more intersectional contests. *Liberty* reasoned that the players were the "one group that knows more about the values of the gridiron greats' actual performance than sportswriters, radio commentators, coaches, or grandstand quarterbacks."

From ninety-one schools, representing 1,659 players, who covered more than seven hundred fifty games, came the names of eleven men who were the year's best football players. There were two basic rules by which all had to abide: (1) A player could not name a member of his own team, and (2) he could select only a player against whom he had actually competed during the past season in a scheduled game.

Liberty ran the results in the January 6, 1940, issue:

Only one player of the 664 named received the vote of every player who opposed him. He was Kenny Washington, UCLA's great halfback. One hundred and three players who competed against the Negro star agreed in the returns that he was the outstanding backfield man they met.

Woodrow Strode and Jackie Robinson made honorable mention in some polls in 1939.

In 1940 Washington and Strode had departed, and Ray Bartlett was in the halfback post, having been moved from end. UCLA had a disastrous season, winning only one game. However, Robinson, despite

Left: Jackie Robinson, UCLA four-sport star, in practice session in the 1940 season. Right: Woody Strode, shown in 1939 as UCLA All-Coast end. He would later, on May 7, 1946 sign a pro contract with the Los Angeles Rams, and still later become a successful motion picture actor.

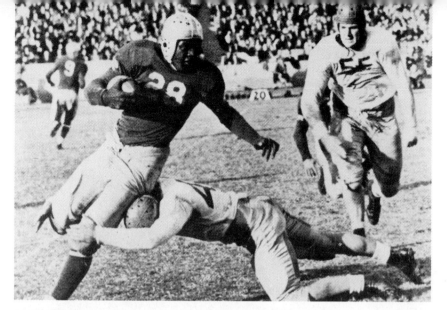

Jackie Robinson in game on November 30, 1940 against USC at the Los Angeles Coliseum. USC's Lewis Hindley makes tackle as Ben Sohn (55) also closes in on Jackie. USC won, 28–12.

being nagged with injuries, enjoyed some good days. He also had punting and kick runback averages of twenty-one yards, to lead the nation of players with an average of a minimum of fifteen runbacks.

On November 2, 1940, Jackie Robinson grabbed a punt on his own twenty-three-yard line and ran it to Stanford's thirty-two-yard line, a forty-five-yard run. He also ran one back forty-three yards from his own fourteen-yard line to Stanford's forty-three-yard line. He capped a brilliant offensive day with a twenty-six-yard run and a twenty-yard pass to Milt Smith. UCLA lost, 20–14.

In 1940 Robinson would complete forty-one of ninety-eight attempted passes, for 435 yards, a 41.8 percent average. UCLA's lone win came on November 16. Typically, it was engineered by Jackie Robinson:

ROBINSON RUNS WILD—U.C.L.A. BACK SCORES 22
POINTS AS TEAM RALLIES FOR VICTORY

With a final score of UCLA, 34, Washington State, 26, Robinson scored three touchdowns on a one-yard run in the first quarter, a sixty-yard punt return in the third quarter, and a seventy-five-yard run

Major professional football becomes "reintegrated" in 1946. From left to right: Woody Strode, Adam Walsh (coach of the Los Angeles Rams), and Kenny Washington.

from his own twenty-five-yard line in the fourth quarter. Besides these eighteen points, Robinson kicked four extra points and passed for a fourth touchdown, having a direct hand in twenty-eight of the thirty-four points scored.

John Roosevelt "Jackie" Robinson would in seven years meet his destiny on a major-league baseball diamond. Kenneth Stanley Washington and Woodrow Wilson Strode would meet their destinies on a major-league football gridiron in seven years as well. Past merged with present.

The Negro athlete was no instant phenomenon. His roots were deep and a large portion was buried in the athletic programs of the Negro colleges. But the Robinsons, Strodes, Lillards, and others would have played with little recognition were they not on white college football teams. Nevertheless, the nation's Negro college football teams, though ignored for the most part by the mass-circulation dailies and the wire services, have shown by their alumni that they were worthy proving grounds.

6

Football in the Black Colleges

The first Negro intercollegiate football game was played on Tuesday, December 27, 1892, between Biddle University and Livingstone College on the Livingstone campus in Salisbury, North Carolina. Biddle University won, 4–0.[1]

Biddle Memorial Institute was formally inaugurated on April 7, 1867, by the Catawba Presbytery held in Charlotte, North Carolina. The college was named in honor of Mary D. Biddle's late husband, Major Henry J. Biddle, in appreciation of a "generous gift" of $1,400 donated by the northern white woman. In 1877 the name was changed to Biddle University and finally in 1923 to Johnson C. Smith University, this time in appreciation of gifts from a white woman, Mrs. Mary Jane Smith, living in Pittsburgh, Pennsylvania, to honor her husband, Johnson C. Smith.

Livingstone College was formed by a small band of black ministers who gathered in Concord, North Carolina. They met in an African Methodist Episcopal Zion Church parsonage and formed the Zion Wesley College in 1879. In 1882 the institution was removed to Salisbury, and on October 3, 1882, with three teachers, three students, and a matron, the college was named after Dr. David Livingstone, the

---

[1] The value of scores in the chronological history of college football follow: 1883–1896: safety, 2 points; touchdown, 4 points; goal after touchdown, 2 points. 1897–1903: touchdown, 5 points, goal after touchdown, 1 point; field goal, 3 points. 1912: touchdown, 6 points. (Some of the early scores of the Negro college football contests did not strictly follow the above and were often at variance. Some sources list the Biddle-Livingstone final score as 5–0.)

missionary, philanthropist, and explorer, who penetrated the massive continent of Africa.

The Freeman, a weekly newspaper published in Indianapolis, Indiana, ran an item from their Biddle correspondent on December 3, 1892:

Our football eleven has received a challenge from the one of Livingstone College to play a match game of ball . . . the challenge will most likely be accepted, and the boys are now kicking the leather bag over the field, and are preparing for the encounter.

On the day after Christmas, Monday, December 26, 1892, the Biddle University football team entrained for Salisbury. The team included C. H. Shute, W. L. Metz, H. L. Peterson, L. B. Ellerson, Bright Funderbunk, T. R. Veal, M. Prather, H. H. Muldrow, Calvin Radford, W. H. Haig, George E. Caesar, Will Morrow, J. H. Hutton, and S. M. Plair.

Football was the principal sport on the Biddle campus, and several teams had been formed in 1892. But when the Biddle team arrived in Salisbury, the weather kept attendance down on the day of the game. A snowstorm had raged in southern Virginia and the Carolinas throughout the day and night of December 27.

Meanwhile, at Livingstone, the team had been formed in September. Each player had chipped in to order a regulation football from the Spaulding Sporting Goods Company. The uniforms were made by the young women of the industrial department out of ten-ounce white ducking cloth. The padding was sewn into old clothes furnished by the players.

The first Livingstone team was composed of J. W. Walker (captain), R. J. Rencher, Henry Rives, C. N. Garland, J. R. Dillard, J. B. A. Yelverton, Wade Hampton, Charles H. Patrick, J. J. Taylor, F. H. Cummings, and W. J. Trent.

William Trent, who was later to become president of Livingstone College, scored on that cold, dreary, snowy field. Walker forced a fumble by tackling a Biddle runner. Trent recovered the ball and ran it across the goal line. The line markings, however, were completely covered by the snow, and the referee disallowed the points, ruling that when Walker had tackled the Biddle runner, he was out of bounds. Biddle scored in the first half of a game that consisted of two forty-five-minute halves.

In 1892 Howard University played interclass football for the first time. The Detroit *Plaindealer* of October 28, 1892, reported:

Professor C. C. Cook . . . comes fresh from Cornell to succeed Professor William V. Tunnell in the chair of Belles Lettres and is already making a good impression upon students. Professor Cook is a splendid athlete and in the chase after the football is one of the swiftest . . . men on the campus.

Charles C. Cook has been called the father of sports at Howard University. He was Howard's first football coach, although he did not play varsity football while an undergraduate at Cornell.

Cook's name had been entered for class orator at Cornell, the only one submitted. After his automatic election, he resigned, giving his reason: "My election reflected no especial credit upon the university or upon me. I shall at once withdraw to private life, where I belong."

The New York Times visited the campus at Ithaca and observed that "Cook is a very good-looking, well-dressed, and well-mannered fellow, who studies hard and keeps much to himself. In his relation with classmates his color has never been considered, and he is a good fellow well met among all."

Under Cook's direction in 1893 Howard beat the Washington YMCA, 40–6, and also defeated Annapolis and several other athletic clubs.

In 1894 Howard and Lincoln universities engaged in their first intercollegiate football game. Lincoln, one of the first Negro colleges, had been founded in 1854 as the Ashmun Institute in Lower Oxford Township, Chester County, Pennsylvania. The name was changed in 1865.

In the 1893 football season there had been forty serious injuries on the nation's gridirons. Consequently, the professors at Lincoln had misgivings about permitting the team to journey to the Howard campus to engage in what many of them regarded as a brutal sport. The

The Howard University football team of 1893. Professor Charles C. Cook, Howard's first football coach, is shown third from left (in sleeveless sweater).

faculty finally relented, with the admonition that any serious injury would end football at the university.

On Thanksgiving Day, November 29, 1894, Howard and Lincoln began what in time would become a classic rivalry. Lincoln won, 6–5. However, a player's leg was broken and he had to be hospitalized, as his victorious mates returned to the Lincoln campus. Once on campus, the entire team was isolated for two weeks because, while in Washington, some of the players had visited a house that was under quarantine. The Howard-Lincoln encounters were therefore canceled for a decade.

On Monday, January 1, 1894, Tuskegee Institute and Atlanta University engaged in their first football game. Atlanta won, 10–0. A youth six days shy of his seventeenth birthday, William Clarence Matthews, was the student-coach of the Tuskegee Institute football team.

That New Year's Day, the Negroes had staged a big parade in downtown Atlanta to celebrate Emancipation Day. Unfortunately, it was scheduled at the same time as the football game. The receipts were small, and Tuskegee manager J. B. Washington had to wire for return railroad fare for the team. Enough money was received later

The Howard University football team of 1894. Note the pumpkin-like football of the early era.

that night to enable the team to get as close to Tuskegee as Chehaw, five miles away. A bunch of tired and hungry athletes straggled on campus at daybreak in time for breakfast.

In 1897 Charles Winter Wood, a Beloit College graduate, became Tuskegee's first nonstudent football coach, but Tuskegee did not field another varsity football team until 1899.

Problems of another sort loomed for Alabama's northern neighbor, Tennessee, in 1897. *The New York Times* reported on a Thanksgiving Day game, November 25:

Knoxville, Tenn. Nov. 25—The first football game ever played by Negroes in Tennessee took place here this afternoon between local teams. The game was not finished on account of the fatal wounding of Fred Staples and the serious injury of half a dozen other players. A riot concluded the game, when several drunken white men attacked the players because they could not make a touchdown. Hasty summons of the police prevented murder. . . .

Fred Staples died in 1902, but whether as a result of the 1897 "fatal wounding" is not known, although he suffered a "badly injured" spine in the game.

The Howard University football team of 1896. Bottom row, on ground, left to right (3): Joseph Carroll, George Weaver, and Coach Charles Cook. Second row, left to right (8): Thomas Flowers, Benjamin Jackson, Robert Jones, Cornelius Ridgeley, unidentified player, Zeal Brookens, George Brewer, and, standing with hands on hips, William Ford. Third row, left to right (4): George DeReef, James Ellis, William Nelson, and Joseph Rapier. Fourth row, left to right (6): unidentified player, Dwight Oliver Wendell Holmes, unidentified player, Wylie Crocker, Garnet Johnson, and unidentified player. (The Howard University Alumnus *of November 15, 1924*)

This Thanksgiving Day game was played between an amateur team, John Singleton's Tigers, and Knoxville College. The game ended after the first half in a 4–4 tie.

In the early days, contests were scheduled with whatever opposition was available. *The Colored American,* published in Washington, wrote on December 2, 1899:

HOWARD *VS.* ANNAPOLIS

The football game Saturday, November 18, between Howard University and the Crescent Athletic Club of Annapolis, Md., resulted as follows: Howard 22; Annapolis 0.

Howard played three games in 1899 and won all of them, including victories over Storer College, 40–0, and Morgan College, 71–0.

The Morgan College game was played on Thanksgiving Day, November 30, 1899, on the Howard campus before almost a thousand fans.

Howard completely outclassed Morgan. Scott had runs of sixty, thirty-five, and thirty yards. Carroll had a twenty-five-yard run. Ganaway had runs of twenty-five and fifteen yards. The lineups follow:

HOWARD (71)		MORGAN (0)
Craighead	C	Lockerman
McGuire—Chaney	RG	Johnston
Carter—Butler	LG	Wise
Washington	RT	Brown
Burnett—Hopson	LT	Grey
N. Ridgely—Mitchell	RE	Hughes—Young
Fox—Ganaway	LE	White
Jackson	RHB	McCullough—Wright
Alexander—Scott	LHB	Wright
A. Ridgely	FB	Banks—McCullough
Oliver—Carroll	QB	Young—Denver

Football was formally organized at the Atlanta Baptist College (now Morehouse) in 1900. Benjamin Griffith Brawley, class of 1901, was the first manager; Charles H. Willis was the captain. In the first game in 1900, Atlanta Baptist lost to Atlanta University, 35–0.

Atlanta Baptist started slowly. It was not until 1904 that it won its first game, a victory over the Atlanta YMCA, but in 1905, 1906, 1907, and 1908, Atlanta Baptist won consecutive championships.

Football, spreading in popularity, was moving to other Negro colleges. In November 1900, over four hundred fans in Petersburg saw Virginia Union University leave the field while losing to Virginia Normal and Collegiate Institute, 11–0.

Referee Estes had ruled that Virginia Normal, the hometown team, had successfully made enough yards for a first down and placed the ball on the one-yard line of Virginia Union.

The Virginia Union players protested vigorously that they had stopped the opposition short of the first down. When the referee overruled them, the Virginia Union players left the field with five minutes remaining in the game. Estes awarded the game to the Virginia Normal and Collegiate Institute, 16–0.

On December 15, 1900, Atlanta University beat Tuskegee Institute, 17–12, before over five hundred fans in Atlanta. Atlanta University's 1900 season's record follows:

Atlanta University, 35—Atlanta Baptist College, 0
Atlanta University, 56—Clark University, 0
Atlanta University, 10—Claflin College, 0
Atlanta University, 17—Tuskegee Institute, 12

In 1898 George R. Smith College was founded in Sedalia, Missouri, with twenty students in the college departments and 137 in the high school.

On October 19, 1901, George R. Smith, playing in Sedalia, beat Plaza High School of Fort Scott, Kansas, 33–0.

In Atlanta University's final game of the 1901 season, it defeated Claflin College, 10–0. Atlanta had not allowed any team to score upon its team all season.

In 1902 Atlanta Baptist College played two games—and lost two.

The same year, Hampton Institute began its varsity football history by winning the single game played. The Hampton Normal and Agricultural Institute was founded by General Samuel Chapman Armstrong in 1868 for the "education of Negro and Indian youth." One of Hampton's illustrious alumni was Dr. Booker T. Washington, who went on to found Tuskegee Institute in 1881.

Tuskegee in 1902 won two of three football games. Howard University played one game against Morgan College and won, 23–0. Howard now had a streak of thirteen straight victories without being scored upon—over five seasons.

In Jefferson City, Missouri, Lincoln Institute was beginning its varsity athletic program in 1902. A game was scheduled against Sumner High School of St. Louis. Negro high schools were scheduled because they were accessible, the other Negro colleges being some distance away. The game was played on October 20, 1902, at Jefferson

City, but the high school team left the field before the game ended, accusing Lincoln of "slugging." Lincoln led by two touchdowns when Sumner departed.

On November 17, 1902, Lincoln Institute met Fisk University in Nashville. Fisk won, 11–0.

Nashville around this period had three Negro colleges, Fisk University, Roger Williams University, and Walden University, as well as a professional school, Meharry Medical College. The Walden players were actually composed of students of Meharry Medical College, and Walden (Meharry) had lost only one game in three years.

Alabama State Teachers College (then Alabama State Normal) began its varsity athletic program in 1902. One game was played that first year against Tuskegee. Tuskegee won, 85–0.

The greatest football game up to this point—and certainly the most thrilling—was played in 1903 between Fisk University and Talladega College at a neutral site, Westside Park, in Birmingham, Alabama.

Steele of Fisk kicked off, and Terry of Talladega returned the ball to the thirty-yard line. A sustained drive by Talladega carried fifty yards to Fisk's twenty-yard line. Fisk held and Talladega was forced to punt.

Fisk mounted a drive from her forty-yard line. A series of line plunges carried to Talladega's ten-yard line. Talladega's defenses stiffened. The first half ended after an exchange of punts and two aborted drives by both teams.

In the second half, Talladega kicked off. Fisk returned the ball to midfield, but lost it on the first play from scrimmage via a fumble. Talladega recovered on Fisk's forty-yard line. In a series of straight-line plunges, over center, Talladega moved the ball to Fisk's eight-yard line. Again Fisk's defense dug in and held and took possession on downs on their own one-yard line.

After two running plays, the ball still rested on the one-yard line. Steele was called on to punt out of danger.[2] But "Terrible" Terry, of

---

[2] In 1903 a team was allowed three downs to make five yards for a first down.

Talladega, broke through and blocked the punt and Dick Hubbard fell on the ball as it bounded into Fisk's end zone for a safety.[3] Score: Talladega, 2; Fisk, 0.

Twelve minutes now remained in the game. Talladega's partisans were jubilant, as the brass band broke into their victory march. Another series of drives was thwarted by one side and then the other. Fisk now mounted a drive as time ticked away. Two minutes remained. Fisk had the ball on Talladega's twenty-five-yard line. Two line plunges were stopped at the line of scrimmage. On the third down, Steele dropped back to the thirty-five-yard line and received a direct snap from center. He drop-kicked the ball. It sailed high and straight, clearing the cross-bar by ten yards.

The Fisk partisans, who had journeyed from Nashville, went wild with joy. Final score: Fisk, 4; Talladega, 2.

Later, Coach Robinson, of Oberlin fame, acknowledged that it was the greatest game he had ever witnessed. His counterpart, Coach DeCatur, of Talladega, murmured his assent.

In 1904 two Negro colleges which had suffered football "injuries" in the late nineteenth century returned to the gridiron.

On Friday, October 28, 1904, before over four hundred fans, Morristown Normal and Industrial College and Knoxville College, both in Tennessee, played on the latter's home grounds. Knoxville College won, 20–0.

In 1904 Howard and Lincoln universities resumed their rivalry after a ten-year interruption. Lincoln won, 1–0, owing to a "forfeit."

On November 11, 1904, at 10:00 A.M., Howard University's football team entrained for Raleigh, North Carolina, for a 3:00 P.M. game on November 12. They beat Shaw University, 17–3.

In a return engagement on Thanksgiving Day, November 24, 1904, the two teams battled to a scoreless tie. This game, played on the Howard Campus, was witnessed by upward of two thousand fans.

---

[3] A safety is made when the ball in possession of a player guarding his own goal is declared dead by the referee, any part of the ball being on, above, or behind the goal line, provided the *impetus* which causes it to pass from outside the goal line to or behind the goal line was given by the side defending the goal.

In the deep South, Tuskegee Institute ran roughshod over Alabama State Teachers College in 1904. Tuskegee won, 65–0.

On November 3, 1906, Fisk beat Lincoln Institute, 11–9, at Nashville. On Saturday, December 1, 1906, Tuskegee Institute beat Fisk University, 4–0. At half time both teams were scoreless, but near the end of the game, Tuskegee's Newberne kicked the winning field goal.

In 1907 Alabama State Teachers College won its first football game, beating Talladega, 10–5.

On Thursday, November 7, 1907, Tuskegee's football team embarked on a six-game trek northward. It was to turn out disastrously.

At Washington, D.C., on November 9, Howard beat Tuskegee, 16–0. The other results follow:

Tuskegee Institute, 0—Hampton Institute, 10
Tuskegee Institute, 5—West Virginia Institute, 6
Tuskegee Institute, 0—Meharry Medical College, 28
Tuskegee Institute, 0—Talladega College, 7
Tuskegee Institute, 0—Louisville Baptist State University, 16

On November 28, 1907, Thanksgiving Day, the Louisville Baptist State University beat the Indianapolis Eagles, 44–0.

On the same day in Nashville, Meharry beat Fisk, 6–0. In Meharry's starting lineup was Clarence Agee "Terrible" Terry, who had played on the Talladega team, and would have an extensive football career, ending with the Howard University team from 1909–11.

Atlanta Baptist College and Fisk University, two titans, battled to a scoreless tie on November 2, 1907. The next week, on November 9, South Carolina State College, at Orangeburg, went down before Atlanta Baptist, 45–0.

By 1908 Alabama State Teachers College was improving. The season's record follows:

Alabama State Teachers College, 5—Talladega College, 0
Alabama State Teachers College, 6—Talladega College, 0
Alabama State Teachers College, 0—Tuskegee Institute, 6
Alabama State Teachers College, 6—Atlanta University, 0

On Thanksgiving Day, Thursday afternoon, November 26, 1908, Fisk and Meharry played before a large and enthusiastic crowd. The game was called at precisely 2:45 P.M. by referee Cobson. Meharry kicked off. Jackson received the punt and ran it back to the thirty-yard line. After two plays, Fisk was forced to punt. Johnson, of Meharry, muffed the kick and Fisk's Smith recovered the ball and ran it in for a score. The point-after-touchdown attempt failed. Fisk, 5; Meharry, 0.

In the second half, Fisk kicked off to Meharry, who returned the ball to the twenty-five-yard line. Finally Meharry had to punt. This time a Fisk player muffed the punt and it was recovered by Meharry, who ran thirty yards for the touchdown. The point-after attempt failed. Fisk, 5; Meharry, 5.

After an exchange of punts on thwarted drives, Upshaw of Fisk tried a place kick from thirty yards away. It failed.

Following another exchange of punts, Upshaw connected, this time on a thirty-yard drop-kick. Fisk, 9; Meharry, 5.

After another exchange of punts, and with time running out, Upshaw tried an inside kick from the twenty-five-yard line. Jackson recovered the ball as it bounced away from a Meharry player and dashed seventy yards for the final tally on this surprise play. The point-after attempt failed. Fisk, 14; Meharry, 5. The lineups follow:

FISK (14)		MEHARRY (5)
Jackson	RE	Johnson—Selby
McMillan	RT	Saunders
Thompson	RG	Dixon
Warren	C	McDew—Butler
McKissack	LG	Davis
Smith	LT	Scott
Washington—Payne	LE	Hurt
Upshaw	RHB	West
Dawson	LHB	Canady
Clark	FB	Thompson
Stitch	QB	Hickman—Johnson

Another big Thanksgiving Day contest was held in Atlanta in

1908. Atlanta Baptist College beat Talladega College, 33–0.

Four days later, on Monday, November 30, 1908, Atlanta Baptist beat Atlanta University, 12–0, on a muddy, slippery field.

The complete record of the 1908 Atlanta Baptist College team follows:

Atlanta Baptist College, 51—Athens, 0
Atlanta Baptist College, 27—YMCA, 0
Atlanta Baptist College, 11—Fisk University, 4
Atlanta Baptist College, 17—Tuskegee Institute, 0
Atlanta Baptist College, 33—Tuskegee Institute, 0
Atlanta Baptist College, 12—Atlanta University, 0

In 1909 Alabama State Teachers College, won its first championship, and the season's record follows:

Alabama State Teachers College, 6—Talladega College, 0
Alabama State Teachers College, 6—Atlanta University, 0
Alabama State Teachers College, 18—Americus Institute, 0
Alabama State Teachers College, 65—Florida A & M College, 0
Alabama State Teachers College, 2—Tuskegee Institute, 0

On Saturday, October 2, 1909, Fisk University defeated Knoxville College, 12–7, and on November 13, 1909, Meharry Medical College romped over Kentucky State College, 23–0.

In 1909 the Atlanta Baptist College and Hampton engaged in a rare intersectional contest. Hampton Institute won, 17–5.

In 1910 Fisk and Meharry both were undefeated as they met on Thanksgiving Day, November 24, 1910. Each team had their bands out, bedecked in fine array. The weather was ideal and a big crowd was in the stands at Nashville. Both team captains were confident. Captain Zuber of Meharry said: "We are going to play a hard clean game, but we are going to win and that is all there is to it. I know that all the boys feel just as I do about the matter, and we are going to start from the first whistle to win and win we must."

Captain Upshaw, of Fisk said: "I think my boys should bring home the bacon. But we are all in good condition. And I have nothing more to say but that we are going to play football and play hard and clean."

Fisk was doubly determined, having lost the last "Turkey Day" encounter in 1909. Meharry had scored in five minutes after recovering the kickoff, and when Zuber increased the lead with a field goal, that shut out Fisk, 9–0.

But now it was 1910. The annual game in Nashville was attended by some six thousand fans in a festive mood. Automobiles, carriages, and "vehicles of all kinds" encircled the playing field.

The game started at 2:30 P.M., and the opponents battled on even terms until the third quarter. Then Brown of Meharry grabbed a fumble and romped in for the score from twenty-five yards out. Zuber kicked the point afterward. Meharry, 6; Fisk, O.

Fisk received the kickoff and carried the ball to Meharry's fifteen-yard line, then lost the ball. Meharry lost five yards in attempts to carry the ball out. Zuber got back and attempted a forward pass. Fisk interfered with what seemed a perfect pass and grabbed the tumbling ball as it rolled in the end zone. The Fisk fans burst out in a paroxysm of wild shouts of happiness, thinking their player had made a touchdown.

The referee ruled that it was a safety and not a touchdown. The final score: Meharry, 6; Fisk, 2. The lineup follows:

MEHARRY (6)		FISK (2)
Madison	RE	Kendall
Canady	RT	Suggs
Wade	RG	McBeth
Bass	C	Warren
Whittaker	LT	Howell
Brown	LG	G. Howell
Rickey	LE	Payne
Zuber	QB	Weslegt
West	RHB	Merchant
Landry	LHB	Upshaw
Scott	FB	King

The Freeman proclaimed: "This still leaves Meharry the undisputed champion of colored football, especially southern, where are found nearly all of the great teams."

Meharry Medical College was coached by the ex-Beloit College great Sam Ransom. Ransom, an all-round athlete in college, played on the Hyde Park High School team in Chicago before entering Beloit.

In 1909 Howard University beat Hampton Institute, 5–0, and in their annual Thanksgiving Day game, beat Lincoln University, 5–0.

Meantime in 1909, Tuskegee had battled to a scoreless tie against Atlanta Baptist College and had defeated Hampton Institute, 6–0, deriving a measure of satisfaction from the fact that it had beaten Hampton by a greater score than had the perennial football power, Howard.

In 1909 Howard's season record was four victories without a defeat. One of the wins was a 17–0 victory over Shaw University on November 13, 1909.

In 1909 Roger Williams University took up the increasingly popular game of football. The *Nashville Globe* noted that the "boys have purchased a football outfit at a cost of eighty dollars and more than half that amount was paid cash."

On Friday, October 29, 1909, Roger Williams journeyed to Shelbyville, Tennessee, and defeated Turner Normal College, 6–0. The following Friday, they beat Walden University, 6–0.

On Friday, November 11, 1910, at Raleigh, North Carolina, Shaw went down to defeat before Howard, 21–0. Edward Benjamin Gray ran for a fifty-five-yard touchdown and was reported to have "played a good game for Howard, getting more than his share of tackles and gaining continually through the line and skirting Shaw's ends for long gains."

On Saturday, November 12, 1910, Tuskegee beat Montgomery State Normal College, 6–0, on the institute's campus.

The Howard-Lincoln annual game was alternated in a home and home series. The 1910 game on Thanksgiving Day, November 24, was played on the Lincoln campus.

Some three thousand fans jammed the campus grounds. The weather was ideal and the hometown fans looked forward to their fourth victory—one game ended in a tie—but instead received their second loss.

Edward Gray, the former Amherst star and Howard captain, sustained a broken arm in the hard-fought contest. Howard won, 5–0.

With their leading ground gainer and captain injured, Howard played its final game on December 3, 1910. Tuskegee Institute was the opposition, in a rare intersectional contest. Despite a steady drizzling rain that lasted throughout the game, one thousand fans were in attendance on the Howard campus. Howard won, 17–0.

In 1910 Howard won five games and lost none. For the second straight year Howard had not been scored on by the opposition, totalling 105 points to its opponents' zero. Still, some speculated that if more intersectional games had been scheduled by Howard, its record would not have been so imposing. The critics knew that C. Eugene Allen, the 180-pound fullback; Edward Benjamin Gray; and George Brice were outstanding athletes, but they wondered if a steady diet of Fisk, Meharry, or Atlanta Baptist College might not have pinned a defeat or two upon the Howard team.

A few comparisons in 1910 were offered.

Tuskegee won over Montgomery State Normal, 6–0, but lost to Meharry, 6–0. However, Howard won easily over Tuskegee, 17–0, and without Gray, their captain and the best player in the lineup.

The Lincoln University (Pa.) football team of 1910. Dr. Lewis (1), G. Bullock (2), Thompkins (3), S. Bullock (4), Redd (5), Bibb, Mgr. (6), Morris (7), Bird (8), Collins (9), Roberts, Coach (10), Perry (11), Midgette (12), Jacobs (13), Walker (14), Evans (15), and B. Morris (16).

The twenty-year-old Mordecai Wyatt Johnson as a member of the 1910 Atlanta Baptist College football team. The future Howard President was the team's quarterback.

Fisk University had beaten Atlanta Baptist College, 15–10, and lost to Meharry, 6–2. A game between Howard and Fisk or Howard and Meharry would have gone a long way toward setting a mythical crown upon the winner's head.

For whatever reason—distance and expense involved—Howard did not schedule these teams when it was a power in Negro college football.

On October 7, 1910, Meharry Medical College opened its football season against the local school, Pearl High, before more than two hundred fans. They defeated the other team, 5–0. The next day, Pearl High battled Fisk University to a 0–0 deadlock. About one thousand "paid admissions" witnessed the contest.

Tuskegee Institute journeyed to Nashville to play Meharry. And on Saturday, November 5, 1910, Meharry won, 6–0. Meharry's Scott scored the lone touchdown in the fourth quarter with less than five minutes left in the game. Zuber kicked the point after touchdown.

On Saturday, November 4, 1911, Howard opened its football season with a 26–0 win over the Annapolis Athletic Club.

Frank Forbes starred for Howard with two touchdowns of forty-five yards and eighty-five yards, and Gray, Forbes, and Nixon tore through the Annapolis line at will for gains of from five to fifteen yards.

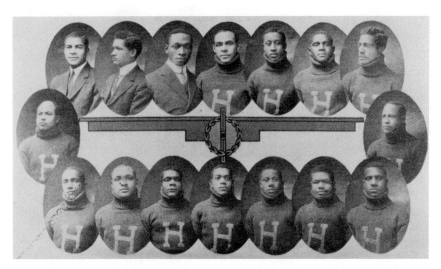

*The Howard University football team of 1911. Top row, left to right (7):
Curley (Mgr), Brent, Marshall (Coach), Allen, Brice, Terry, and Tyson.
Bottom row, left to right (9): Moore, Gray, Durrah, Clelland, Slaughter,
Howard, Smith, Nixon, and Bell.*

On November 11, 1911, Tuskegee beat Atlanta Baptist College,
6–0. Atlanta had a new coach, Matthew Washington Bullock, of
Dartmouth football fame.

On Thanksgiving Day, November 30, 1911, Hampton beat Shaw,
2–0, and on the same day, Howard and Lincoln engaged in their
annual "Turkey Day" encounter that was now being billed as a
"classic." Before more than five thousand spectators on the Howard
campus, the teams fought to a scoreless tie. The game that started at
2:30 P.M. was played on a field splattered with mud.

On Tuesday, November 7, 1911, Fisk journeyed to Talladega and
won, 16–0. On November 11 at Athletic Park in Nashville, Meharry
beat Talladega, 13–0.

In the Fisk-Meharry Thanksgiving Day game in 1911, Fisk won,
11–8. After receiving the kickoff, Fisk quickly drove for a touchdown after only one minute, with Merchant going over for the score.
Kindle kicked the point after the touchdown. Fisk, 6; Meharry, 0.

Shortly before the first half ended, Merchant again scored from close in. Failing to make the point, Fisk now led, 11–0.

Finally, Meharry scored late in the game via a Canady touchdown and a Zuber field goal. Final score: Fisk, 11; Meharry, 8. The lineups follow:

FISK (11)		MEHARRY (8)
Washington	RE	Ritie
Wesley	LE	Matison
Suggs	RT	Brown
Powell	LT	Canady
McBeth	RG	Dixon
Howard	LG	Mittico
Jones	C	Bass
Lewis	QB	Zuber
Sublett	RHB	Cochran
Kindle	LHB	Asbury
Merchant	FB	Hamilton

Professor Benjamin Brawley, the first manager of the Atlanta Baptist football team and in 1912 the dean at the college, posed a question in the *New York Age* of November 23, 1912, as to what section of the country really had the best football teams.

In the *New York Age* on December 19, 1912, Charles T. Lunford, former athletic editor of the *Howard University Journal*, gave his response:

Howard has claimed the Colored championship for the last four years by virtue of her unbroken string of victories over Lincoln, Hampton, Shaw, Livingstone, Annapolis, and Tuskegee. There is Atlanta Baptist College in Atlanta, with a good team, but the first year Howard defeated Tuskegee, 18–0, Tuskegee had played a scoreless tie with A.B.C. The next time Howard played Tuskegee, her team was the undisputed champion of the South, and Howard played all over her and defeated her 22–0. . . . Harvard claimed the championship this year not by winning from all the white colleges in the country but by virtue of her unbroken string of victories over the best college teams in the East. Howard has the same record as, if not a better record than Harvard. Why can't she claim the championship?

Professor Brawley's question would remain moot as long as sec-

The West Virginia Institute football team of 1912. Hughes (1), Fulks (2), Hunter (3), Davis (4), Patterson (5), B. Fulks (6), Noel (7), Cunningham (8), Kincaid (9), J. B. Brown, Coach (10), Hill (11), Ross (12), Young (13), Burke (14), Clarke (15), Marshall (16), Jones (17), C. W. Smith, Mgr. (18).

tional loyalties were strong and intersectional contests infrequent. Howard had never in fact engaged in a contest against Atlanta Baptist College. However, tremendous followings were being generated by annual Thanksgiving Day encounters. In 1912, however, one intensely spirited contest would be no more—the Fisk-Meharry annual Thanksgiving Day game in Nashville.

The *Nashville Globe* of September 27, 1912, reported:

NO FOOTBALL AT MEHARRY

ANNUAL SOCIAL EVENT CANCELLED

The dean of the Meharry Medical College, George W. Hubbard, and the board of directors, had decided to end football beginning with the 1912 season.

The sudden announcement was met with a "wailing and gnashing of teeth" by the players, fans, and alumni. Many moaned about the paucity of athletic contests, particularly after Pearl High School had also ended its football program in 1912. Many appeals were made to Dean Hubbard to reconsider, but he was firm, saying only that the athletes needed all their spare time for "their studies."

Another Thanksgiving Day rivalry was budding in the deep South. In 1912 Rust College beat the Mississippi Industrial Institute, 12–6, on the Rust campus in Holly Springs.

In 1912 an illustrious name was added to the Fisk University football team at fullback. *The Freeman* noted on November 16: "Booker T. Washington, Jr., was captain for Fisk, and played a consistent game for his team at fullback."

The Atlanta Baptist College won all five of its games in 1912, scoring 205 points against its opponents' 9.

The same year Howard University won all five of its games, scoring 72 points against its opponents' 7. Hampton Institute was the only team to score on Howard in three seasons.

The Howard-Hampton series dated back to 1908, and Howard had won all five of the games played, but in 1913, Hampton won, 8–6.

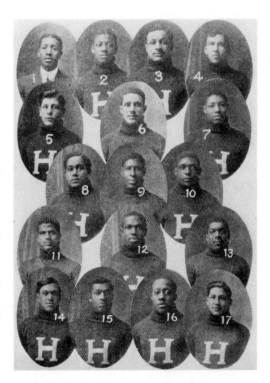

The Hampton Institute football team of 1912. Williams, Physical Education Director (1), Dudley (2), Scott (3), Stony (4), Bender (5), Oliver (6), Wildy (7), Aiken (8), Warner (9), B. Scott (10), Atkins (11), Hall (12), Gayle (13), Smith (14), Flynt (15), Shearer (16), and Jamison (17).

Hampton scored first when Beamen made a bad snap from center, and a safety was scored. Later, Howard scored when Brice hit Slaughter with a pass for a touchdown. The point after attempt was missed. Howard, 6; Hampton, 2.

Then, with time running out and on fourth down and seven, the ball was on Howard's thirty-yard line. Bender crossed up the Howard defense when he faked a kick and passed for the winning score.

In 1913 Atlanta Baptist College was renamed Morehouse College; it continued as powerful as before. On Saturday, October 18, 1913, Morehouse whipped Morris Brown College, 38–0. On October 25, Morehouse overwhelmed Clark University, 98–0. Many believe this victory to have been the largest ever scored between Negro football teams, larger than the 87–0 score Atlanta Baptist (Morehouse) had run up against Morris Brown in 1912.

The *New York Age* summed up the feelings of many:

It is to be regretted that on account of the great distance between Washington and Atlanta, plans for a game this year between this brilliant eleven [Morehouse] and that of Howard will not be successful.

But on Friday, October 31, 1913, Morehouse and Talladega col-

The Livingstone College football team of 1912. Benjamin B. Church, Coach (1), William Clinton (2), Robert Long (3), Richard Sherrill (4), George Sherrill (5), Arthur Sherrill (6), Eugene West, Mgr. (7), Arthur Platt (8), Herman Holt (9), William Michael (10), Price McCain (11), Joe Robinson (12), Charles Henderson (13), and Felix Anderson (14).

leges played to a 0–0 tie on the Talladega campus. When Fisk beat
Morehouse, 25–9, on Friday, November 21, 1913, the *New York
Age* commented:

Fisk established a record by defeating Morehouse, being the only team
that has ever won a football game on the Maroon's gridiron during the
last fourteen years that she has played.

The records of the leading Negro college football teams in the 1913
season follow:

	Won	*Lost*	*Tied*
Livingstone College	5	0	0
Jackson College	4	0	0
Hampton Institute	4	0	0
Haines Institute	3	0	0
Fisk University	4	0	1
Howard University	3	1	1
Morehouse College	3	1	2
Tuskegee Institute	2	0	1
Atlanta University	2	1	0

In 1914 the Howard-Lincoln game was moved back from Thanksgiving Day to November 7. The game, played on Lincoln's campus,
was won by the Pennsylvania team, 12–0.

Lincoln played Hampton on November 16 and lost on a forfeit,
1–0. The ball was on Lincoln's three-yard line in the last quarter.
Flynt, Hampton's fullback, appeared to get across on a line smash for
the score, but Lincoln protested that he had been held short of the
goal line. When the referee, B. B. Church, upheld Hampton's claim
to the score, Lincoln angrily left the field. Church awarded the game
to Hampton.

On January 1, 1914, the *New York Age* commented on the progress of football in Negro colleges in Mississippi and Louisiana:

The season just closed has shown material progress in the great college
game of football in the State of Mississippi and Louisiana. . . . In a game

The Tuskegee Institute football team of 1912. Thomas, Coach (1), Washington, Mgr. (2), Logan (3), Stanton (4), Patillo (5), Bonner (6), G. Gray (7), Jacobs (8), Johnson (9), S. Hunter (10), E. Gray (11), Smith (12), Wesley (13), Burgridge (14), Harper (15), Graham (16), and V. Hunter (17).

between Jackson College and Rust University played at Jackson during the Mississippi Fair, a representative white paper stated that a large number of whites attended out of curiosity to see what a Negro football game was like. . . . It stated that a better exhibition of football had never been seen at Jackson. . . . For two years now Jackson College has set the pace in athletics for the school of the State, having as close rivals Rust University, Tougaloo University, and Straight University of New Orleans. Campbell College has also organized and played games this year.

On Thursday, June 11, 1914, philanthropist Julius Rosenwald met with Booker T. Washington in Chicago to assure Dr. Washington that he would match southern monies raised for the erection of additional schoolhouses for Negroes in the South. The details and locations, Rosenwald left up to Washington.

In November 1914, the school that had started in a single converted chicken coop, Tuskegee Institute, beat Fisk University, 9–7, on the institute's grounds, the margin of victory coming on a thirty-yard field goal by Tuskegee's Harper.

In the 1914 opening game, Morehouse beat Morris Brown, 13–6. A recovered fumble by Morris Brown in the last quarter was the first touchdown ever registered by Morris Brown over Morehouse. Morehouse defeated Talladega, 19–0, in 1914. The game was less than two minutes old when Brock hit Ely with a touchdown pass. In the second quarter, Morehouse displayed a little razzle-dazzle. Brock received the center snap and flipped the ball back to Weaver, who threw downfield to Ely, covering forty-five yards to the one-yard line. Lewis scored on a plunge on the next play and also kicked the point after touchdown.

The last touchdown was made late in the fourth quarter. James Jove, a sub, twisted, scrambled, and straight-armed his way twenty-five yards for the score. The starting lineups follow:

MOREHOUSE (19)		TALLADEGA (0)
Ely	LE	Savage
Richardson	LT	Frazier
Dickson	LG	Cole
Harris	C	Woods
Carter	RG	Jordon
Ross	RT	Brown
Weaver	RE	Shanks
Brock	QB	Moore
McKay	LHB	Proctor
Jackson	RHB	Beh
Lewis	FB	Bryant

George D. Brock, all-time great Morehouse College quarterback, in 1917.

In Biddle's season opener on October 30, 1914, Biddle beat Bennett College, 6–0, at Charlotte, North Carolina. Downing scored the lone touchdown on a delayed pass.

In Georgia State College's first game on October 30, it played to a 0–0 tie against South Carolina State College in Orangeburg.

Rust College, on the same date, started its season with a 6–6 tie against Mississippi Institute.

On November 7, the Morehouse machine rolled over Atlanta University, 40–0. Weaver scored two touchdowns, Brock scored two, Jones scored one, and Lewis scored one. Davis kicked three points after touchdowns, and Brock kicked one.

On November 21, before two thousand spectators, Morehouse beat Tuskegee, 13–7. On Thanksgiving Day 1914 Fisk beat Morehouse, 7–0, and in Salisbury, North Carolina, on the same day, Shaw beat Livingstone College, 7–0.

On November 13, 1915, Morehouse and Tuskegee played to a 6–6 tie on the institute's grounds. The next day, Tuskegee's founder, Booker T. Washington, died. Death came to the educator at 4:40 A.M., Sunday, from hardening of the arteries, following a nervous breakdown.

On February 2, 1912, a meeting had been held at Hampton Institue, Hampton, Virginia, out of which the Colored Intercollegiate Athletic Association was formed.

On December 30, 1913, representatives of ten Negro colleges had met in Atlanta, Georgia, on the Morehouse College campus, and formed the Southeastern Intercollegiate Athletic Conference. In 1929 the name was changed to the Southern Intercollegiate Athletic Conference.

A tightening up of rules and eligibility standards was now being regulated under the watchful eye of conference officials. But some informal aspects of the game as it was played in the halcyon period of the late nineteenth century and the early 1900s persisted. The days of professional school varsity players and grade school varsity athletes were not yet completely in the past.

In 1915 Collins, a former Lincoln University quarterback, coached

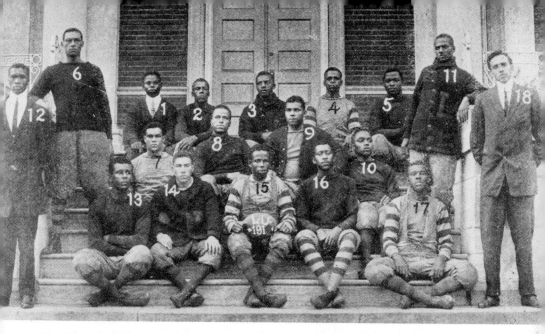

*The Lincoln University football team of 1913. Harry James, Trainer (1),
Walter Anderson (2), Alfred White (3), George Bullock (4), Arthur Langa
(5), Ralph Dunn (6), John Barnum (7), Philip Hilton (8), David Wallace
(9), William Townsend (10), Frank Raiford (11), Clarence Wood, Trainer
(12), Frank Wheaton (13), Chalmer Harley (14), William Jones (15), Ralph
Wickes (16), Henry Goss (17), and Henry Pellam, Assistant Manager (18).*

at Kittrell College. On occasion he would also play under the alias
"Glassport."

On October 22, 1915, at Greensboro's Cone Park, Greensboro
A & T beat Shaw, 7–0, the lone score coming on a sixty-yard run by
halfback Jackson. On the Howard campus on October 30, Virginia
Union went down to defeat, 18–3. One of Howard's scores was via a
Brice-to-Grinnage pass. Union's Huckles, who two decades later
would coach at his alma mater, kicked a thirty-five-yard field goal for
its only tally.

Rust College opened its 1915 season on October 29th with a 6–0
win over Mississippi Industrial Institute at Holly Springs.

On November 3 Rust left Holly Springs for Jackson, Mississippi,
and beat Jackson College on November 4, 3–0.

On November 12, in Greensboro, Shaw's second team beat Bennett
College, 3–0. The next day, at Durham, Shaw's second team beat
the National Religious Training School, 6–0. On the same day,

St. Paul's Normal and Industrial School ran roughshod over the Collins-coached Kittrell College team, 65–0, at Lawrence, Virginia.

In 1915, for the first time in eight years, the Howard-Lincoln annual game would not be played. Howard would play Hampton Institute on Thanksgiving Day, November 25, and Lincoln would travel to Pittsburgh to play the amateur team, the Delaney Rifles.

At Hampton, Howard went down to defeat, 18–0. Some other 1915 Thanksgiving Day games follow:

Georgia State College, 21—Allen University, 0
Rust College, 47—Mississippi Industrial Institute, 0
Livingstone College, 6—Biddle University, 0

South Carolina State had a good 1915 football season's record:

South Carolina State College, 37—Voorhees Industrial Institute, 0
South Carolina State College, 0—Allen University, 0
South Carolina State College, 12—Georgia State Teachers College, 7
South Carolina State College, 37—Haines Institute, 0
South Carolina State College, 13—Paine College, 6

In 1915 Livingstone College and Greensboro A & T College tied for the state collegiate championship. Livingstone's season's record follows:

Livingstone College, 42—High Point, 0
Livingstone College, 3—Bennett College, 0
Livingstone College, 0—Greensboro A & T College, 0
Livingstone College, 6—Biddle University, 0
Livingstone College, 12—Greensboro A & T College, 12

In 1916 Hampton Institute opened its season on Saturday, October 21, against the Roanoke Athlete Club and beat Roanoke overwhelmingly, 87–0. The second team played the entire second half.

In Morehouse's opening game in 1916, Morehouse beat Clark University, 47–0. In the second half, mostly "scrubs" were playing for Morehouse. Morehouse's 1916 season's record follows:

Morehouse College, 48—Clark University, 0
Morehouse College, 32—Morris Brown College, 0
Morehouse College, 26—Talladega College, 0
Morehouse College, 23—Tuskegee Institute, 0
Morehouse College, 17—Atlanta University, 10

Howard played a rare intersectional game in 1916 in Nashville, against Fisk University. Howard won, 16–0.

On November 16, 1916, Edward Walters College beat the Florida Baptist Academy, 12–6, and claimed the championship of the state of Florida and the southern part of Georgia.

In the Thanksgiving Day game against Fisk on November 30, Morehouse won, 14–0, and became the undisputed champion of the South. (This was the first time that a team-by-team comparison could be made between Howard and Morehouse, based on their meeting a common opponent, Fisk. Howard had beaten Fisk by two points more than had Morehouse.)

On November 24, 1916, Biddle University journeyed to Orangeburg and beat South Carolina State College, 7–0. With the ball on the South Carolina State forty-yard line in the last quarter, Francis circled right end for thirty-five yards. Williams cut over left tackle for four yards, and a moment later, C. O. Hilton bucked over for the single score. He also kicked the point after touchdown.

In a 1916 Thanksgiving Day game, the two historic adversaries, Biddle University and Livingstone College, met, with Biddle University the victor, 21–0.

Tuskegee Institute opened its 1917 season by decisively beating Birmingham High School, 86–0. With a draft-riddled team, Hampton Institute was beaten for the first time by Virginia Union, 3–0, at Hovey Park, in Richmond.

The First World War affected college football programs throughout the nation as young men answered the nation's call to service. The *New York Age*, on December 23, assessed the 1917 football season:

Football has suffered this season along with other sports because of the war; but there have been many surprises and much interest taken in the game. Among the surprises were remarkably strong teams developed by Virginia Union University. Another surprise was the weak team turned out by Howard University. Having been the leading school in the football world for a number of years, Howard this season was somewhat disappointing.

In a biennial series first started in 1900 against Virginia Union, Howard had won all nine games, but in 1917 Virginia Union beat Howard, 16–0.

In 1918 many of the college athletic teams were comprised of Student Army Training Corps personnel. Howard's SATC football team met Hampton's SATC team on November 16 in Washington. A large crowd witnessed the home team go down to its sixth straight defeat, 6–3.

The draft-riddled, weakened teams saw many of the once mighty fall. On November 23 Talladega College beat Morehouse, 7–0.

By 1919 football began to return to normalcy. On November 11, 1918, the First World War had ended. On October 11, 1919, in its first game of the season, Howard beat Virginia Theological Seminary and College, 40–0. Earlier, the Howard-Lincoln Thanksgiving Day encounters had been resumed.

A clamor for the game had gone up after the 1915 season, when the series had been interrupted. Resuming the contest in 1916, Howard beat Lincoln, 26–0. In 1917 Lincoln won, 6–0, and in 1918—with the games still being played on each other's campuses—Lincoln won, 13–0. The ever increasing crowds at the Howard-Lincoln games made it necessary for school officials to seek larger facilities.

In Washington, D.C., at the American League stadium, Griffith Park, the Army Medico team played the Seamen Gunners, in a 10:30 A.M. contest. In the afternoon, the Marines played the Army Gun Factory team at 2:30 P.M. There was no scheduled game in the stadium in 1919; this was the year that the Howard-Lincoln game would be at the site furnished by Lincoln University.

For 1919 Lincoln officials obtained a lease on Philadelphia's thirty-three-thousand-seat Shibe Stadium. The stadium was being shared during the baseball season by the National League's Philadelphia Phillies, and the American League's Philadelphia Athletics.

More than eighteen thousand fans showed up, a record attendance for two Negro college teams. They saw Howard and Lincoln play to a scoreless tie.

Lincoln University was coached by the former All-American, Brown University halfback, Frederick Douglass "Fritz" Pollard. His team outplayed Howard throughout the game and five times had the ball on Howard's ten-yard line, but could not gather the punch to score.

Tuskegee opened its 1919 season with a 79–0 win over Birmingham's Industrial High School, and that year Howard played West Virginia Collegiate Institute for the first time. Before some two thousand colored and white fans, the two teams fought to a 0–0 tie at Lakin Field, Institute, West Virginia.

In 1919 a game between Morehouse and Tuskegee ended in a forfeit. The score at the end of the first half was 7–6 in favor of Morehouse. In the third quarter, a fumble by Tuskegee was recovered by Morehouse's Harris. The referee, Shaw, ruled it a touchdown for Morehouse. A heated argument ensued, then the Tuskegee players stormed off the field when Shaw would not change this ruling.

On a chilly, windy Thanksgiving Day afternoon, 1919, at Institute, West Virginia, a crowd of twenty-five hundred fans gathered to see the home team play Wilberforce University. West Virginia Collegiate Institute won, 41–0.

The 1920 Howard-Lincoln game was again played on Howard's Washington campus. Plans to lease Griffith Park had fallen through, but the jammed campus grounds was the only discomfort returning Howard grads had to endure. Howard walloped Lincoln, 42–0.

Many critics blamed Lincoln's coach. Frederick Douglass "Fritz" Pollard had been installed as head football coach in 1918. He had let it be known that with a family to support he could not give up his career as a professional football player with the Akron (Ohio) Steels. It was on condition of this part-time arangement that he acceded to the head coach position. But the 42–0 score sent critics howling for

Pollard's scalp, or more precisely for his dismissal. The former All-American halfback said: "Much blame has been placed upon the coaching system, I being the target of much attack. I wish to state here that I have no apologies to make for the showing made by Lincoln. I have led them to victory and honorable athletic achievement during the previous two years. Working entirely with raw material, I was successful in defeating Howard and Hampton once and in tying them once."

John Shelburne, Dartmouth, Class of 1919, replaced Pollard for the 1921 football season.

The largest score by Howard over Lincoln reverberated about campus. The Howard yearbook, *The Enopron*, reported:

After being presented with a floral design by the President, the team went forth to battle. When the roar of the crowd ceased and the sun set in the west, it was evident that Howard had successfully vanquished Lincoln, 42–0.

In 1921 the Howard-Lincoln game returned to Philadelphia. Committees were set up to welcome incoming crowds, and greeted specially run chartered trains from Washington, Baltimore, New York—and even from some points in the deep South. Dances, banquets, and a press breakfast were scheduled. The black press provided full coverage. The *Pittsburgh Courier*'s Robert Vann, William Nunn, Chester Washington, Ira Lewis, and Rollow Wilson; the *Chicago Defender*'s Frank Young, William White, Russell Caution, and J. H. Gray; and the Associated Negro Press's Nahum Brascher—all were there, along with sportswriters on the Washington and Baltimore *Afro-American*, the *New York Age*, the New York *Amsterdam News*—and, of course, the local black paper, the *Philadelphia Tribune*.

The Howard team arrived on Wednesday—a day before hostilities —and was quartered at the local YMCA on Christian Street. The Lincoln team would arrive on Thursday morning from its nearby campus.

Lincoln came to the big game with an imposing season's record:

Lincoln University, 13—Hampton Institute, 0
Lincoln University, 20—Wilberforce University, 6
Lincoln University, 6—Annapolis Crescent Athletic Club, 0
Lincoln University, 26—Bordentown Training School, 0
Lincoln University, 0—Virginia Union University, 1 (forfeit)

But Howard had a spotless record:

Howard University, 24—Shaw University, 0
Howard University, 3—West Virginia Collegiate Institute, 0
Howard University, 33—Greensboro A & T College, 0
Howard University, 21—Virginia Normal and Industrial Institute, 0
Howard University, 10—Virginia Theological Seminary and College, 0

The game was beset by bad weather. A steady rain pounded throughout play, as more than twenty thousand fans stoically braved the elements.

In the first quarter Lincoln's captain, Jimmy Law, passed thirty-five yards to Stanley Skinker for a touchdown. The point-after-touchdown attempt failed. Lincoln, 6; Howard, 0.

In the second quarter, after several thwarted drives by each side, Howard finally mounted a sustained march that carried to the Lincoln one-yard line. Payne bucked over behind a block from his center. Doneghy kicked the point after touchdown. Howard, 7; Lincoln, 6.

Each team played on even terms in the third quarter. In the last quarter, a twenty-yard lateral pass from Seldan Parr to James Law registered the final score. Law grabbed the ball at his own forty-yard line and behind two key blocks outran virtually the entire Howard team.

Lincoln fans, unmindful of the elements, ran onto the field, many of them sliding, falling, and rolling in the mud happily with upstretched arms. The police finally had to clear the field so the game could continue. Final score: Lincoln, 13; Howard, 7.

In 1922 Hampton Institute won the CIAA championship. Captain Edward Dabney led his team to six wins out of seven games:

Hampton Institute, 3—St. Paul Normal and Industrial Institute, 0
Hampton Institute, 6—Virginia Normal and Industrial Institute, 12

Hampton Institute, 9—Lincoln University, 7
Hampton Institute, 1—Shaw University, 0 (forfeit)
Hampton Institute, 13—Howard University, 0
Hampton Institute, 8—Virginia Union University, 6

Coach Gideon Smith's Hampton lettermen were David Burrell, W. W. Cardozo, T. T. Coleman, E. L. Dabney, C. W. Frye, S. L. Gayle, D. L. Gunn, Herbert Hardwick, B. C. Jacobs, J. H. Jones, S. H. Scott, A. R. Ruffin, J. S. Ruffin, J. W. Greene, and W. D. Dixon,
On November 30, 1922, the following Thanksgiving Day scores were registered:

Fisk University, 20—Morehouse College, 19
Hampton Institute, 8—Virginia Union University, 6
West Virginia Collegiate Institute, 6—Wilberforce University, 0
Atlanta University, 18—Morris Brown College, 6

The Howard-Lincoln Thanksgiving Day game was *the* attraction that was awaited by most fans. The "Flapper Special" was already bringing trainloads from New York City, and other special trains were arriving from Pittsburgh and from Philadelphia.

Howard, like Lincoln, finally built a stadium large enough to seat the crowds. Lincoln also hired a new coach. John Shelburne had departed for the professional ranks, and James Law, who had graduated, replaced him as coach.

In 1921—when the Howard-Lincoln game was in Philadelphia—Georgetown had defeated Bethany College, 13–0, at Griffith Stadium. When Emmett J. Scott, secretary-treasurer at Howard, started negotiations for a Thanksgiving Day lease for 1922, he was informed that Georgetown and George Washington universities already had contractual rights to an afternoon game for November 30. Scott talked stadium officials into a morning game, and the lease was granted.

The stage was set for the biggest sporting extravaganza for Negro Americans. The early starting time seemed to double the incoming crowds, as the probable starting lineups of both teams were announced:

HOWARD UNIVERSITY

Number	Player	Position	Weight
16	Long	RE	155
21	Smith	RT	191
22	Doakes	RG	165
18	Holton	C	160
23	Nurse	LG	175
19	Crawford	LT	165
20	Williams	LE	175
15	Carter	QB	170
4	Dodson	HB	145
17	Contee	HB	158
40	Doneghy	FB	165

LINCOLN UNIVERSITY

Number	Player	Position	Weight
21	Skinker	LE	170
1	Coston	LT	180
14	Walls	LG	166
32	Morgan	C	205
36	Poindexter	RG	180
20	Diggs	RT	175
6	Crudup	RE	175
2	McLean	QB	130
33	Politt	HB	165
7	Trigg	HB	175
13	Johnson	FB	170

The lineups were set, the warriors primed for battle, and some twenty-five thousand fans poured into Griffith Stadium on the morning of Thursday, November 30.

The score was 0–0 midway into the second quarter when "Jazz" Byrd went in to replace R. W. Johnson at fullback. The *Chicago Defender* described the action on December 1:

Two of Lincoln's backs hit the left side of Howard's line, drawing the defense to that spot, while Byrd and another backfield man started for the right side of Howard's line. Byrd, seeing a hole near Morgan open, shot through and with splendid interference by some of his mates got clear for a 77-yard run for a touchdown.

Franz Alfred "Jazz" Byrd, off on his 77-yard touchdown run in Washington's Griffith Stadium on Thursday, November 30, 1922. Lincoln University defeated Howard University, 13–12.

The two teams battled to a standoff. Then, in the last quarter, a fumble on an attempted punt was picked up by Brooks of Howard, who ran twenty-five yards for the touchdown. The point after touchdown was missed. The score stood Lincoln, 7; Howard, 6.

Lincoln got the ball on Howard's twenty-three-yard line via a fumble recovery by Wyche. McLean shook off three would-be tacklers and swept around his end and outran the secondary. The touchdown was good for twenty-three yards. The point-after-a-goal attempt by Johnson was wide. The score was Lincoln, 13; Howard, 6.

Howard ran the kickoff back to their own twenty-yard line. Doneghy completed two passes for twenty yards each, and ran for twenty-three yards on a fake pass play. Melton earned twelve yards over center, to move the ball to the five-yard line. The crowd was now near hysteria. One enthusiastic alumnus had to be restrained from running onto the playing field. Fifty-eight seconds remained in the game, as Melton scored off tackle. Doneghy quickly called time out. After time out, fifty thousand eyes trailed the extra point attempt. The ball sailed high and straight, but swerved to the outside of the cross-bar, bringing a loud groan from Howard partisans. The final score: Lincoln, 13; Howard, 12.

Afterward, in a less dramatic contest, with a smaller turnout, Georgetown beat George Washington University, 46–6.

The 60–40 hometeam share of receipts gave the Howard athletic department a profit—and one lucrative contest had accomplished this.

In 1922 the Howard-Lincoln series stood at:

Games Played	Howard Won	Lincoln Won	Ties
18	4	9	5

Below: Sometimes in uniforms that were almost identical, the early Negro college teams nevertheless were aware of whom to tackle. Charles Doneghy (40) of Howard is shown rushing for short yardage against Lincoln University in the 1922 Thanksgiving thriller. Right: Doneghy is shown again being tackled after nearly breaking for a touchdown in the 1922 Thanksgiving game.

Left: Captain Charles Doneghy, full-back of the 1923 Howard University football team. Right: Franz Alfred "Jazz" Byrd, called the "black Red Grange" is shown in the 1924 season of Lincoln University.

In 1923 the Howard-Lincoln Thanksgiving Day game was played in Philadelphia's National League stadium, Baker Field, on Thursday, November 29. The *Pittsburgh Courier* front-paged on December 8, 1923:

BYRD'S 83-YARD RUN THRILLED 25,000 AS
LINCOLN TIES HOWARD

For the second straight year, Byrd had provided the thrills that virtually represented the height of college football entertainment for black Americans in the 1920s.

The weather was ideal, but the ground was slippery from an overnight rain as Howard took the field first at 2:30 P.M. Lincoln followed and kicked off. Howard's captain, Charles Doneghy, five feet eight inches and 167 pounds, from Danville, Kentucky, engineered a long drive from his own twenty-yard line, scoring from close in on an off-tackle plunge. The drive had taken ten minutes. The point-after attempt by Doneghy failed. Howard, 6; Lincoln, 0.

The first quarter was nearing the end when Doneghy kicked off to Lincoln. The fleet-footed Byrd, as was later reported, "gathered the oval in his hands, standing on his own five-yard line. Swinging to his right he started on his journey down the field. Given superb interference by his mates, each of whom took off an oncoming tackler, Byrd was on his way."

"Jazz" Byrd was finally hauled down by Sam Peyton at the twelve-yard line of Howard for an eighty-three-yard run.

Lincoln fans went wild. Referee Gibson had to halt play until the din subsided. The players could not hear the signals.

Two plays into the line gained ten yards as the quarter came to an end. On the first play in the second quarter, Byrd rammed the ball in from the two-yard line. The try for the point after touchdown by Crudrup failed. Howard, 6; Lincoln, 6. There was no more scoring.

The lineups follow:

HOWARD UNIVERSITY (6)		LINCOLN UNIVERSITY (6)
Williams	LE	Lancaster
Smith	LT	Coston
Anderson	LG	Poindexter
Priestly	C	Morgan
Kelley	RG	Parker
Doakes	RT	Jason
Long	RE	Crudrup
Blackmon	QB	Byrd
Doneghy	LHB	Johnson
Contee	RHB	Brown
Peyton	FB	Lee

The dreaded specter of serious injury always hovered about the gridiron. However, in the 1920s serious injuries—and deaths—were appearing less often. But on occasion. . . .

Haywood "Speed" Johnson was born on May 8, 1904. In June 1924 he received his degree from Howard University. In September 1924 he entered Howard's Medical College. In Howard's first varsity football game against Greensboro A & T College on October 3, 1924, Johnson was fatally injured.

Johnson was running down the field on a kickoff in the first half when the injury occurred. On October 6 he died in Freedman's Hospital. Howard's next scheduled game against St. Paul College, for Saturday, October 11, was canceled.

The annual Thanksgiving Day game went on as scheduled with the following two-day planned activities:

Wednesday

5:30 P.M.	Press Reception
8:00 P.M.	Grand Reception—Campus Dining Hall
9:00 P.M.	Student Demonstration and Pep Rally
10:00 P.M.	Chi Delta Mu Fraternity Dance

Thursday

9:00 A.M.–	Arrival of Trains and Buses from New York,
11:00 A.M.	Baltimore, Atlantic City, and Points South
11:30 A.M.	Breakfast Promenade
2:30 P.M.	Howard-Lincoln Football Classic Game
6:00 P.M.–	Dance

Howard University on occasion had a player or two from the professional schools[4] on its varsity athletic teams.[5] Unlike many Negro institutions with college divisions, Howard, in the 1920s, did not maintain grade and secondary departments, but competed against institutions which sometimes fielded athletes from their grade and secondary schools, as well as from their college divisions, in varsity competition.

[4] In 1928 the CIAA barred professional school athletes from varsity competition, and a four-year varsity eligibility rule was enacted.

[5] The first Negro selected as an All-American, William Henry Lewis, was in Harvard Law School the two years he won the honors, in 1892 and 1893.

In December 1924, Howard withdrew from the CIAA because Howard's 205-pound left guard, Robert Miller, had not been eligible for play in the Howard-Lincoln game. G. B. Miller, Robert's 215-pound brother, was already a member of Howard's football team. He played in the Howard-Lincoln game at left guard.

Robert Miller had played with Virginia Union University in 1923. He left the Richmond school and entered Dunbar High School in Washington, D.C., in February 1924. In September he entered Howard.

Hampton Institute, Virginia Normal and Industrial Institute, and Lincoln University protested that Miller should have been barred from play under CIAA regulations. These regulations stated that a college student who had competed in varsity competition at a secondary level

Left: Captain Raymond Doakes, right guard, on the 1924 Howard University football team. Right: Robert Miller as he appeared on the 1923 Virginia Union University team.

had to wait a year before he could compete at the college level.

A good showing against Lincoln University would have salvaged some degree of respectability for Howard's 1924 football season, which was not up to that of past Howard teams. Howard brought a record of two wins, no losses, and three ties into Washington's Griffith Stadium.

Howard University, 0—Greensboro A & T College, 0
Howard University, 0—West Virginia Institute, 0
Howard University, 7—Hampton Institute, 3
Howard University, 0—Virginia Normal and Industrial Institute, 0
Howard University, 7—Wilberforce University, 0

Lincoln University brought her high-scoring machine into Griffith Stadium ready to do battle against Howard. Lincoln had scored 208 points to its opponents' three. The only blotch on Lincoln's record was a 0–0 tie against Virginia Union University.

Lincoln University, 48—Bordentown Manual Training School, 0
Lincoln University, 63—The Delaware Giants, 0
Lincoln University, 21—Virginia Theological Seminary and College, 0
Lincoln University, 0—Virginia Union University, 0
Lincoln University, 7—Hampton Institute, 3
Lincoln University, 33—St. Paul Polytechnic Institute, 0
Lincoln University, 36—Shaw University, 0

A crowd of twenty-seven thousand eagerly awaited the action. The *Washington Post,* speculated: "Washington will try to stop "Jazz" Byrd, terror of the Lions."

Lincoln University won, 31–0, scoring four touchdowns, four points after touchdowns, and a field goal. Lancaster scored two touchdowns, Taylor scored one, Crudrup kicked four points after touchdowns, and Lancaster kicked a field goal. And yes, "Jazz" Byrd scored a touchdown, reported as follows:

Byrd . . . got away for a 45-yard run being tackled apparently five times on the journey up the field, but "jazzing" out of every tight situation like a revolutionist dancing the Carmagnole.

The *Washington Post* called the five-foot seven-inch, 143-pound star of three Howard-Lincoln classics "the Negro Red Grange."

Franz "Jazz" Byrd was born on June 28, 1905, the son of the Reverend W. A. Byrd, pastor of Lafayette Presbyterian Church, Jersey City, New Jersey. He obtained his college degree in 1925, and in 1926 became director of athletics at Florida A & M in Tallahassee, where he received a master's degree.

Early in 1925 Howard University felt it was being unfairly treated by the CIAA because of a CIAA ban against Robert Miller. The university bitterly withdrew from the association, which prevented Howard from playing any association teams.

On February 2, 1925, at Lincoln University, a committee reviewed the restriction on Howard in relation to the highly lucrative Howard-Lincoln Thanksgiving Day game and decided that the contest should be played as scheduled—in effect rebuffing the CIAA. But not for long. The *Washington Tribune* of February 24, 1925, reported: "Lincoln Ousted by CIAA."

Lincoln officials argued that since they had signed a "two-year" contract for the annual game, they were compelled to honor the pact.

In 1925 Howard's seven games would include Morgan College, Livingstone College, Johnson C. Smith University, West Virginia Institute, North Carolina College at Durham, Wilberforce University, and Lincoln University, in a new schedule that would take the team to Maryland, North Carolina, West Virginia, Ohio, and Pennsylvania.

Howard's 1925 schedule of longer trips would not work an undue hardship. It was 1925 and the postwar boom was at its peak, while thousands of miles away events were fermenting that would eventually affect the United States—and the entire world.

During the 1925 Negro college football season, however, thoughts were not on a possible world crisis, but instead on a 183-pound, six-foot halfback, Harry "Wu Fang" Ward, who was creating a special kind of crisis for opponents of the Wilberforce University team. The Wilberforce University starters were: ends—Allen, Wooldridge, Burrell; tackles—Slater, Calloway; guards—Bickett, Evans; center—Buchanon; backs—Harding, Williams, Richie, Longdon, Stout, and Harry "Wu Fang" Ward.

Wilberforce opened its 1925 season with a 68–10 victory over Lindon Center, of Dayton, Ohio. The awesome Wilberforce machine grounded out 446 yards from scrimmage. Playing about a quarter, Ward gained ninety-eight yards, including a seventy-five-yard touchdown run.

Next, Wilberforce beat Lincoln University, 25–0. Ward scored three touchdowns; one on a one-yard plunge, one on a sixty-yard pass interception, and one on a thirty-five-yard run with a punt.

On Thursday, October 1, 1925, Howard University began its fifty-seventh academic year. Dr. J. Stanley Durkee, president, addressed students and faculty in Andrew Rankin Memorial Chapel on the subject "Science and Life."

Wilberforce continued its winning streak. Against Kentucky State Normal, Ward scored three touchdowns, as Wilberforce won, 25–0. The *Pittsburgh Courier* of November 14, 1925, reported:

Ward is never completely stopped. Aside from his running, Ward is a deadly tackler, a good punter, and a good passer, and is first on the interference.

But on November 6, Howard University stopped Wilberforce—and Ward. Howard won, 6–0, in a game played ᵼn Griffith Stadium.

Before eighteen thousand fans at Philadelphia's Shibe Park, Howard and Lincoln played to a scoreless tie in the annual Thanksgiving Day classic in 1925. On the same date, Tuskegee beat Talladega College, 55–0, and claimed the southern title.

Dr. Mordecai Wyatt Johnson became the first black president of Howard University on September 29, 1926. Also in 1926, Howard had a new athletic field, a new gymnasium, and a fifteen-thousand-seat stadium. On October 9 Howard beat Livingstone College, 31–0, in the first game in the stadium.

At Neil Park, in Columbia, Ohio, Wilberforce scored on a thirty-five-yard drop-kick in the first quarter against West Virginia Institute. With time running out, Wilberforce had the ball on its own three-yard line and touched the ball down back of the line, taking a safety rather than a chance of having a punt blocked on the slippery, muddy grid-iron, to win 3–2.

Wilberforce's great star was also at it again in 1926. The *Pittsburgh Courier* of October 16, 1926, reported: "Wu Fang Ward runs 98 yards for touchdown; Wilberforce beats Bluefield Institute." Wilberforce won, 16–0.

Over sixteen hundred fans looked on at the game played in Wilberforce, Ohio. Ward's heroics continued, he intercepted a pass, and ran fifty yards for the only touchdown of the battle. Wilberforce beat Lincoln University, 7–0.

Another triple-threat breakaway runner was also showing his wares in 1926. On October 29, at Franklin Field in Philadelphia, Tuskegee Institute beat Lincoln University, 20–16. Benjamin Franklin Stevenson scored all twenty points in the City of Brotherly Love.

Stevenson scored on a short-line plunge as well as a sixty-five-yard run, and he kicked both extra points and two field goals.

Some other 1926 results follow:

Benjamin Franklin Stevenson, 6 ft. 3 in., 215 pounds, Tuskegee Institute all-time great back, in 1927. He starred from 1926–1930.

A throng of 12,000 fans jammed Howard University's new stadium on Thanksgiving Day, November 25, 1926. They saw their heroes defeat Lincoln University, 32–0.

Tuskegee Institute, 14—Alabama State Normal, 7

Tuskegee Institute, 28—Talladega College, 27 (Stevenson ran 40 yards for a touchdown, and kicked four extra points.)

Tuskegee Institute, 23—Southern University, 0

Tuskegee Institute, 14—Atlanta University, 0

Tuskegee Institute, 47—Fisk University, 13

Hampton Institute, 14—Greensboro A & T College, 6

Hampton Institute, 12—Virginia Union University, 0 (Hampton won CIAA title)

Virginia Union University, 12—Virginia Normal and Industrial Institute, 0

Voorhees Institute, 18—Harbison College, 0

Talladega College, 2—Alabama State Normal, 0

Samuel Houston, 74—Texas College, 0

Samuel Houston, 25—Bishop College, 0

South Carolina State College, 32—Haines Institute, 0

South Carolina State College, 13—Allen College, 0

Claflin College, 16—Benedict College, 6

Johnson C. Smith University, 13—Livingstone College, 0

Paine College, 53—Harbison College, 0

Greensboro A & T College, 13—Shaw University, 2

Virginia Normal and Industrial Institute, 12—St. Paul College, 0

Morehouse College, 7—Fisk University, 6

Howard University, 7—Atlanta University, 0

Howard University, 52—Morehouse College, 0

Howard University, 14—West Virginia Institute, 6

Howard University, 32—Lincoln University, 0

The 1926 Howard-Lincoln Thanksgiving Day game was played in the new university stadium before upward of twelve thousand fans. Howard won, 32–0.

On October 28, 1927, fourteen thousand fans looked on at Shibe

Park as Tuskegee Institute beat Lincoln University, 30–0. For the second straight year, Tuskegee's Ben Stevenson, 6 feet 3 inches and 215 pounds, was the star. The *Chicago Defender* reported:

Ben Stevenson, the crack half back of the Alabama eleven lived up to his reputation as the best back in our colleges today, when he played a whale of a game both on the offense and defense. Time and time again he carried the ball for large gains . . . shook off five and six tackles at a time. His clever dodging and change of pace made it possible for him to get around the right end in the last quarter for 32 yards and a touchdown.

Some other 1927 results follow:

Tuskegee Institute, 32—Fisk University, 0
Tuskegee Institute, 14—Morehouse College, 0
Tuskegee Institute, 16—Lincoln University, 3
Tuskegee Institute, 0—Alabama State Normal, 0
Tuskegee Institute, 47—Straight College, 0
Tuskegee Institute, 21—Knoxville College, 6
Tuskegee Institute, 28—Clark University, 12
Tuskegee Institute, 31—Florida A & M College, 13
Greensboro A & T College, 20—Lincoln University, 0
Greensboro A & T College, 13—Hampton Institute, 0 (A & T won 1927
    CIAA Title)
Greensboro A & T College, 28—North Carolina College at Durham, 13
Virginia State College, 51—North Carolina Normal at Fayetteville, 0
North Carolina College at Durham, 26—Claflin College, 0
North Carolina at Durham, 12—Johnson C. Smith University 12
North Carolina College at Durham, 33—Kittrell College, 0
Wilberforce University, 38—Lincoln (Mo.) University, 6
Wilberforce University, 12—West Virginia Institute, 12

Virginia Theological Seminary and College, 38—Shaw University, 0
Virginia Theological Seminary and College, 13—Hampton Institute, 13
Virginia Theological Seminary and College, 36—St. Paul Polytechnic
   Institute, 7
Virginia Theological Seminary and College, 13—Lincoln University, 0
Morehouse College, 6—Morris Brown College, 0
South Carolina State College, 17—North Carolina Normal at Fayette-
   ville, 0
South Carolina State College, 22—Benedict College, 0
South Carolina State College, 10—North Carolina College at Durham, 6
South Carolina State College, 68—Walker Baptist College, 0
Claflin College, 37—Allen University, 0
Claflin College, 67—Haines Institute, 0
Claflin College, 40—North Carolina Normal at Fayetteville, 0
Claflin College, 13—Benedict College, 13
Atlanta University, 61—Haines Institute, 0
Atlanta University, 26—Morehouse College, 0
Atlanta University, 6—Howard University, 0
Atlanta University, 0—Fisk University, 0
Alabama State Normal, 19—Miles Memorial Institute, 0
Alabama State Normal, 6—Atlanta University, 0
Alabama State Normal, 12—Talladega College, 6
Alabama State Normal, 6—Clark University, 6
Hampton Institute, 12—Lincoln University, 0
Hampton Institute, 6—Virginia State College, 0
Hampton Institute, 12—Virginia Union University, 7
Hampton Institute, 21—St. Paul Polytechnic Institute, 0
Talladega College, 44—Alabama A & M College, 0
Talladega College, 7—Miles Memorial Institute, 0
Talladega College, 20—Knoxville College, 0
Clark University, 31—Morris Brown College, 12
Clark University, 27—Talladega College, 7
Clark University, 43—Paine College, 0
Clark University, 38—Morehouse College, 0
Virginia Union University, 6—Lincoln University, 0
Storer College, 13—Morgan College, 13
Fisk University, 13—Howard University, 13
Fisk University, 0—Tennessee A & I College, 0
Fisk University, 42—Lincoln (Mo.) University, 0
Paine College, 45—Benedict College, 0

Paine College, 19—Georgia State College, 6
Paine College, 27—Johnson C. Smith University, 12
Paine College, 44—Allen University, 0
St. Paul Polytechnic Institute, 12—Johnson C. Smith University, 0
St. Paul Polytechnic Institute, 20—St. Augustine College, 0
Florida A & M College, 12—Daytona-Cookman College, 6
Lincoln University, 53—Shaw University, 0
Langston University, 14—Alabama State Normal, 0
Livingstone College, 27—Johnson C. Smith University, 26
Bluefield Institute, 27—Greensboro A & T College, 7
Bluefield Institute, 18—Howard University, 7
Bluefield Institute, 14—Virginia Theological Seminary and College, 13
Howard University, 7—Morehouse College, 7
Howard University, 26—Morgan College, 0
Howard University, 19—Livingstone College, 0
Howard University, 20—Lincoln University, 0

Howard won the annual Thanksgiving Day classic against Lincoln University, 20–0. The game was played in Shibe Park before ten thousand fans, but at season's beginning there was doubt if the game would be played at all. On September 15, 1927, at Howard, forty-five players reported for practice. On September 30, they discovered that their free training table in the cafeteria had been removed, and were subsequently informed that room payments would be required. Athletic scholarships were abandoned. On October 3 the football players went on strike.

On October 5 the Board of Athletic Control met and voted to keep its proceedings secret. On October 6 the board met and voted to cancel the entire 1927 schedule unless the players would report to practice no later than 5 P.M. on October 11. On October 7, the players met with President Johnson, who advised the athletes to return to the team, and made a general call for football candidates. On October 8 twenty-four players reported for practice, thus forestalling cancellation of the 1927 football season.

Howard University's season record of three wins, two losses, and two ties, was commendable under the adverse circumstances.

In 1928 Charles West, of Washington and Jefferson fame, was the coach at Howard University, and Robert Miller, who had graduated, was assisting as line coach.

In 1928, a new power stepped upon the football stage—Bluefield Institute of Bluefield, West Virginia. Bluefield's season record follows:

Bluefield Institute, 31—Virginia Union University, 7
Bluefield Institute, 3—Wilberforce University, 0
Bluefield Institute, 26—Morgan College, 0
Bluefield Institute, 0—Howard University, 0
Bluefield Institute, 13—West Virginia Institute, 0
Bluefield Institute, 12—Virginia Theological Seminary and College, 7
Bluefield Institute, 40—Morehouse College, 0
Bluefield Institute, 129—Morristown (Tenn.) College, 0

In the Morristown game, the second string played all but the first quarter. The only player who stayed in the entire game was George Sandridge, the quarterback. The regular quarterback, Herbert Cain, had suffered a broken leg earlier. Cain would also sustain a broken arm in the first game of the 1929 season. The awesome statistics in the Morristown game follow:

	Bluefield	*Morristown*
Points after touchdowns	15	0
Passes completed	9	5
Passes attempted	15	12
Average per punt	35-yds.	25-yds.
Yards gained	1,215-yds.	253-yds.
First downs	33	5
Touchdowns	19	0
Punts	2	8

A power also came to the fore in Texas in 1928—Wiley College, whose record follows:

Wiley College, 64—Philander-Smith, 0
Wiley College, 49—Arkansas Baptist College, 0
Wiley College, 7—Langston University, 7
Wiley College, 26—Sam Houston College, 0

Wiley College, 14—Texas College, 0
Wiley College, 33—Southern University, 6
Wiley College, 45—Philander-Smith College, 6
Wiley College, 23—Paul Quinn College, 0
Wiley College, 19—Prairie View A & M College, 15
Wiley College, 12—Bishop College, 0

The standings of the teams in the Southeastern Intercollegiate Athletic Conference for 1928 follow:

	Won	*Lost*	*Tied*
Tuskegee Institute	5	1	2
Clark University	5	1	1
Atlanta University	4	1	1
Fisk University	4	1	0
Knoxville College	2	1	3
Morris Brown College	3	2	1
Alabama State Normal	4	3	1
Morehouse College	2	3	0
Tennessee A & I College	1	3	1
Florida A & M College	0	4	0
Miles Memorial College	0	4	0

Some other 1928 results were:

Shaw University, 2—St. Paul Polytechnic Institute, 0
Hampton Institute, 13—Virginia Theological Seminary and College, 0
Hampton Institute, 27—St. Paul Polytechnic Institute, 0
Hampton Institute, 16—Virginia State College, 0
Hampton Institute, 36—Lincoln University, 6
Hampton Institute, 38—North Carolina College at Durham, 7
Hampton Institute, 66—Shaw University, 0
Hampton Institute, 25—Virginia Union University, 0
Talladega College, 12—Knoxville College, 12
Alabama State Normal, 32—Selma University, 6
Lincoln University, 6—Virginia Theological Seminary and College, 6
Johnson C. Smith University, 22—Shaw University, 0
Johnson C. Smith University, 49—North Carolina Normal at Fayetteville, 0
West Virginia Institute, 21—Howard University, 7

Greensboro A & T College, 19—Virginia Union University, 12
Knoxville College, 13—Tennessee State College, 0
Langston University, 7—Alabama State Normal, 0
Claflin College, 6—Livingstone College, 0
South Carolina State College, 39—Georgia State College, 0
South Carolina State College, 6—Johnson C. Smith University, 0
South Carolina State College, 31—Benedict College, 0
South Carolina State College, 26—Greensboro A & T College, 0
Livingstone College, 7—North Carolina College at Durham, 0
Livingstone College, 18—Paine College, 7
Morgan College, 7—Lincoln University, 0
Morgan College, 19—Storer College, 0
Fisk University, 13—Talladega College, 0
Fisk University, 12—Tennessee State College, 0
Virginia State College, 13—Greensboro A & T College, 6
Howard University, 7—Morehouse College, 0
Howard University, 7—Fisk University, 0
Howard University, 0—Morgan College, 0
Howard University, 19—Johnson C. Smith University, 6
Howard University, 32—Livingstone College, 0
Howard University, 12—Lincoln University, 0

The annual Howard-Lincoln Thanksgiving Day classic had historically been the number one attraction in Negro college football, but
attendance had begun to drop by the late 1920s. The reasons were
many: Howard and Lincoln were no longer the chief attractions in
Negro college football; the general state of the economy; and other
competition for the sports entertainment dollar, such as pro baseball,
basketball, and track.

In 1929 Howard returned to the CIAA and lost its first two games
by identical scores of 19–0 against Johnson C. Smith University and
Morehouse College.

Meanwhile, on November 2, 1929, Hampton Institute and Lincoln
University played the first football game between major Negro col-
leges in New York City, at the Polo Grounds. Ten thousand fans saw
Lincoln University beat Hampton Institute, 13–7.

Attendance figures exceeded those of the Howard-Lincoln classic,
and, besides, Howard and Lincoln were no longer the powers in Negro

college football. In fact, Howard came into the annual Thanksgiving Day game without a victory or even without having crossed an opponent's goal line. The Thanksgiving Day game seemed to reflect Howard's failures that season, as it ended in a scoreless tie. The game was played in Philadelphia's Municipal Stadium, and for the first time—probably because of the state of the economy—fans began openly complaining about the $2 general admission tickets. The *Pittsburgh Courier* of December 7, 1929, commented:

And now to these games in big stadiums. Soldiers Field, Chicago; the Polo Grounds, New York; and the Municipal Stadium, Philadelphia, were the scenes of our big games. Soldiers Field has a capacity of 110,000; the Polo Grounds, 50,000, and the Municipal Stadium, 80,000. . . . Why is it that Promoters don't realize it is better, for several reasons, to place 25,000 people in the stands at a dollar admission (general) than to demand $2 and get 10,000 people.

Some 1929 results follow:

Morgan College, 27—Storer College, 0
Morgan College, 47—Bordentown Manual Training School, 0
Morgan College, 0—Howard University, 0
Clark University, 14—Benedict College, 0

The Clark-Benedict game was played in Columbia, South Carolina. Eric Roberts took a pass from Elmer Baker and ran twenty-one yards for the first touchdown. Roberts later had a forty-six-yard run that carried to the two-yard line to set up the final tally.

Later, in the Clark game against the 24th Infantry of Fort Benning, Georgia, Elmer Baker started the scoring with a forty-four-yard dropkick. Clark University won 9–0. A description of the final score stated: "The soldiers fumbled and Hughes recovered on Clark's 22-yard line. Ric Roberts then feinted on a cutback, avoided two tacklers, and outsprinted the entire soldiers secondary for 78 yards and a touchdown."

Some other 1929 results follow:

Tuskegee Institute, 34—Bluefield Institute, 0
Tuskegee Institute, 21—Greensboro A & T College, 0
Tuskegee Institute, 24—The 24th Infantry, 7
Tuskegee Institute, 21—Clark University, 0
Tuskegee Institute, 6—Wilberforce University, 0

The Tuskegee-Wilberforce game was played before twenty thousand fans in mammoth Soldiers Field. Big Ben Stevenson scored on a twenty-five-yard pass for the sole tally of the day.

And before seven thousand fans in Atlanta, Stevenson had a magnificent touchdown run of sixty-five yards. He twice reversed his field before reaching paydirt. Tuskegee beat Morris Brown College, 32–19.

Some other 1929 results:

Bluefield Institute, 13—Wilberforce University, 13
Bluefield Institute, 20—Morgan College, 0
Bluefield Institute, 20—Howard University, 0
Bluefield Institute, 47—Knoxville College, 7
Bluefield Institute, 32—Virginia Theological Seminary and College, 0

The Bluefield-Seminary game was played in Princeton, West Virginia, on November 23, 1929. It was the first night football game that these two schools had ever played and was contested on four inches of snow.

Some other 1929 results follow:

Virginia State College, 12—Greensboro A & T College, 6
Virginia State College, 19—North Carolina College at Durham, 0
Virginia State College, 14—Morgan College, 0
Virginia State College, 6—Hampton Institute, 0
Virginia State College, 6—Virginia Union University, 0 (won 1929 CIAA title)
Hampton Institute, 6—Howard University, 0
Hampton Institute, 20—St. Paul Polytechnic Institute, 0
Johnson C. Smith University, 19—Howard University, 0
Johnson C. Smith University, 13—South Carolina State College, 6
Johnson C. Smith University, 20—Morehouse College, 8
Johnson C. Smith University, 13—Benedict College, 0
Johnson C. Smith University, 26—Shaw University, 0

Johnson C. Smith University, 44—Laurenburg Institute, 0
Johnson C. Smith University, 0—Livingstone College, 0
Alabama Teachers College, 6—Florida A & M College, 0
Alabama Teachers College, 0—The 24th Infantry, 0
Alabama Teachers College, 2—Morris Brown College, 0
Alabama Teachers College, 13—Langston University, 13
Fisk University, 25—Lane College, 0
Fisk University, 7—Morehouse College, 0
Fisk University, 20—Tennessee A & I College, 0
Fisk University, 26—Knoxville College, 0
Fisk University, 19—Talladega College, 6
Fisk University, 31—Howard University, 0
Fisk University, 13—Lincoln (Mo.) University, 0
Wiley College, 81—Straight College, 0
Wiley College, 10—Bishop College, 8
Langston University, 22—Bishop College, 0
Virginia Union University, 13—North Carolina College at Durham, 0
Virginia Union University, 13—Lincoln University, 6
Virginia Union University, 6—Hampton Institute, 0
Prairie View A & M College, 73—Jarvis Institute, 0
Wilberforce University, 23—West Virginia Institute, 0
Wilberforce University, 13—Bluefield Institute, 13
Wilberforce University, 12—Fisk University, 7
Greensboro A & T College, 25—Shaw University, 0
Knoxville College, 19—Simmons College, 0
Knoxville College, 0—Livingstone College, 0
Claflin College, 7—Livingstone College, 0
Morris Brown College, 20—Miles Memorial College, 0
West Virginia Institute, 12—Hampton Institute, 6
Talladega College, 24—Alabama State A & M College, 0
Talladega College, 6—Knoxville College, 0
Talladega College, 13—South Carolina State College, 0
Livingstone College, 19—Brick Junior College, 0
Livingstone College, 51—Paine College, 7
South Carolina State College, 27—Benedict College, 0
South Carolina State College, 21—Paine College, 0
South Carolina State College, 24—Haines Institute, 0
St. Paul Polytechnic Institute, 20—Greensboro A & T College, 0
Morehouse College, 12—Knoxville College, 0
Tennessee A & I College, 7—Morris Brown College, 0
North Carolina College at Durham, 39—North Carolina Normal at Fayetteville, 0

As Lincoln and Howard awaited their annual Thanksgiving Day confrontation, their seasons' records showed:

Lincoln University, 7—Virginia Union University, 13
Lincoln University, 12—Greensboro A & T College, 7
Lincoln University, 12—St. Paul Polytechnic Institute, 6
Lincoln University, 32—North Carolina College at Durham, 6
Lincoln University, 13—Hampton Institute, 7
Lincoln University, 19—Morgan College, 7

Howard's somewhat less imposing season's record follows:

Howard University, 0—Hampton Institute, 6
Howard University, 0—Johnson C. Smith University, 19
Howard University, 0—Wilberforce University, 13
Howard University, 0—Fisk University, 31
Howard University, 0—Morehouse College, 19

The Howard-Lincoln classic ended in a scoreless tie in 1929. The *Amsterdam News* of November 22, 1929, reported:

The public expects the best in everything from Howard; the best scholarship, the best sportsmanship, and the best athletic competitions. Why not? Is not Howard "the capstone of Negro education?" Should she not set the pace in all of these things? Certainly she should! President Johnson alone is to be blamed for the miserable football team that represents Howard University this year. He cut out the training table a couple of years ago because he feared the survey being made by the Carnegie Foundation. Then he began to ballyhoo sportsmanship in order to justify his act. I believe, however, that he was sincere in what he did. But sincerity or no sincerity, the effect is just the same. The miserable showing of his mediocre team has created a spirit of sullen indifference among the students and sour indignation among the alumni.

In 1930 Morgan College, led by its freshman Thomas "Big Tank" Conrad, swept to the CIAA championship. Some results follow:

Morgan College, 13—Hampton Institute, 7
Morgan College, 26—Lincoln University, 6
Morgan College, 18—Greensboro A & T College, 6

Conrad caught forward passes of twenty-five and sixty-five yards for touchdowns in the A & T game, won by Morgan College, 18–6.

Some other 1930 results follow:

Tuskegee Institute, 0—Wilberforce University, 0
Tuskegee Institute, 31—Knoxville College, 6
Tuskegee Institute, 19—Morehouse College, 6
Tuskegee Institute, 40—Talladega College, 6
Tuskegee Institute, 57—Alcorn A & M College, 0
Tuskegee Institute, 42—24th Infantry, 0
Tuskegee Institute, 26—Wiley College, 0
Tuskegee Institute, 19—Clark University, 7
Tuskegee Institute, 32—Alabama State College, 6
Tuskegee Institute, 41—Lane College, 6

Before a crowd of four thousand fans, Ben Stevenson ran for touchdowns of forty-nine, sixty, and fifty-nine yards, as Tuskegee beat Lane College, 41–6.

Playing his last game, a week later, Stevenson had a thirty-seven-yard run against Morris Brown College. He also had touchdowns of forty-five and thirty-two yards. Tuskegee beat Morris Brown College, 12–0.

Cleve L. Abbott was a twenty-nine-year-old coach and director of athletics at Kansas Industrial and Educational Institute, Topeka, in 1919. He observed a youngster whom he thought had all the potential for future greatness. And when the former Dakota State College all-round athlete assumed his duties at Tuskegee, in 1923, the first athlete he sought out was the Kansas youngster, Ben F. Stevenson.

Some other 1930 results follow:

Fisk University, 21—Johnson C. Smith University, 6
Fisk University, 25—Kentucky State College, 0
Fisk University, 12—Wilberforce University, 6
Fisk University, 51—Talladega College, 6
Fisk University, 31—Bluefield Institute, 6
Greensboro A & T College, 12—Hampton Institute, 7
Greensboro A & T College, 14—Shaw University, 13
Greensboro A & T College, 19—St. Paul Polytechnic Institute, 2

Paine College, 21—Claflin College, 6
South Carolina State College, 26—Allen University, 7
South Carolina State College, 24—Talladega College, 0
South Carolina State College, 19—Haines Institute, 0
South Carolina State College, 42—Paine College, 0
South Carolina State College, 21—Benedict College, 7
Shaw University, 12—Livingstone College, 6
Wilberforce University, 43—Lincoln (Mo.) University, 0
Wilberforce University, 20—Clark University, 0
Wilberforce University, 13—Bluefield Institute, 0
Wilberforce University, 39—North Carolina College at Durham, 0
Benedict College, 6—Morris Brown College, 0
Benedict College, 0—Allen University, 0
Wiley College, 53—Sam Houston College, 7
Wiley College, 76—Texas College, 0
Wiley College, 7—Bishop College, 0
Wiley College, 36—Straight College, 0
Wiley College, 43—Xavier University, 0
Wiley College, 17—Prairie View A & M College, 13
Wiley College, 6—Southern University, 0
Hampton Institute, 0—Lincoln University, 0
Hampton Institute, 14—Virginia Union University, 7
Hampton Institute, 40—St. Paul Polytechnic Institute, 0
Hampton Institute, 25—Virginia State College, 12
Hampton Institute, 19—Bluefield Institute, 18
Hampton Institute, 13—Howard University, 6
West Virginia Institute, 7—Howard University, 0
West Virginia Institute, 10—Fisk University, 7
West Virginia Institute, 12—Virginia State College, 7
Morehouse College, 32—Johnson C. Smith University, 7
Morehouse College, 19—Knoxville College, 13
Morehouse College, 25—Benedict College, 0
Morehouse College, 32—Talladega College, 2
Morehouse College, 3—Alabama State College, 0
Morehouse College, 32—Allen University, 0
Morehouse College, 13—Hampton Institute, 6
Virginia State College, 27—Greensboro A & T College, 0
Virginia State College, 6—Johnson C. Smith University, 6
Virginia State College, 20—St. Paul Polytechnic Institute, 8
Virginia State College, 16—Howard University, 13
Virginia Union University, 26—Shaw University, 7

Virginia Union University, 7—Greensboro A & T College, 6
Virginia Union University, 34—St. Augustine College, 0
Virginia Union University, 13—Morgan College, 0
Virginia Union University, 2—Lincoln University, 0
St. Paul Polytechnic Institute, 6—North Carolina College at Durham, 0
Alabama State College, 40—Paine College, 13
Alabama State College, 46—Alabama A & M College, 6
Alabama State College, 13—Florida A & M College, 7
Alabama State College, 13—Clark University, 0
Johnson C. Smith University, 6—Virginia Theological Seminary and College, 0
Johnson C. Smith University, 0—Howard University, 0
Knoxville College, 19—Livingstone College, 0
Knoxville College, 19—Talladega College, 6
Kentucky State College, 7—Knoxville College, 6
Morris Brown College, 0—Clark University, 0

Before the annual Thanksgiving Day classic, Lincoln University's record follows:

Lincoln University, 46—St. Paul Polytechnic Institute, 0
Lincoln University, 6—Johnson C. Smith University, 0
Lincoln University, 34—North Carolina College at Durham, 0
Lincoln University, 26—Greensboro A & T College, 6

Howard University's record, going into the classic, follows:

Howard University, 0—Johnson C. Smith University, 0
Howard University, 40—St. Paul Polytechnic Institute, 0
Howard University, 44—Livingstone College, 7
Howard University, 6—North Carolina College at Durham, 2
Howard University, 20—Prairie View A & M College, 20
Howard University, 13—Virginia Theological Seminary and College, 6

On a cold day in mammoth Griffith Stadium, fewer than ten thousand fans saw Howard defeat Lincoln, 2–0. The lone score came late in the third quarter when eighteen-year-old substitute center Tom Walker leaped high in the air and blocked a punt. The ball rolled back of the goal, where Howard's halfback LeMarr recovered it for a safety.

Hampton Institute's 1931 C.I.A.A. Champion football team. Identifiable players are, from left to right, first row: "Big Tom" Thomas, J. P. Scott, "Cutes" Carter, Ted Edwards, Glover, Gaines, "Heavy" Rivers, Anderson, Jimmy Unthank, and "Ox" White. Second row, left to right: "Hi" Harris, Joe Brodus, Crocket, Powell, Lafaye, Al Farmer, unidentified player, Portfield Harris, Arnett Beam, and Campbell. Third row, left to right: Alfred Ham, Sam Cole, Longsworth Quinn, Al White, Major Jones, Harvey Freishman, Dirk Bell, Sylvius Moore, and unidentified player. Fourth row, left to right: unidentified player, unidentified player, "Weasel" Hunt, Jim Goldsboro, Bob Church, Reginold Jackson, unidentified player, unidentified player, unidentified player, unindentified player. Fifth row, left to right: C. H. Williams, Della Campbell, "Duck" Moore, Harold Gates, Gideon Smith, "Buck" Neilson, Robert Pendell, and Ed Queen.

In 1931 Benjamin Stevenson was teaching agriculture in Tuskegee High School and coaching the football team. Hampton Institute and Wilberforce University had the top football teams in the Negro colleges.

Some 1931 football results follow:

Hampton Institute, 26—Howard University, 0
Hampton Institute, 26—Morgan College, 0
Hampton Institute, 13—Lincoln University, 6
Hampton Institute, 44—Livingstone College, 0
Hampton Institute, 0—Virginia State College, 0
Hampton Institute, 21—Greensboro A & T College, 0

Hampton Institute, 24—North Carolina College at Durham, 0
Hampton Institute, 20—St. Paul Polytechnic Institute, 0
Hampton Institute, 14—Virginia Union University, 0
Wilberforce University, 14—Lincoln University, 6
Wilberforce University, 32—Bluefield Institute, 0
Wilberforce University, 62—Kentucky State College, 0
Wilberforce University, 24—Virginia State College, 0
Wilberforce University, 15—Tuskegee Institute, 6
Wilberforce University, 24—Kentucky State College, 6
Tuskegee Institute, 13—Wiley College, 0
Tuskegee Institute, 32—Alabama State College, 7
Tuskegee Institute, 31—Morehouse College, 0
Tuskegee Institute, 18—Knoxville College, 7
Tuskegee Institute, 31—Fisk University, 0
Tuskegee Institute, 21—Prairie View A & M College, 0
West Virginia Institute, 22—Fisk University, 12
West Virginia Institute, 18—Bluefield Institute, 0
Virginia State College, 77—St. Augustine College, 0
Virginia State College, 43—Johnson C. Smith University, 0
Virginia State College, 42—Virginia Union University, 6
Virginia State College, 19—St. Paul Polytechnic Institute, 0
Virginia State College, 32—Shaw University, 0
Virginia State College, 7—West Virginia Institute, 6
Morgan College, 26—North Carolina College at Durham, 12
Morgan College, 19—Howard University, 8
Morgan College, 12—Greensboro A & T College, 0
Morgan College, 25—Morehouse College, 0

In 1931 Tom "Big Tank" Conrad starred in Morgan's opener against Greensboro A & T. He ran for touchdowns of seventy-five and thirty-five yards. Morgan won, 12–0.

Howard University won its 1931 opener in impressive fashion, beating Johnson C. Smith, 69–6. Hampton Institute won the 1931 CIAA championship. But attendance continued to fall at the Howard-Lincoln Thanksgiving Day game. Fewer than eight thousand fans saw Lincoln beat Howard, 7–6, at Shibe Park. Some 1931 results follow:

Howard University, 69—Johnson C. Smith University, 6
Howard University, 13—West Virginia Institute, 0

Howard University, 6—Lincoln University, 7
Howard University, 9—Virginia Theological Seminary and College, 0
Howard University, 8—Morgan College, 19
Howard University, 6—Virginia Union University, 25
Howard University, 0—Virginia State College, 19
Lincoln University, 12—Greensboro A & T College, 0
Lincoln University, 12—Johnson C. Smith University, 0
Lincoln University, 27—St. Paul Polytechnic Institute, 0
Lincoln University, 7—Virginia Union University, 0

In 1932 the top teams in Negro college football finished as follows:

	Won	Lost	Tied
Wiley College	8	0	0
Morgan College	7	0	1
Virginia State College	7	0	1
Kentucky State College	7	0	2
Tuskegee Institute	5	0	0
Wilberforce University	5	0	3
Alabama State College	6	1	1
Virginia Union University	6	1	1
Hampton Institute	6	2	1
Clark University	4	1	0
Morris Brown College	5	1	1
Langston University	4	2	0

Thomas "Tank" Conrad, had another outstanding season for Morgan College in 1932, as Morgan won the CIAA championship. Against Howard University, Conrad ran for a seventy-yard touchdown in the second quarter, and Morgan won, 13–6. In Morgan's 38–0 victory over Cheyney College, Conrad had a twenty-five-yard touchdown run and a twenty-yard touchdown run in the 24–0 victory over Virginia Union University.

Some other 1932 results follow:

Morris Brown College, 12—South Carolina State College, 6
Morris Brown College, 21—West Virginia Institute, 0
North Carolina College at Durham, 21—Johnson C. Smith University, 0
North Carolina College at Durham, 13—Shaw University, 0

Fisk University, 6—Knoxville College, 0
Fisk University, 2—West Virginia Institute, 0
St. Paul Polytechnic Institute, 20—Johnson C. Smith University, 6
St. Paul Polytechnic Institute, 13—Greensboro A & T College, 0
Morehouse College, 13—Fisk University, 6
Morehouse College, 6—Paine College, 0
Bluefield Institute, 19—St. Paul Polytechnic Institute, 0
Bluefield Institute, 43—St. Augustine College, 0
Wiley College, 52—Bishop College, 0
Wiley College, 5—Fisk University, 0
South Carolina State College, 12—Claflin College, 0
St. Augustine College, 7—Shaw University, 7
Hampton Institute, 19—Howard University, 6

Hampton beat Howard, 19–6, at New York's Polo Grounds before five thousand fans. The anticipated attendance had been estimated at twenty thousand. And in the annual classic Howard beat Lincoln, 12–0, at Howard's University Stadium in 1932.

Morgan College joined the CIAA in 1930, and Coach Edward Paulette Hurt started right off leading his team to the championship. Morgan won seven and lost one game in 1930, a 13–0 loss to Virginia Union University.

In 1931 Hampton Institute won the CIAA championship, but Morgan, led by a convoy of big swift backs, won the championship during the next four years. Quarterback Howard "Brutus" Wilson, fullback Otis Troupe, and left halfback Thomas "Big Tank" Conrad, led the attack. During the period 1930–1935, Morgan compiled a record of forty-one wins, three losses, and four ties. Looking further into the future of Eddie Hurt's dynasty, his team lost to Hampton Institute, 26–0, in 1931, and would not lose another game until sixty-one contests later. Along the way, seven ties were included.

The final CIAA standings for 1932 follow:

	Won	*Lost*	*Tied*
Morgan College	6	0	0
Virginia State College	6	1	1
Virginia Union University	6	1	1

	Won	*Lost*	*Tied*
Hampton Institute	5	2	1
Bluefield Institute	3	2	0
St. Paul Polytechnic Institute	3	5	0
North Carolina College at Durham	3	5	0
Howard University	2	4	0
Lincoln University	0	2	0
Shaw University	0	4	0
Johnson C. Smith University	0	4	0

The chief attraction in Negro football in 1933 was the Hampton and Morgan contest. The student bodies and alumni were still enthusiastic over the annual Howard-Lincoln classic, but the general public was somewhat less so. The thirty-three-thousand-seat Shibe Park would have to be abandoned for a smaller, and cheaper, stadium. Still, Lincoln officials wanted a park close to Philadelphia, Washington, Baltimore, and New York. When Convention Hall in Atlantic City, New Jersey, sent its bid, the offer was snapped up. The hall was near the large cities, and weather would have no bearing, as the hall would accommodate indoor football under floodlights.

For the first time since the series began in 1894, the Howard-Lincoln game was not played on either school campus or in a Philadelphia or Washington major-league stadium. Fewer than five thousand fans showed up in the twenty-thousand-seat Atlantic City hall to watch Howard beat Lincoln, 13–6. An era had ended.

The classics would continue, but the crowds would never again approach the nearly thirty thousand fans of the past, due partly to the economy and partly to the caliber of the Howard-Lincoln teams of the 1930s. The spotlight of Negro college football no longer focused on the Howard-Lincoln Thanksgiving Day game. It had moved on.

The 1933 CIAA final conference standings follow:

	Won	*Lost*	*Tied*
Morgan College	8	0	0
Hampton Institute	7	1	1
Bluefield Institute	4	1	2
St. Paul Polytechnic Institute	4	2	2

	Won	Lost	Tied
Virginia Union University	4	2	3
North Carolina College at Durham	4	4	0
Howard University	3	3	0
Greensboro A & T College	3	3	3
Johnson C. Smith University	1	5	0
Lincoln University	0	4	1
Shaw University	0	6	0

At the end of the 1934 football season, the CIAA standings were released as follows:

	Won	Lost	Tied
Morgan College	4	0	3
Bluefield Institute	7	0	1
Greensboro A & T College	7	1	1
Howard University	3	1	2
Virginia Union University	4	2	2
Virginia State College	3	3	2
North Carolina College at Durham	4	4	0
Hampton Institute	3	5	0
St. Augustine College	1	2	1
St. Paul Polytechnic Institute	2	6	0
Shaw University	1	6	0
Johnson C. Smith University	0	4	1
Lincoln University	0	5	0

It was later discovered that Howard University had used an ineligible player, and all the games in which this player participated would have to be forfeited. Paul Perkins, halfback, was a freshman in the first quarter at Washington and Jefferson College in 1932–1933. He was also a freshman in the first quarter at Washington and Jefferson in 1933–1934. He left Washington and Jefferson, shortly after enrolling in September, and entered Howard University. Howard's registrar, Frederick D. Wilkinson, did not receive Perkins's records from Washington and Jefferson until November 24, 1934. Only then did he learn that Perkins had been "dropped for poor scholarship."

The final revised 1934 CIAA standings, and Dickinson Rating System points follow:

	Won	Lost	Tied	Dickinson Rating
Morgan College	5	0	2	23.57
Bluefield Institute	7	0	1	22.81
Greensboro A & T College	7	1	1	21.87
Virginia Union University	4	2	2	19.37
Virginia State College	4	3	1	18.43
Hampton Institute	4	4	0	15.00
North Carolina College at Durham	4	4	0	15.00
St. Paul Polytechnic Institute	3	5	0	13.75
St. Augustine College	1	2	0	13.75
Howard University	1	5	0	11.66
Shaw University	1	6	0	11.66
Johnson C. Smith University	0	4	1	11.00
Lincoln University	0	5	0	10.00

In 1935 Morgan College was again the power in the CIAA, followed closely by Hampton Institute. All eyes watched their confrontation. Both were undefeated, Morgan with a 5–0–0 record, Hampton with a 6–0–0 record. In a cold driving rain, on Hampton's Armstrong Field, Morgan won, 13–0. Two thousand fans watched the battle of the two teams slipping and sliding in the quagmire. Morgan had now rolled to its thirty-second victory—with only four ties marring a perfect slate.

On October 20, 1935, *The New York Times* had dispatched a writer to cover the Morgan-Lincoln game, reporting:

MORGAN CAPTURES 29TH GAME IN A ROW
DEFEATS LINCOLN ELEVEN, 26–0, BEFORE 10,000 TO EXTEND
THREE YEAR STREAK

The game was played at New York's Dyckman Oval on Saturday, October 19. Morgan scored when, as reported,

Simpson carried through the line for 3 yards and before completely stopped he tossed for a short lateral to Troupe, who dashed the remaining 28 yards for the first score.

In 1935 the "national championship" award was voted to Kentucky State College by the writers on the *Chicago Defender*. Kentucky's season record follows:

Kentucky State College, 14—West Virginia Institute, 0
Kentucky State College, 15—Wilberforce University, 0
Kentucky State College, 6—Tuskegee Institute, 2
Kentucky State College, 21—Morris Brown, 0
Kentucky State College, 45—Fisk University, 0
Kentucky State College, 34—Lincoln (Mo.) University, 0
Kentucky State College, 33—Wiley College, 0

The standings of the CIAA teams for the 1935 football season were:

	Won	*Lost*	*Tied*
Morgan College	8	0	1
Hampton Institute	7	1	0
Greensboro A & T College	6	2	1
Bluefield Institute	5	3	0
Virginia State College	4	3	1
Virginia Union University	4	3	1
North Carolina College at Durham	4	3	0
Shaw University	3	3	0
Lincoln University	1	3	1
Johnson C. Smith University	1	4	0
Howard University	1	5	1
St. Augustine College	0	5	0
St. Paul Polytechnic Institute	0	8	0

The standings of the SIAC teams for the 1935 football season follow:

	Won	*Lost*	*Tied*
Alabama State College	6	0	1
Morehouse College	5	1	1
Tuskegee Institute	5	2	0

	Won	*Lost*	*Tied*
Clark University	2	1	2
Morris Brown College	2	2	2
LeMoyne College	3	2	0

Suddenly the *Washington Afro-American* blared forth on December 21, 1935:

MORGAN SUSPENDED FROM CIAA

William "Wildman" Simpson, star halfback, had been given a "deferred examination," which he had passed. This was to make up for the "seven weeks" he had been away from Morgan. The CIAA let it be known that Morgan had not broken any specific association regulation, "except in spirit," noting that it frowned upon deferred examinations in principle. Morgan College was reinstated in February 1936.

Morgan College, located twenty minutes from downtown Baltimore and forty miles from Washington, had been chartered in 1867 as the Centenary Biblical Institute, renamed Morgan College in 1890, and renamed again when it became Morgan State College in 1939.

In 1936 Chester Washington, sportswriter for the *Pittsburgh Courier*, assessed the big game:

With a better record than Michigan and Minnesota, Morgan College, after 40 consecutive games without a loss, will march into the battle with Virginia State confident of another victory. Statistics show that adept grid pupils of coach . . . Hurt have won five CIAA championships since 1930. They also reveal that in five years they have piled up 925 points to their opponents 63 . . . maybe Morgan . . . will fool us, but I'm expecting the Trojans to "truck on down" to victory Thursday.

Morgan kept its streak intact, as the game ended in a 6–6 tie.

Virginia State College won the 1936 CIAA championship, and Tuskegee Institute won the SIAC championship. Attendance at black college football games in 1936 ranged from a few hundred to the largest crowd of twenty thousand and ninety-nine at Dallas's Cotton Bowl, which gathered to watch Wiley College beat Prairie View A & M College, 6–0. The only score was registered by freshman and substitute center Johnny Brooks. He intercepted a pass and ran fifteen yards for the touchdown.

There was no Howard-Lincoln Thanksgiving Day game in 1936, the second time in the long history of the series, since it had resumed in 1904, that the annual classic had not been played.

On Monday, November 16, 1936, the Howard University football team went on strike, and 85 percent of the student body of two thousand supported them by staging a one-day sympathy strike. Instead of going to classes they picketed, carrying their placards through the buildings, and held a mass meeting at eleven o'clock.

Meanwhile, the players were outlining their terms. They met in the gymnasium with John H. Burr, head of the department of physical education, and the coach, Harry Payne. They presented five demands: (1) campus jobs, which would be repayable in room and board, including breakfast, lunch, and dinner; (2) good playing equipment; (3) adequate and experienced training staff, including a team physician, head trainer, and two assistant trainers; (4) adequate medical supplies; and (5) the appointment of a graduate manager, with a publicity staff of undergraduate students.

The players thought that their demands were not being taken seriously, so instead of playing against Virginia Union University, the entire team went to the Howard Theater and saw comedian "Pigmeat" Markham on stage, and a horse-racing picture, *Down The Stretch*.

The Howard-Lincoln game was also canceled.

The abolition of grants-in-aid for the athletes had led to the strike; there had even been reports that some of the athletes were suffering from malnutrition. The Carnegie Report had stated that in light of the Depression, a deemphasis of athletics would probably effect a savings. Howard officials had no doubt overreacted. The training table for athletes had been long established at most colleges, and the Howard-Lincoln annual classic, while not as lucrative as it had been in the 1920s, did draw some money into the coffers.

The identifiable 1937 Morgan College football team members, from left to right, front row: Cheatham, Walter Mosby, Gordon, Ryan, Hawkins, Sowell, Holley, Roberts, Lampkins, Kee, and Smith. Second row, left to right: Head Coach Edward Paulette Hurt, Smith, Jones, Hurtt, unidentifiable player, Watkins, Hampton, Cain, Patterson, unidentifiable player, Tucker, and Owens. Last row, left to right: Manager Brown, Hill, Walker, Gross, Gibson, Johnson, McNeil, Bowie, Ree, Thomas, Hall, Bradon, Williams, and two unidentified assistant coaches. (Courtesy of Mr. Talmadge Hill)

In 1937 Morgan and Virginia State colleges had the leading Negro football teams. After six games, Morgan had won all its games and scored 146 points to its opponents' 13.

Virginia State College, after seven games, had won all of them and scored 251 points against its opponents' 13.

Morgan beat Virginia, 21–6, in their confrontation. The final CIAA 1937 standings follow:

	Won	*Lost*	*Tied*
Morgan College	7	0	0
Virginia State College	7	1	0
Virginia Union University	7	2	0
Johnson C. Smith University	4	2	0
Lincoln University	3	2	1
Shaw University	4	3	0

	Won	*Lost*	*Tied*
North Carolina College at Durham	2	4	1
Hampton Institute	2	5	0
Howard University	1	3	0
Bluefield Institute	1	3	2
St. Paul Polytechnic Institute	1	6	0
St. Augustine College	0	4	0

Texas College won the southwestern football championship in 1937 with a 5–0–1 record. Florida A & M won the Southern Intercollegiate Athletic Conference football championship in 1937 with a record of 5–0–1, and also won a postseason Orange Blossom game against Hampton Institute, 25–20.

The Howard-Lincoln game was back. Lincoln won, 9–0. The game was played in Shibe Park before ten thousand fans.

In 1937 Tougaloo College won the South-Central Conference championship, as it had done in 1935 and 1936, and Morgan College's winning streak had now reached forty-eight games.

The leaders in the midwestern conference in 1937 were as follows:

	Won	*Lost*	*Tied*
Kentucky State College	3	0	0
Lincoln (Mo.) University	2	1	2
Tennessee A & I College	2	1	1
Wilberforce University	2	2	1
West Virginia Institute	2	3	0
Louisville Municipal College	0	4	0

The *Pittsburgh Courier* on November 12, 1938, eyed Morgan's continuing victory streak with the headline:

MORGANS UNBEATEN STREAK TO 53; TOPS A & T

Greensboro A & T College was defeated, 12–0, at Morgan College Stadium. Then the inevitable happened as reported by the *Pittsburgh Courier* of December 3, 1938:

First row, left to right: Elridge Pankey, Horace Robinson, George Lamb, James Terrell, Joseph Rose, Henry Briscoe, Louis Ballard, James Nelson, Conway Downing, David Holmes, Alexander Cook. Second Row: Stanley Land, Joseph Hall, William Bennett, Marshall Brown, James Brewer, Russell Burr, Leo Woods, Larry Bartee, Colman Lewis, Joseph Echols, John Brewer. Third row: James Moore (Athletic Director), Teddy McClain, Jefferson, William Bond, Richard Cobb, Donald Harris, D. Travis, "Rabbit" L. Taylor, "Red" J. Jackson, Granston. Fourth row: Thomas Verdell (Coach), "Red" Harris, Willie Hurst, Chandler, Fred Kersey, James Harris, "Pat" Patterson, R. Glasker, Thompson. Fifth Row: George Hardy, James Young, Coleman, Rowe, William Bailey, Elmer Taylor, W. Denny, Victor, Reid, Mitchell. Sixth row: Harry Jefferson (Head Coach), Joseph Lynch, James Slade, "Bust" Tull, Bimp McClain. Virginia State 1938 football squad that broke Morgan's winning streak.

VIRGINIA STATE SHATTERS MORGAN'S GRID RECORD
8,000 SEE STATE COP CIAA CROWN AND HALT BEARS' BID FOR GRID FAME

At Rogers Field, Petersburg, on Thanksgiving Day, Morgan lost, 15–0. Morgan's fifty-four-win streak was two short of tying the national record. The University of Michigan had a winning streak from the first game in 1901 to the thirteenth game in 1905, of fifty-six straight wins, scoring 2,826 points during this period, against its opponents' forty.

The standings in the Midwest Conference in 1938 follow:

	Won	Lost	Tied
Kentucky State College	4	0	0
Tennessee A & I College	2	1	0
Wilberforce University	2	2	1

	Won	Lost	Tied
West Virginia Institute	2	2	1
Lincoln (Mo.) University	2	3	0
Louisville Municipal College	0	4	0

The leaders in the Southwestern Athletic Conference in 1938 follow:

	Won	Lost	Tied
Southern University	4	1	1
Langston University	3	0	3
Prairie View A & M College	2	2	2
Wiley College	2	3	1
Texas College	2	3	1
Arkansas State College	2	3	1
Bishop College	1	4	1

The 1937–1938 Kentucky State College's champion football team. Identifiable players are, from left to right, first row: unidentified player, Frank Gregory, Melvin Bailey, unidentified player, Redford Rogers, Sterling Hancock, Asbury Ransaw, unidentified player, unidentified player. Second row, left to right: Joe Thomas, Eugene Tooner, unidentified player, unidentified player, Azberry Jones, Randolph Blackburn, unidentified player, Roscoe Chambers, unidentified player, and Dawson. Third row, left to right: Paul White, unidentified player, unidentified player, unidentified player, unidentified player, unidentified player, and Lorraine Miller. (All the rest of the players, including the ones in the fourth row, are unidentifiable).

The standings in the SIAC for 1938:

	Won	*Lost*	*Tied*
Florida A & M College	6	0	0
Morris Brown College	6	1	1
LeMoyne College	4	1	0
Morehouse College	4	1	1
Xavier University	3	2	0
Lane College	3	2	0
Alabama State College	4	4	1
South Carolina State College	2	3	0
Fisk University	2	2	1
Talladega College	2	2	2
Tuskegee Institute	1	4	2
Knoxville College	0	5	1
Clark University	0	6	0

The CIAA 1938 final standings:

	Won	*Lost*	*Tied*
Virginia State College	6	0	1
Morgan College	5	1	1
Shaw University	5	1	2
Virginia Union University	4	2	2
Hampton Institute	3	3	1
Bluefield Institute	3	4	1
Johnson C. Smith University	2	2	1
Greensboro A & T College	2	4	0
Howard University	2	4	0
North Carolina College at Durham	2	4	1
Lincoln University	2	5	0
St. Paul Polytechnic Institute	2	5	0
St. Augustine College	0	4	0

The 1939 leaders in the Southwestern Athletic Conference were:

	Won	Lost	Tied
Langston University	5	0	1
Wiley College	3	2	0
Arkansas State College	3	2	1
Prairie View A & M College	2	2	1
Bishop College	1	2	2
Southern University	1	3	1
Texas College	1	5	0

Florida A & M won the SIAC championship with a 6–2–1 record in 1939.

Virginia State won the CIAA championship in 1939. The final standings follow:

	Won	Lost	Tied
Virginia State College	7	0	1
Lincoln University	5	1	1
Bluefield Institute	4	1	3
Johnson C. Smith University	4	2	0
Greensboro A & T College	3	2	2
North Carolina College at Durham	4	3	0
Hampton Institute	3	3	1
Virginia Union University	3	4	0
Morgan College	2	3	2
Shaw University	3	5	0
St. Paul Polytechnic Institute	2	6	0
St. Augustine College	0	3	0
Howard University	0	7	0

The 1939 Howard-Lincoln Thanksgiving Day game was declared "no contest." The classic was played in Philadelphia's Drexel Park before twelve thousand fans, the largest turnout in a decade.

Howard had held the highly favored Lincoln team to fourteen points and had scored a touchdown. The score was 14–7 going into the last quarter. Howard put together a drive, with two minutes remaining, that carried to the Lincoln twenty-yard line.

A swarm of Howard enthusiasts, overcome with joy, and perhaps even amazement, could not restrain themselves. They poured onto the field—at least half of the twelve thousand in attendance. The game was held up because police simply were unable to clear the field. Darkness was falling. Finally, the referee called the game.

Both teams claimed victory, but two weeks later the CIAA ruled the game "no contest." Despite the fact that Lincoln was ahead, a forefeit was not ruled because Lincoln, as the home team, was responsible for maintaining order, and it could not be determined how many of the unruly spectators who refused to leave the playing field were Howard or Lincoln partisans.

On March 15, 1939, German troops marched into Czechoslovakia, then Lithuania. And in April, Mussolini invaded Albania. On May 22, Mussolini and Hitler signed a ten-year military pact. On August 24, a Russo-German pact was signed. Then on September 1, fourteen German mechanized divisions sped deep into the Polish plains.

On September 3 Great Britain and France declared war on Germany. On November 30 Russia invaded Finland. In a surprise attack, on April 9, Denmark and ports in Norway were occupied by Germany. On May 10, 1940, Holland was attacked by Germany and capitulated four days later. An attack on Belgium was next, then France. On May 15 Holland surrendered. On May 16 Germany invaded France. Belgium surrendered on May 27. On June 3 Italy declared war and joined Germany as an ally and invaded France. On June 22 France surrendered to Germany at Compiegne.

On July 30, 1940, Secretary of War Henry L. Stimson warned the House Military Affairs Committee that a "grave danger" existed of a direct attack by Hitler on the United States.

On September 7, 1940, the House passed the Burke-Wadesworth Compulsory Selective Service Bill. It called for the registration of males from twenty-one to thirty-one years of age. On September 16 President Roosevelt signed the bill into law. On September 27 Germany, Italy, and Japan signed a ten-year military pact.

Nations were girding for world conflagration, while in another world, some were wondering if the color of a man's skin hampered his ability to play a "game."

Ray Kemp was born in Cecil, Pennsylvania. He had played on the Duquesne University varsity football team, and had made "honorable mention" for All-American. Kemp also played major professional football during a session with the Pittsburgh Steelers in 1933. Now in the coaching ranks, he had been at Bluefield Institute for a year, and later at Lincoln University (Mo.).

Kemp was interviewed by the *Pittsburgh Courier*'s Chester Washington, on November 9, 1940:

Washington: Taking individual players, do you think we have ever produced grid stars to compare with such immortals as Red Grange, Charles Cagle, Benny Friedman, Howard Harpster, Larry Kelly . . . and Davey O'Brien?

Kemp: Yes, I think we have, for example I think that Tarzan Kendall was a greater player than Davey O'Brien, Tank Conrad and Doneghy rank with Grange and Cagle, and Stevenson of Tuskegee and Art Wilson of Wilberforce were the equal of Kelly.

Washington: Why do you think they have barred our boys from the pro ranks?

Kemp: I don't think they want colored boys to make that kind of money.

Washington: Do you think Negro stars would be advantageous in pro football?

Kemp: Yes. Take a city like Chicago with a large colored population. The Chicago Cardinals realized what a drawing card Duke Slater was with both whites and colored—in addition to his playing ability—and they kept him with the club.

On August 29, 1940, before 84,567 fans, the Green Bay Packers beat the College All-Stars, 45–28, at Chicago's Soldiers Field.

The *Chicago Daily Tribune* answered the question as to how an outstanding Negro athlete would do in the pro ranks:

Buckets Goldenberg, the stocky guard who met Kenny Washington head-on on the one-yard line, but was bowled over for a touchdown, termed the dusky UCLA star the finest man on the college squad.

The *Chicago Daily News* concurred:

Kenny Washington, UCLA's Negro star, also figured prominently in the night of thrills, twice threatening to break loose on kickoff returns and firing his sharp hard-to-handle passes pretty accurately.

After a two-year hiatus, Morgan State College returned to the top. The *Amsterdam News* of November 30, 1940 reported:

MORGAN TOPS VA. STATES WINS CIAA CROWN

Morgan beat Virginia State, 12–0. Earlier, Morgan's powerhouse machine had overwhelmed Lincoln University, 31–7, as three thousand fans shivered in the sleet and snow in Wilmington (Del.) Park.

There were few highlights by the outclassed Lincoln team, but one was a fumble by Morgan's fullback, Walter Mosby, on the sixteen-yard line. It was scooped up and run back forty-nine yards to the Morgan State thirty-five-yard line by Ralph Oves.

Ralph Oves, 200-pound center, was the only white player on a black college football varsity team in 1940.

The final 1940 standings of the CIAA follow:

	Won	*Lost*	*Tied*
Morgan State College	5	0	1
North Carolina College at Durham	4	1	0
Johnson C. Smith University	4	1	0
Lincoln University	3	1	0
Virginia Union University	3	2	2
Hampton Institute	3	3	1
Virginia Union University	2	2	2
Greensboro A & T College	2	2	1
Bluefield Institute	2	3	0
Shaw University	1	4	1
St. Paul Polytechnic Institute	2	5	0
Howard University	1	6	0
St. Augustine College	0	2	0

Left: Florida A & M's Alonzo S. "Jake" Gaither, one of the all-time great college coaches, in the 1940's. Right: John Clifford "Big Train" Moody, all-time Morris Brown backfield great, only missed seven games in four seasons (1938–1941) and averaged over eleven yards per carry from scrimmage on 295 carries and 3,336 yards gained. He scored 39 touchdowns, 32 extra points, and three field goals—a total of 275 points.

In 1940 the Howard-Lincoln annual Thanksgiving Day encounter returned to Griffith Stadium in the nation's capital. It was the first time that the game had been played in the massive ball park since 1930. Lincoln beat Howard, 63–0.

Howard's drubbing drew no consolation from the *Amsterdam News* on November 30, 1940 (the *Washington Afro-American* did not even run an account of the game):

We wonder whether the ignominious 63 to 0 defeat of Howard University by Lincoln will make the Bisons realize that they should either get a football team or do like the University of Chicago, "throw in the sponge." Possibly it has never occurred to Howard's officials that mediocrity in football or any other form of intercollegiate competition doesn't help the school's prestige.

In 1940 Morris Brown College emerged as a power in the deep South. It won the Southern Intercollegiate Athletic Conference championship and repeated the victory in 1941.

On December 28, 1940, the *Amsterdam News* wrote of Morris Brown's five-feet seven-inches, 216-pound star from Freeport, Pennsylvania, John "Big Train" Moody:

In addition to being the leading scorer in the nation, with 96 points scored personally and setting a new record in sepia football, Moody is a triple-threat man, a great punter, a potent passer, and a pile-driving punter. Dixie's critics have compared him to the immortal Ben Stevenson. A few of them have rated him as even greater.

North Carolina College at Durham dethroned Morgan College in 1941. The standings at the end of the season follow:

	Won	*Lost*	*Tied*
North Carolina College at Durham	6	0	1
Morgan State College	6	1	0
Hampton Institute	6	2	0
Virginia State College	4	2	1
Johnson C. Smith University	3	2	1
Shaw University	4	3	1
St. Augustine College	1	1	0
Bluefield Institute	3	4	0
Virginia Union University	2	4	0
Greensboro A & T College	2	5	0
Howard University	1	3	0
Lincoln University	1	4	0
St. Paul Polytechnic Institute	0	8	0

The only mar on North Carolina College's record was a tie against Virginia State College.

For the first time in the history of Negro college football, the top team in the CIAA would meet the top team in the SIAC in a post-season game, Morris Brown's unbeaten and untied team against North Carolina College's aggregation in the Peach Blossom Classic, at Memorial Stadium, in Columbus, Georgia, on December 6, 1941.

The North Carolina Eagles jumped off to an early lead in the first quarter, when Ray Moore, end, a twenty-year-old senior, blocked Moody's punt and raced twenty-five yards with the recovery for a score. Six thousand fans looked on in stunned disbelief, for Morris Brown was heavily favored. The try for the extra point failed. Score: North Carolina College, 6; Morris Brown, 0.

Both teams battled on even terms. Then, in the third quarter, Morris Brown mounted a sustained drive and Moody scored from the four-yard line. Moody also kicked the extra point. The final score: Morris Brown, 7; North Carolina College, 6.

The North Carolina College players were en route to Durham by special train the following day. They were talking happily and in general enjoying themselves. The game had been a great "moral" victory, for Morris Brown had been acclaimed as the national champion by many Negro newspapers and was rated from three to five touchdowns favorites over a team that had won its first CIAA title, ever.

Then one of North Carolina College's coaches entered the car and informed the young athletes that Pearl Harbor had been attacked. United States involvement in the war was imminent. A pall immediately fell over the assembled athletes as each player seemed caught up in his own thoughts. Thirteen of the thirty-three man squad were eligible for the draft.

North Carolina College received more bad news a few days later. It forfeited the CIAA championship, and Morgan State College was declared the 1941 CIAA champions.

Henry Thomas, end, from Farrell, Pennsylvania, had been declared ineligible. Thomas had graduated from Farrell High School in 1939. In September 1939 he enrolled in Lincoln University (Mo.). After the football season, he returned to Farrell and obtained employment.

When Thomas enrolled at North Carolina College, he did not list on his application that he had attended Lincoln, but a rival conference coach tipped off the CIAA that a "Henry Thomas" had played football for Lincoln University. North Carolina had to forfeit the Bluefield, St. Paul, Lincoln (Pa.), Shaw, and Johnson C. Smith University victories.

The revised 1941 CIAA standings were:

	Won	*Lost*	*Tied*
Morgan State College	6	1	0
Johnson C. Smith University	4	1	1
Virginia State College	4	2	1
Bluefield Institute	4	3	0
Hampton Institute	6	2	0
Shaw University	5	2	1
Virginia Union University	2	4	0
North Carolina College at Durham	1	5	1
Greensboro A & T College	2	5	0
St. Paul Polytechnic Institute	1	7	0
St. Augustine College	1	1	0
Lincoln University	2	3	0
Howard University	1	3	0

The powerful Morris Brown team had a 9–0–1 record in 1940, including wins over Kentucky State College, 28–0, in the 1940 Peach Blossom Classic, and Wilberforce University, 19–3, on New Year's Day. Their only loss in the 1941 season was a 13–0 victory by Langston University on New Year's Day.

Germany's nonaggression pact with Russia was not honored. Hitler launched an attack on Russia on June 22, 1941. And with the Japanese attack against the United States, the world was caught up in the Second World War. Young men and women would soon be leaving the college campuses to engage in another type of training.

The nation had been at war nine months as the 1942 football season got under way. The *Washington Afro-American* of October 3, 1942, reported:

W. VA. STATE-UNION CONTEST CANCELED

Lawrenceville, Va.—A total of twelve contests were canceled within the last two weeks, according to a release by J. L. Whitehead, secretary-treasurer of the CIAA, Monday. Besides the Lincoln-North Carolina . . . game, the seven games canceled by St. Paul and the three called off by Shaw this week, Whitehead revealed that the Union-West Virginia contest was canceled.

The manpower shortage resulting from the draft was already severely limiting football squads in 1942. But Howard University had thirty-five candidates report for practice, and Coach James H. Rowland was pleased: "We are going to have a football team here. I think Howard is fortunate when we observe the uncertainty which faces many schools with regard to athletics."

Of Howard's football aspirants, twenty-six were between the ages of seventeen and twenty, and nine were between the ages of twenty-one and twenty-four. So Howard was assured—barring ineligibility in some other way or injury—that twenty-six players would be able to finish the season. Other schools had problems. The *Washington Afro-American* of October 31, 1942, noted:

CANCELS SEASON'S SCHEDULE

ONLY 15 PLAYERS ON SQUAD AFTER SIX ARE INDUCTED

Shaw University had played only one game, a 7–6 loss to Fayetteville State Teachers College, when it had to cancel the remainder of the schedule. Only Shaw University, St. Paul Polytechnic Institute, and St. Augustine College, dropped football "for the duration" in the CIAA. The final CIAA standings for 1942 follow:

	Won	*Lost*	*Tied*
Morgan State College	5	1	1
Johnson C. Smith University	4	1	1
Virginia State College	5	2	1
Bluefield Institute	2	1	3
Hampton Institute	3	1	3
West Virginia Institute	2	2	0

	Won	Lost	Tied
Lincoln University	1	1	1
North Carolina College at Durham	1	3	0
Virginia Union University	1	4	0
Greensboro A & T College	1	6	0
Howard University	0	3	0

The annual Howard-Lincoln game in 1942 was played before four thousand fans at Griffith Stadium. Lincoln won, 20–6.

The final Southwestern Athletic Conference standings for 1942 follow:

	Won	Lost	Tied
Texas College	4	0	0
Prairie View A & M College	3	1	0
Langston University	1	2	1
Wiley College	1	3	0
Southern University	0	3	1

In the Southern Intercollegiate Athletic Conference, the Florida A & M College football team won the 1942 championship.

In 1943 Livingstone College suspended varsity football for the duration, and in the SIAC, varsity programs were "curtailed." But at the annual CIAA meeting the pledge was for college athletic programs to "carry on in 1943." The realities of the war years soon began to be felt, however. The *Washington Afro-American* of October 2, 1943, reported:

BLUEFIELD AND UNION DROP FOOTBALL FOR DURATION
7 CIAA COLLEGES QUIT FOR DURATION
LINCOLN ALSO OUT; HOWARD EXPECTED TO FOLLOW;
HAMPTON OPENS SUNDAY

The CIAA colleges which had canceled for the 1943 season and/or the duration were Virginia Union University, Bluefield Institute, Lincoln University, North Carolina College at Durham, St. Augustine,

St. Paul Polytechnic Institute, Shaw University, and Howard University.

Twenty-four football candidates reported at Morgan, the smallest number in its history, and twenty candidates reported at Delaware State College, where Thomas "Big Tank" Conrad was in his first year as coach.

Morgan State College opened the 1943 season with a 25–0 victory over the 1390th Service Unit of the Camp Holabird Signal Depot. Next Morgan beat Wilberforce University, 43–0. Virginia State College beat Camp Butner, of Durham, 33–0. And Johnson C. Smith University lost to Camp Pickett, 9–6. Morgan State College was now scheduled to meet Florida A & M College, champions in the SIAC. The Rattlers had been very successful in their intersectional contests:

1933: Florida A & M College, 9—Howard University, 7
1934: Florida A & M College, 13—Virginia State College, 12
1937: Florida A & M College, 13—Greensboro A & T College, 7
1937: Florida A & M College, 25—Hampton Institute, 20
1938: Florida A & M College, 13—Greensboro A & T College, 0
1939: Florida A & M College, 0—Greensboro A & T College, 0
1939: Florida A & M College, 20—North Carolina College at Durham, 7
1940: Florida A & M College, 7—Greensboro A & T College, 0
1940: Florida A & M College, 7—North Carolina College at Durham, 7
1941: Florida A & M College, 19—Greensboro A & T College, 0
1942: Florida A & M College, 9—Greensboro A & T College, 0

In 1943 Morgan State College overwhelmed Florida A & M College, 50–0, at Griffith Stadium before fourteen thousand spectators.

Because of cancellations, make-up games, and decimated schedules, the CIAA had not since 1942 listed official standings of the teams. However, everyone knew that Morgan State College, which had not been defeated in two years, was the power in Negro college football.

The year was 1944. Muriel Rahn and Hilda Simms were starring on Broadway in *Carmen Jones* and *Anna Lucasta*, respectively. *Stormy Weather*, starring Lena Horne, Bill Robinson, and Cab Calloway, would have an advance showing on January 8, 1944; price, 60 cents. *The Ox-Bow Incident* and *Oklahoma Kid* were playing at neighborhood theaters. President Roosevelt was reelected for a fourth term on November 7; and a thirty-six-year-old Harlem Minister, Adam Clayton Powell, Jr., was sworn into the Seventy-ninth Congress.

In 1944, the Tuskegee Army Air Force football team won the Negro Servicemens' Gridiron championship. On Saturday night, November 11, 1944, the best Negro Service team met what was possibly the top Negro college football team, Morgan State College. The game was played at Griffith Stadium before twenty-two thousand spectators.

In the first quarter, Bob Carson lofted a forty-three-yard punt, which Morgan's Terry Day let roll and then suddenly scooped up, while trying to evade a swarm of onrushing Air Force players. His wide sweep carried him into the end zone, and he was tackled by Ernie Hill for a safety. Day was shaken up and had to leave the game. He would not return. Tuskegee Army Air Force, 2; Morgan State College, 0.

At half time the fifty-four-piece 613th Army Air Force band took the field. The stadium lights were shut off and there appeared a dazzling sight of bands' uniforms bedecked in electric illumination of red, white, and blue bulbs. After a series of formations, the band played "God Bless America." When they marched off the field, they were greeted by a standing ovation that lasted several minutes.

The final score of the game stood at 2–0. It was Morgan State College's seventh loss in thirteen seasons. But somehow, on this night, there was a sense that Negro college football would never be the same again, and indeed that the nation would never be the same. This change would probably be symbolized in Morgan State's big left end, Leonard Ford. In a year he would be in the Big Ten. And in six months the nation's headlines would shout:

GERMANY SURRENDERS UNCONDITIONALLY

THE WAR IN EUROPE IS ENDED! SURRENDER IS UNCONDITIONAL;
V-E WILL BE PROCLAIMED TODAY; OUR TROOPS ON OKINAWA GAIN

On September 2, 1945, the war in Asia ended:

JAPANESE SIGN FORMAL ARTICLES OF SURRENDER; MACARTHUR
ACTS FOR ALLIES, PLEDGES FIRM JUSTICE; TRUMAN HAILS VICTORY
IN ADDRESS TO NATION

It had been over half a century since the first Negro college football teams took the field in homemade uniforms on a snowy day in North Carolina. Now at Griffith Stadium in the nation's capital, another era was beginning and one was ending. The trek toward the college campus and the athletic field would return. The game, however, not unlike the world, was changed for all time.

No other Negro college football team would run up a continuous victory streak as had Morgan College. Just how had a small school, with barely three hundred students, established such a dynasty? They had had no gymnasium, meager equipment, and a limited coaching staff.

Otis Troupe tells how: "The coaches and alumni were completely dedicated. Coach Hurt went out and got the best athletes from both white and black high schools. Even then we had the same plays that I see on television today. Only today they are specialists—and we were full-time players."

Troupe played on Morgan's basketball team that had to "go into town" one or two nights a week to practice at the New Albert Casino. When a player's football jersey was ripped off, he simply took one from a bench-warmer. Meanwhile, Morgan alumni were looking for material all over.

Troupe had graduated from Thomas Jefferson High School in Elizabeth, New Jersey, in June 1930. He was in a poolroom playing a "stranger in town," in February 1931. Suddenly the stranger said, "How would you like to go to school at Morgan College?"

The nineteen-year-old youngster had no intention of going to college, and besides, he had not even heard of Morgan, but in February he found himself on the Morgan campus.

Otis Emanuel Troupe, five feet eight inches and 206 pounds, went on to become one of Morgan College's "immortals."

His credentials at the Hall of Fame ceremonies for Morgan athletes in 1972 read:

Morgan immortal—without a doubt Morgan's greatest Triple-Threat Ace . . . had blinding speed and unlimited power. No. 1 Morgan best, "Tank" Conrad or "Whataman" Troupe, may never be settled, but anyone else will be second best—stand second best to no football player ever to play for Morgan.

The past merged with present. The beginnings of Negro college football had been: six thousand fans at a Thanksgiving Day game in Nashville, Tennessee. It had been the Student Army Training Corps in 1918. It was the postwar boom. It was outstanding black football coaches, Cleveland L. Abbott, Matthew Washington Bullock, and Edward Paulette Hurt; and as the 1950s and 1960s approached, Alonzo Smith "Jake" Gaither, who carried the mantle to an incredible one hundred twenty-one football victories in one hundred forty-one contests at Florida A & M College.

The sturdy pioneer players were Will Morrow, Bright Funderburk, Wade Hampton, William Trent, Clarence Agee "Terrible" Terry, Edward Benjamin Gray, Harry "Wu Fang" Ward, Robert Miller, and Franz "Jazz" Byrd. And, yes, among the pioneers was also Haywood McPherson Johnson, dying from football injuries at Washington's Freedmens Hospital.

The pioneers were also love of country. A Greensboro A & T College quarterback, Samuel M. Bruce, being shelled by enemy flak and dying when his parachute failed to open "somewhere in Italy." The beginnings were gaiety. Defeats. Victories. Press receptions. Breakfast promenades. And fraternity dances. It was thirty thousand fans in Shibe Park and fifty students cheering on a cold November afternoon.

The early game was a Morrison College losing 129–0, and the team's tackle refusing to leave the game despite an injury. It was Benjamin Stevenson reversing his field an incredible three times on the way to a 90-yard touchdown run.

These were the beginnings. The pioneers. Negro college football. Tough, full-time players. Asking no quarter and giving none. And all proud to be members of a Negro college football team.

7

Early Black Stars in Track and Field

Track and field is steeped in the literature of the ages, as the Twenty-Third Book of the *Iliad*'s narration of the Funeral Games in honor of Patroclus and the graphic description of the footrace between Odysseus and Ajax so vividly depict. And it is not only in Greek literature that track and field events have been extolled, but also in Latin literature as well with such epic heroes virtually bulging from the pages of Virgil's *Aeneid* as Nisus, Euryalus, Salius, Helymus, and Diores, all engaged in the competition of the games. The Anglo-Saxon variety of track and field events was known as early as A.D. 1100, in London, England.

It is in America that track and field events are of relatively recent vintage. American track dates back to the close of the Civil War; or more precisely, to 1876, when both the Amateur Athletic Union and the Intercollegiate Association held their first meetings.

It is not known who the first black track and field athlete was. But perhaps "A. Wharton, a Negro in the VII AAA Championships at Stamfort Bridge, London, in 1886" was one of the first. He was also one of the first athletes to run a hundred-yard dash in ten seconds.

Also in the nineteenth century, several Negro athletes won fame in track and field at a few white eastern universities.

William Tecumseh Sherman Jackson was born in Alexandria, Virginia, on November 18, 1865. He received his early education in the public schools of Petersburg, Virginia, later attending Virginia Normal and Collegiate Institute, at Petersburg. He entered Amherst Col-

William Tecumseh Sherman Jackson as he appeared on the 1892 Amherst College track and field team.

lege as a sophomore in September 1889.

In 1890 Jackson was on the track and field team, after having been on the varsity football team the previous fall. A dispatch to *The New York Times* from Amherst on June 1, 1890, noted:

Nothing this year has given such satisfaction as the fact that last Wednesday Amherst a second time won the championship in track athletics.

Amherst was content to rest on its laurels, despite a challenge from elsewhere. Again *The New York Times* reported:

It is doubtful whether Amherst will accept the challenge of Hamilton College to contest with her in track athletics on neutral grounds. Hamilton is champion of New York State, while Amherst is champion of the New England Intercollegiate Athletic Association.

The annual meet of the New England Intercollegiate Athletic Association (NEIAA) was held on Wednesday, May 28, 1890.

Over fifteen hundred fans attended at Worcester, Massachusetts, on a cold showery day. Members of the NEIAA were Amherst, Dartmouth, Brown, Wesleyan, Trinity, Williams, Worcester Polytechnic Institute, and the University of Vermont.

Amherst won the meet, having ten first-place victories, to runner-up Dartmouth's four first-place wins. Jackson won his event, the half-mile, in 2 minutes 8⅕ seconds.

But three days later, on May 31, at New York's Berkeley Oval, five thousand fans cheered a meet sponsored by the Intercollegiate Association of Amateur Athletes of America and Harvard College's victory of thirty-two points. Amherst was fifth runner-up (twelve points) behind Columbia, Princeton, Yale, and Harvard.

Jackson was entered in his customary event, the half-mile. The field lined up with a total of ten starters. The runners set off in a bunch, but H. I. Dadmun, of Worcester Polytechnic Institute, led the pack from the outset. E. A. Taylor, also of Polytech, stayed with him for a while and outbattled Jackson for second place. Dadmun ran a 2-minute 1⅗-second half-mile. Jackson finished third.

In 1891 the NEIAA held its meet on May 27 in Hampden Park, Springfield, Massachusetts. The air was festive; the weather cool. Permission had been granted for the public schools to hold half-day sessions, so the teachers and students could see the games. Permission had been sought to have the stores closed, but this was denied. Nearly five thousand fans were present to witness the eighteen events on the track and field program.

Amherst College again won. The winning first- and second-place points follow:

	First	Second
Amherst	9	4
Dartmouth	4	6
Wesleyan	2	1
Worcester	1	5
Williams	1	3
Brown	1	0
University of Vermont	0	1
Trinity	0	0

Dadmun of Worcester again won the half-mile run, this time in

2 minutes 1⅖ seconds. Jackson failed to place. But the next year, at the sixth annual NEIAA held on May 25, 1892, at Springfield, Jackson won his specialty. The *Boston Globe* of May 26 noted:

In the half-mile run Jackson of Amherst, the colored runner, had things his own way and at no time was pushed, although Price of Dartmouth struggled hard to head him.

Jackson's time in the half-mile was 2 minutes 5⅖ seconds. G. D. Price of Dartmouth finished second.

Walter Lamont Tower, Amherst, class of 1893, wrote a book in 1935 entitled *A Glance At Amherst Athletes*. He placed Jackson at "honorable mention" on the all-time Amherst teams in track and field.

After W. T. S. Jackson graduated in 1892 (the year a nineteen-year-old freshman named John Calvin Coolidge entered Amherst), he became an instructor in Greek and Latin at the Virginia College and Seminary in 1892–1893. From 1893 to 1906 he was an instructor in mathematics at the M Street High School (now Dunbar High School), in Washington, D.C., of which he later became principal. Jackson retired in December 1930. In 1943, at the 50th anniversary of his graduation from Amherst, William Jackson was honored by that institution for his work as an educator.

The next black track and field athlete at a white college during the nineteenth century was Napoleon Bonaparte Marshall, Harvard College, class of 1897. He was on the track team four years.

On Saturday, May 26, 1894, N. B. Marshall finished third in the 440-yard run in the Yale-Harvard meet. Yale won the meet with 37 points to Harvard's 24¼.

In June 1895 the Harvard graduate magazine noted that after the April recess, N. B. Marshall and other members of the track team had been assigned to the training table. The magazine also noted that Marshall's time in the 440-yard run was 51⅕ seconds.

In 1896 N. B. Marshall was a member of the 440-yard run team with W. H. Vincent, H. Hollister, H. H. Fish, W. R. Mansfield, C. H. Williams, Mel Butler, and J. Boardman.

The 1895 Harvard University track and field squad. Shown at right (next to back row) is Napoleon Bonaparte Marshall.

But for the big track meet in May, Harvard sent only twenty-five athletes to New York, and N. B. Marshall did not make the trip.

On May 28, 1897, N. B. Marshall made the trip to the intercollegiate track championships, being held on Berkeley Oval, New York.

On the first day of the preliminaries of the two-day events, Marshall was entered in the second heat of the 440-yard run. He finished third, running behind W. H. Vincent and T. E. Burke of Boston University. Burke's time was 50⅘ seconds. S. K. Gerard of Yale was fourth.

The following field in the 440-yard-run finals lined up the next day: T. E. Burke, S. K. Gerard, G. F. Luce, F. B. Garvin, W. H. Vincent, H. H. Fish, N. B. Marshall, and R. D. Hoffman.

Burke finished first in 50⅖ seconds. Garvin, of Yale, finished second, and Hoffman, of the University of Pennsylvania, finished third. Marshall did not place.

The University of Pennsylvania went on to win the meet with 34 points. Yale was second with 24½ points, and Harvard third with 15¾ points.

After graduation, Marshall became an attorney with a long and distinguished career in the nation's capital.

In 1896 S. Dickerson was on the track team at the University of Chicago. On June 6, on the grounds at Thirty-fifth Street and Wentworth Avenue, Chicago, twelve institutions of higher learning were entered in the annual Western Intercollegiate Athletic meet. They were Center College, Grinnell College, Beloit College, State University of Iowa, University of Minnesota, University of Illinois, Northwestern University, University of Kansas, University of Wisconsin, Lake Forest College, DePauw University, and the University of Chicago.

S. Dickerson was entered in the 440-yard run. J. H. Rush of Grinnell won this event in 50⅘ seconds, Downer of Wisconsin was second, and Jackson of Lake Forest was third. Dickerson failed to place. Wisconsin won the meet with forty-six points. Grinnell finished second with twenty-two points, and the University of Chicago finished third with ten points.

At the turn of the century, track-and-field meet competition had not as yet taken a grip upon the nearly sixty-eight Negro four-year institutions of higher learning.

As far back as 1826, John Russwurm had been the first Negro college graduate, at Bowdoin. And in 1870 Richard T. Greener had become the first Negro to graduate from Harvard College, a college that had been one of the first to open its educational facilities to the Negro. Several Negroes, even before Greener, had taken special courses there, and its professional schools had had Negro students. Yet, partly because track-meet competition first started in American colleges in 1876, W. T. S. Jackson was perhaps the first Negro American to compete in track events.

William Tecumseh Sherman Jackson was named after the then forty-five-year-old Civil War general. Jackson, Napoleon Bonaparte Marshall, and Spencer Dickerson were worthy precursors for the many outstanding black track and field athletes who would follow in ever increasing numbers.

George Poage, at the beginning of the twentieth century, entered the University of Wisconsin. He was the next outstanding Negro track and field athlete. In a dual meet against Beloit College on May 4, 1903, Poage scored a high of eighteen points. Knox of Beloit was the second highest individual scorer with sixteen points. The summaries of Poage's events follow:

100-yard dash, won by Knox in ten seconds. Second place, Poage. Third place, Hayden, of Wisconsin.

200-yard dash, won by Poage in 22⅗ seconds. Second place, Hayden. Third place, Merrill, of Beloit.

220-yard low hurdles, won by Poage in 27 seconds. Second place, Campbell, of Beloit. Third place, Saridakis, of Wisconsin.

440-yard run, won by Poage in 52 seconds. Second place, Merrill. Third place, Mowry.

The University of Wisconsin won the meet with 58⅓ points, to Beloit's 53½ points.

In a handicap meet at Madison, Wisconsin, on May 9, 1903, George Poage, of course, started from scratch in his events. Chapman was given a five-yard lead in the 220-yard dash and just barely won over Poage in 23⅕ seconds. However, in the 220-yard hurdles, Marquisse was given a ten-yard lead but Poage passed him at the taps in 26⅘ seconds.

The University of Wisconsin's varsity track and field team of 1903. First row, left to right: Poage and Kuehmstead. Second row, left to right: Watkins, MacEachron, Keachie, Hean, Hayden, and Hueffner. Third row, left to right: Chapman, Henry, Post, Breitkreutz, Wheeler, Saridakis, and A. Todd. Fourth row, left to right: Glynn, Long, Abbott, Tenner, Conway, and Todd. Back row, left to right: Friend (Manager), Kilpatrick (Coach), and Jackson (Assistant Manager). (Courtesy of the University of Wisconsin)

In a dual meet against the University of Illinois, on May 15, at Champaign, Illinois, Wisconsin won, sixty-two to fifty points. Poage put on a sensational performance on a day in which the weather was perfect—but he got off to a bad start. In the first heat of the 100-yard dash, Poage won in 10⅕ seconds. Hale of Illinois was second. In the second heat, Chapman of Wisconsin won in 10 seconds, and Townsend of Illinois was second. In the finals of the 100-yard dash, Townsend won in 10 seconds. Chapman was second, and Hale third.

Poage won the 440-yard run in 51 seconds. Dunbar of Illinois was second, and Wheeler third. Next Poage won the 220-yard hurdles in 25⅗ seconds. His teammate, Saridakis, was second.

On May 23 the *Wisconsin State Journal* speculated that:

. . . many of the students have picked Poage as a winner in the low hurdles. He has showed good form in practice and it is said he has lots of speed.

The *Chicago Tribune* also liked Poage's chances in the dual meet against the University of Chicago:

Poage will without doubt win the quarter, as he is the strongest man in the west in this event. Poage is also good for a place toward the front in the low hurdles and in the dashes, too, if he runs them.

The University of Chicago won the meet, 72½ points to 43½ points at Madison on Saturday, May 23, but Poage's performance nearly followed the script.

In the 440-yard run, Taylor of the University of Chicago, started off like a shot. At the halfway mark he was ahead of the field. But about one hundred yards from the tape, Poage turned on the speed and overtook Taylor. Poage won by more than six yards. Taylor was second, and Buckwaiter of Chicago was third. Poage's time was 52⅗ seconds.

In the 100-yard dash, Blair of Chicago was first in 10⅕ seconds. Senn of Chicago was second, and Poage was third.

Poage won the 220-yard hurdles in 26⅕ seconds. Catlin of Chicago was second, and Ferris of Chicago was third.

The *Wisconsin State Journal* on June 4, 1903, blared:

POAGE WINS 440-YARD DASH AT CHICAGO MEET

George Poage's time was 50⅘ seconds. Blair of Chicago was second, and Gerrills of Michigan, third.

Poage entered the University of Wisconsin in September 1900. In 1901 he was on the varsity track squad. On May 22, 1902, at Minneapolis, Minnesota, he attracted national attention in a dual meet against the University of Minnesota. He won the 440-yard run in 52 seconds and the 220-yard dash in 22⅘ seconds. He added a third-place finish in the 100-yard dash. The University of Wisconsin won the meet over the University of Minnesota, 66–37.

On June 4, 1904, George Poage closed his track career in a blaze of glory. At Chicago's Marshall Field he won two events. But first, heats were required for the 440-yard run, the first time that this had happened. Entered in the second heat, Poage won in 51⅗ seconds. The other heats were won by Garrels of Michigan, in 52⅕ seconds, and the last heat by Waller of Chicago, in 52⅗ seconds.

In the finals, ten runners lined up, and Poage ran the fastest time of the day to finish first in 50⅘ seconds. He topped off the day by winning the 220-yard low hurdles in 25 seconds.

Poage later became the first Negro Olympian in St. Louis, Missouri, in August 1904.

Jackson, Dickerson, Marshall, and Poage all ran the 440-yard event in track competition, and Jackson also ran the half-mile.

The next outstanding black track athlete was also a quarter-miler. John Taylor was born in Washington, D.C., on November 3, 1882. He received his preliminary education at Central High School in Philadelphia and Brown Preparatory School in 1903.

The *Philadelphia Item* of May 17, 1903, reported:

New Haven, Conn., May 17—J. B. Taylor, a young Negro, the only one who appeared as a contestant in the meet, created a sensation at the second annual inter-scholastic track games under the auspices of Yale University Association at Yale Field yesterday afternoon, by running away from all competitors in the quarter-mile win.

Worcester Academy's J. F. Doyle's record of 51⅗ seconds in the 440-yard run was broken by Taylor. His time was 50⅗ seconds. The thirteen events were run off in one hour and fifty minutes, but Taylor's school got just one first place for their only five points. Mercerburg won with 43½ points.

On May 23, in the Middle States Track and Field Championships at Franklin Field, Philadelphia, "Taylor of Brown Prep School, won the 440-yard dash easily, his mate, Mulligan, getting second." Taylor's time was 53 seconds.

In fall 1903, J. B. Taylor enrolled in the university division of the University of Pennsylvania. When the track season started in 1904, he was on the nineteen-man varsity squad with Dear, Cartmell, Hyman, Orton, Terry, Gunn, Jones, Boyd, Russell, Vernon, Amsler, McClellan, Thayer, Moffet, Gilpin, Hammer, Meede, and Fennell.

The track and field team had two major meets throughout the season, one a dual meet, and the annual intercollegiate championships at the end of May. This was a two-day meet. The University of Pennsylvania had not won the intercollegiate championship since 1900, but it did that year with 39 points. Princeton was second with 25 points, and Yale, third with 20½ points.

But in 1904 the University of Pennsylvania was defeated in its dual meet against Cornell on May 14 at Ithaca, New York, by 76–41 points. Taylor won the 440-yard run in 49⅗ seconds. Hyman was second, and Rogers, third.

The twenty-ninth annual track and field championships of the Intercollegiate Association of Amateur Athletes of America was held on Franklin Field for two days, May 27–28. The *Philadelphia Item* described Taylor's first day, preliminary heat:

> Taylor, the colored boy of Pennsylvania, gave a taste of his quality in the second heat of the quarter-mile in the easiest fashion imaginable, he romped several yards in front of his nearest opponent in 51⅕s.

T. Ewing of Yale finished second, and J. C. Alter, of Princeton, finished third. In the first heat, J. V. Mulligan, of Georgetown, won in

51 seconds. H. A. Hyman finished second, and C. B. Long finished third. In the last heat, J. A. Reilly, of Georgetown, won in 51 seconds. S. R. Burnay, of Yale, was second, and E. J. Dives, of Harvard, finished third.

The *Philadelphia Item* on May 29 blared the results of the 440-yard-run finals:

TAYLOR, A UNIVERSITY OF PENNSYLVANIA ATHLETE, CLIPPED ONE-FIFTH OF A SECOND OFF MAYEY LONG'S FIGURES

Yale won the meet with 34½ points. Harvard was second with 25⅓ points and Pennsylvania finished third with 24 points. Taylor had Pennsylvania's only first-place victory. His win broke the old intercollegiate record of 49⅖ seconds. This was formerly held by M. W. Long of Columbia, set in 1899. Taylor's new mark for the 440-yard run was 49⅕ seconds. C. B. Long finished second, and E. S. Dives, third. S. R. Bernap, of Yale, finished fourth.

John Taylor ran a smart race. With good position and a clear view of all the runners, he stayed well in back. Then, as the field headed for the straight, Taylor suddenly put on a great burst of speed, to a standing ovation, and won by three yards.

As the track season closed, the University of Pennsylvania looked toward 1905 in great anticipation. Nearly the entire squad would be back, and Michael C. Murphy was contemplating returning to Pennsylvania from New Haven.

Michael C. Murphy was the most noted trainer of college athletes in America. He first came to the University of Pennsylvania in fall 1896, and in 1897 Pennsylvania won its first track championship. He subsequently turned out teams that won championships in 1898, 1899, and 1900. In fall 1900 he left for Yale. After a one-year hiatus in the winning streak of championship teams, he resumed his success with Yale. His teams of 1902—Harvard won in 1901 and 1903—and 1904 won track championships. But suddenly, 1905's gloss faded. The *Philadelphia Item* of May 12, 1905, commented:

Whatever chance Penn had of winning the intercollegiate games this spring, or even making a strong bid for first place, was destroyed on Wednesday, when J. B. Taylor, Penn's colored runner, who holds the intercollegiate record for the quarter-mile, was dropped from college.

With Taylor gone in 1905, Cornell University won the championship. In 1906, Taylor returned to the university—but not to the track team. He was not eligible to compete on the team in that year, and Cornell again won the track and field championship.

Finally, on May 29, 1907, Taylor was again on the track and field team at the preliminary trials of the annual track championships at Franklin Field.

The track was heavy, and the weather rainy. A steady downpour had persisted unrelentingly all day, but several thousand fans remained riveted to their seats.

Taylor won his heat in 52⅕ seconds. Deselding, of Harvard, was second, and Carpenter, of Cornell, third. Hendrie, of Swarthmore, was fourth.

The next day, with the favorable weather, and a dry track, Taylor lowered his previous record in the 440-yard run from 49⅕ seconds to 48⅘ seconds.

When the field lined up, all eyes were on Taylor. H. M. Rogers of Cornell had won in 1906, and he was the favorite.

As the field started off, Taylor got mired in a bad position. He was boxed in and could not make his move to the inside or outside. But going into the back stretch, he suddenly shot ahead at an amazing acceleration, that even seemed momentarily to startle Rogers and Coholani, who finished second and third respectively. Atlee, of Princeton, finished fourth.

Murphy had his championship. Cornell won the meet with thirty-three points. Michigan was second with twenty-nine points, and Yale third with twenty-three points.

Taylor had another outstanding track season in 1908. The University of Pennsylvania barely missed the championship, finishing with 29½ points to Cornell's 34 points. Yale was third with twenty-two points.

Dr. John Baxter Taylor in England in 1908 as a member of the Olympic track and field team.

The track season ended, and attention was now focused on the 1908 Olympics scheduled for London. On Saturday, June 6, 1908, the Olympic tryouts were held on Philadelphia's Franklin Field.

The *Philadelphia Item* of June 7, 1908, reported:

TAYLOR'S GREAT RACE

Who of those that witnessed Taylor's wonderful race in the 400-meter event could ever forget; seemingly hopelessly beaten with no chance apparently of winning, but game to the core though his spurt seemed too delayed, he unwaveringly kept on and won amidst the wildest excitement of the day.

When the lineup for the 400-meter[1] race had been fielded, Taylor had drawn a bad position. And as the race started, he found himself bunched in the middle of all the runners. He was still boxed in as the last lap neared and was running in eighth position. But a hundred yards from the tape, Taylor suddenly squeezed through a small opening and turned on some hidden inner reserve of kick speed. He nipped Atlee at the tape with a desperate surge to win in 49⅘ seconds.

[1] 400-meters is equal to 437.2 yards.

W. C. Prout of the Boston Athletic Club ran third.

Taylor was scheduled to compete in the 400-meter run and the 1600-meter relay in London. The 400-meter Olympic squad consisted of ten athletes. The 1600-meter relay team consisted of Cartmell, Huff, Taylor, and Sheppard.

In July 1908 the team sailed for England. Five months later, after returning home from the games, John Baxter Taylor was dead at age twenty-six.

Taylor, a graduate of the University of Pennsylvania School of Veterinary Medicine, had contracted typhoid pneumonia. The shock of his untimely death brought his family hundreds of telegrams from people in all walks of life. Taylor's death was summed up by Harry Porter, acting president of the American Olympic team, in a letter to Taylor's parents:

It was not alone as an athlete of marvelous skill and courage, one of the greatest the world has ever known. Although this was very much. It is far more as the man that John Taylor made his mark. Quite unostentatious, genial, kindly. The fleet-footed, fair-formed red and blue athlete was beloved wherever known. As a member of the American Olympic team, he passed into memory for his modesty and manliness. As a man, John has left behind him a memory fragrant as frankincense and myrrh. He is gone yet he lives. Yes, he lives. He lives still, and always will. Be comforted.

Indeed a great and modest athlete. Few, if any, of the distinguished mourners at his bier knew of the forty-five cups and seventy medals at the 3223 Woodlawn Avenue address of the dead man. John Baxter Taylor, perhaps the best of the early black stars.

In the Negro colleges, intramural competition existed in track athletics, but the first scheduled meets took place on the intercollegiate level. As early as 1906 Howard University and Lincoln University participated in the open events.

Perhaps the first Negro college to hold an intercollegiate track meet was Atlanta Baptist College (Morehouse College) in 1909. Atlanta Baptist won this meet, and the next one, held the following year. In 1911 Atlanta University won the event, and the school officials at

Atlanta Baptist College noted: "The students and people are not yet educated up to track meets, but each year shows improvement." Intramural competition continued. In 1910 Hampton Institute held its first intramural track meet.

Track facilities at Negro colleges were not easy to come by. One theory to explain why black athletes specialized in the sprints holds that sprint events required less running space. It can be noted that with the white colleges' more ample facilities, such as Pratt and Franklin fields, the early black stars nearly all specialized in the half and quarter mile.

A close look at some of the leading Negro colleges of the period shows that in 1910 Howard University had an enrollment of 1,350 students. The college division numbered 347—of whom 147 were freshmen.

Lincoln University (Pa.) had 136 students in its college division and 50 in its theological seminary.

Virginia Union had 35 students in its college division, 30 in its theology department, 120 in its academy, and 40 in its grade school.

Shaw University had 500 students in its preparatory, normal, and college divisions.

As small as these numbers were, there were some who thought that they were still too large. In South Carolina, Governor-Elect Cole L. Bleaze stated: "I am firmly convinced, after the most careful thought and study, that the Almighty created the Negro to be a hewer of wood and drawer of water. I also believe that the greatest mistake the white race has ever made was in attempting to educate the free Negro."

In 1916 former Governor Bleaze was invited to address the students at all-black Allen University in Columbia, South Carolina. He no doubt remembered his 1911 remark, as he informed his audience: "You are coming to higher things. They can't hold you back despite what I or any other man may say."

Two decades later there were 18,980 Negro students in black colleges, with 1,980 degrees conferred. In white colleges, there were about 2,500 Negro students and 280 graduates. In 1913 there had been less than thirty Negro graduates from white colleges, and in 1916 there had been thirty-eight Negro graduates from white colleges.

The 1911 Harvard University track and field squad. Theodore Cable, class of 1913, is shown in third row, second from right.

The number of outstanding Negro track stars was definitely disproportionate to the overall number of Negroes enrolled in white colleges, and as the 1900s progressed, the number of Negro stars increased.

Theodore Cable was born in 1891 and graduated from Shortridge High School, Indianapolis, Indiana, in 1908. In September 1909 he entered Harvard College from Phillips-Exeter Academy. He made the freshman team in hammer throwing and in the 220-yard dash.

In the Harvard-Yale freshman meet, he won the hammer throw with a distance of 117 feet, and in 1911 he won the 56-pound championship for height in Madison Square Garden. Later, in the Harvard-Dartmouth meet, Cable made a record throw of 154 feet 11⅖ inches. This set a Harvard-Dartmouth dual-meet record. In his junior year in 1912, Cable won the hammer throw at the Harvard-Yale meet with a throw of 154 feet 11¼ inches. He also won the broad jump with a leap of 22 feet 10½ inches. On June 1, 1912, he won first place in an intercollegiate meet in Philadelphia, with a hammer throw of 162 feet 4 inches.

On May 31, 1913, Alexander Jackson and Cable were teammates on the Harvard varsity track team. Alexander competed in the 120-

The 1912 Harvard University track and field squad. Shown in second row, second from right, is Theodore Cable, joined by Alexander Louis Jackson, class of 1914 (third from right in second row).

and 220-yard hurdles. He finished second in the 120-yard hurdles, as Cable won the hammer throw against the University of Pennsylvania. However, the University of Pennsylvania won the meet, 24 to 21½ points.

The Jacksons, Poages, Marshalls, Taylors, and Cables may have had their counterparts in the Negro colleges, the few that infrequently scheduled meets or participated in the scholastic meets, but until they entered white schools, they generally remained in the shadows.

In 1910, Henry Binga Dismond was a member of the Smart Set Track Team in New York. In 1911, he was a member of the track squad at Howard Academy. And in 1913 he was setting records at the University of Chicago, his 47.2 seconds for the quarter mile being one of them.

Alexander Louis Jackson (third from right, third row), is shown on the Harvard University 1913 track and field squad.

But AAU track and field officials seldom bothered to attend Negro meets, and any record made was not recognized. It may be said that in the white colleges the athletes were running for records, but that at the Negro colleges the athletes were running for the spirit of competition. But the black stars rolled on.

R. F. Morse, of the Salem Athletic Club in New York, ran a 21⅕-second, 220-yard dash in 1915. There were the likes of Irving T. Howe of Boston, Howard P. Drew of Springfield, Howard Martin of Cincinnati, Jim Ravenelle of New York, W. R. Granger of Dartmouth, Benjamin Johnson of Springfield, W. C. Holmes of Chicago, and Edward Solomon Butler of Dubuque.

Sol Butler was one of the greatest athletes of the early days. His skills and feats could not be contained in track events. Butler was born in Wichita, Kansas, in 1895. He attended Hutchinson High School, and when his coach was transferred to Rock Island High School, the prized star went with him.

In one day at Rock Island, Butler won the 100-yard dash, 220-yard hurdles, 440-yard run, the running high jump, and the running broad jump; five first-place victories. His performance prompted the Illinois State Interscholastic body to rule that no prep school athlete

Jackson, third from left in the second row, on the 1914 Harvard track and field squad.

Roy Morse, winning a 100-yard dash race in 1915. Left to right: Morse, A. B. Kelly, R. J. White, and A. T. Meyer.

could compete in more than two events and the relay in any one meet.

Sol Butler told how he came to enroll at Dubuque when everyone thought that he was headed for the University of Illinois. The story was told by Butler to a classmate, Henry J. Reemtsma, Doctor of Divinity in New Mexico.

Sol and his brother, Benjamin, were then living in Rock Island, and attending high school there. The Reverend Benjamin Lindamen was the pastor of the First Presbyterian Church in Bettendorf, Iowa, across the river from Rock Island. Reverend Lindamen was a graduate of Dubuque's college and theological seminary and was always on the lookout for recruits, particularly those who could run a hundred yards in ten seconds and do the things on a football field that he had seen Sol Butler do.

Butler was shining shoes when Reverend Lindamen approached him about going to Dubuque, and not one, but two Butlers turned up

there. However, Benjamin did not compete in varsity competition at
Dubuque. He was satisfied to act as the team's trainer, but he was a
member of several campus clubs, including the Philophronia Literary
Society. Sol was also a member of the PLS, and the baseball, basketball, football, and track and field teams, as well as the "D" Club, and
the Glee Club.

Sol Butler began his collegiate varsity career in 1915. On September 9 he and fourteen others reported for football practice. Two weeks
later, nearly thirty candidates were engaging in the 4 P.M.–6 P.M.
drills. The team was led by its freshman quarterback, Sol Butler, and
he more than justified Reverend Lindamen's confidence in his athletic
ability. Gifted with amazing running ability, Butler (and Dubuque)
had a highly successful season in 1915. Up to the Thanksgiving Day
game, the record follows:

The Dubuque Germans, 25—Iowa State Teachers College, 7
The Dubuque Germans, 28—Ellsworth College, 0
The Dubuque Germans, 23—Campian College, 0
The Dubuque Germans, 27—LaCrosse Normal, 0
The Dubuque Germans, 13—Upper Iowa University, 6
The Dubuque Germans, 63—St. Ambrose, 0

On Thanksgiving Day, November 26, 1915, the Dubuque German
College and Theological Seminary[2] defeated Dubuque College (St.
Joseph's),[3] 13–7.

Before the largest crowd ever assembled to see an athletic contest
in Dubuque—seven thousand fans—Coach John Chalmer's Dubuque
Germans capped a tremendous season. Coach Charles Dorais's
Dubuque Collegians finished their season with a 7–1, won-lost record,
so the Dubuque Germans won the Hawkeye Championship in 1915.

[2] Organized in 1852 and incorporated in 1871 as The German Theological School
of the Northwest. In 1891 it was renamed The German Presbyterian Theological
School of the Northwest, and since 1911, The Dubuque German College and Seminary.
[3] A Catholic College named St. Joseph's chose to call its athletic teams the Dubuque
Collegians, or simply, Dubuque College, stating that it "did not look right" for the
name St. Joseph to be attached to an athletic team.

The lineups follow:

THE DUBUQUE GERMANS (13)		THE DUBUQUE COLLEGIANS (7)
Cornelius Hooks	C	McCaffrey
Francis Baker	RG	Prospichal
Elmer Baker	LG	Weher
John Deberg	RT	Kipp
Evert Dirks	LT	Flahetry
Amos Niebruegge	RE	Sweeney
Ralph Knapp	LE	Matthews
Sol Butler	QB	Gleason
Stephen Bessemer	RH	Poelier
Clarence Parker	LH	Ryan
Sherman Arends	FB	Balton

Butler was described by the *Des Moines Register* on December 3 as "the fastest man who ever set foot on Hawkeye soil." He and teammate Clarence Parker were selected to the all-state team.

Two months later Butler was performing on the hardwood in a Dubuque win. The *Des Moines Register* of February 13, 1916, reported:

DUBUQUE GERMANS WIN

BEAT IOWA STATE TEACHERS; 25–24

The lineups follow:

THE DUBUQUE GERMANS (25)				IOWA STATE TEACHERS COLLEGE (24)			
	FG	FT	TP		FG	FT	TP
Bessemer, C	2	0	4	A. Dickerson, C	2	0	4
Baker, RF	5	0	10	Cotton, RF	2	4	8
Abrams, LF	3	5	11	Brown, LF	3	0	6
Deberg, RG	0	0	0	Schmidt, RG	3	0	6
Butler, RG	0	0	0	Whitford, LG	0	0	0
Keebs, LG	0	0	0	Bryson, C	0	0	0
				Wright, RF	0	0	0
				R. Dickerson, RG	0	0	0

On April 8, 1916, the busy Butler went to Evanston, Illinois, and set a record in the 50-yard dash in the qualifying heat of 5⅖ seconds, but he lost in the finals to Joe Loomis.

Next, the four man track and field team was off to Philadelphia for participation in the Penn Relays. Butler finished first in his heat of the 100-yard dash in 10⅕ seconds. He also ran a 10½-second semifinal victory. But in the finals he failed to place, finishing fourth. He also finished fourth in the running broad jump.

The Dubuque Germans again had a winning football season in 1916 with a 5–1, won-lost record.

Sol Butler again led the team at quarterback. In the victory against Wisconsin Teachers College, he had a seventy-yard run from scrimmage for a touchdown, and touchdown runs of thirty-five, sixty-five, and ninety-five yards against Upper Iowa University. One player said in astonishment that he had him in his grasp and could see the "whites of his eyes," but Butler ran right out of his arms. Against Buena Vista, Butler ran a kickoff back one hundred yards for a touchdown.

The Dubuque Germans complete 1916 record follows:

The Dubuque Germans, 54—Ellsworth College, 0
The Dubuque Germans, 3—La Crosse Normal, 12
The Dubuque Germans, 35—Wisconsin Teachers College, 0
The Dubuque Germans, 38—Upper Iowa University, 13
The Dubuque Germans, 14—Buena Vista, 0
The Dubuque Germans, 30—Iowa State Teachers College, 2

On January 27, 1917, Sol Butler and Binga Dismond from the University of Chicago scored victories in the fifty-yard dash and the 440-yard run respectively, and a month later, on February 17, Butler was on the hardwood. The *Des Moines Register*'s headline tells the story:

DUBUQUE TEAM COMES FROM BEHIND AND WINS 27–19—THE CLOSE
GUARDING OF PARKER AND BUTLER FEATURES THE GAME

The sport of basketball was twenty-two years old in 1914, when

Dubuque fielded its first varsity team.

On April 9, 1918, the Dubuque Germans opened their baseball season against St. Ambrose College. The *Des Moines Register*'s reporter eyed the Dubuque German's first baseman: "Sol Butler, the German College's Negro star, will be the hope of the Dubuque school when the two teams wearing the blue and white mix."

Butler and his mates went down to defeat, 10–8. Baseball was a pleasant diversion, rather than a major interest at Dubuque. In two games, Butler batted .400 in the cleanup position. He had twelve put-outs without an error.

On April 20 Butler competed in the Ninth Annual Drake Relays at Des Moines. He finished fourth in the 100-yard dash, behind Scholz of Missouri, Johnson of Michigan, and Carroll of Illinois.

It was an impressive field that lined up for the 100-yard dash,

Howard Porter Drew equalling the world's 220-yard dash record of 21⅕ seconds in 1914.

including Howard Drew, a Negro sprinter, then attending Drake University Law School. He was the world's coholder of the 100-yard dash record. The others in the dash were Haddock of Kansas, Zoellin of Michigan, Sylvester of Missouri, and McMahon of Nebraska.

Snow had been shoveled off the track, but the 9⅘ seconds time was fast. Butler did not win, although perhaps he proved he was the world's fastest at 50 yards as reported: "Butler took the lead with the crack of the gun and maintained it for about fifty yards when Scholz pulled up ahead of him."

His college's only entry, Butler ran the anchor leg of the half-mile relay with Yankton College. Although finishing second, he gave the crowd a thrill according to one report:

Sol Butler's sprint in a futile endeavor to catch Hass of Grinnell in the final 220 yards of the half-mile college relay was the only feature of that event. Grinnell had attained too much of a lead, however, and the best the Negro athlete could do was to cut his rival's lead in two and finish second.

Drew had pulled up lame in the 100-yard dash. He was trying to get into shape for the 1920 Olympics. Looking ahead to the tryouts at Harvard Stadium on June 17, Drew tried desperately to earn that one last trip to the Olympics. He had decided to forego the 100-meter dash and concentrate only upon the 220-yard dash, which he now thought was his best event. In his prime he had been tagged the "world's fastest human," and the secret of his many triumphs was his startling acceleration. Once he had taken three strides, he was usually in full flight and running almost as fast as other sprinters would be at the halfway point.

But at the tryouts, a disappointed Drew finished behind Murchison, Woodring, and Kirksey. He took the defeat in stride, only saying that "the youngsters were too fast for me."

Howard Porter Drew had been running a long time, and was approaching thirty years of age.

Drew was born in Lexington, Virginia, on June 28, 1890. He attended Springfield, Massachusetts, High School, Springfield College, the University of California, Lincoln University, and Drake University.

In 1912 Drew was coholder of the 100-yard dash record with Gwin Henry. In 1913 he held the 220-yard dash record at 22⅘ seconds. In 1912 he equaled the American record of 9⅘ seconds in the 100-yard dash and the world's record of 7½ seconds for the 70-yard dash indoors. In 1914 Drew ran 90 yards in 9⅕ seconds and 120 yards in 11⅗ seconds, both new records.

In 1918 Frederick W. Rubien, secretary-treasurer of the AAU, made the selections for the All-American Athletic teams for that year. Howard Porter Drew was selected.

On May 4, 1918, Drew had won four firsts in a meet at Grinnell, Iowa. He won the 100-yard dash in 10⅕ seconds, the 220-yard dash, and the low and high hurdles. Earlier, on May 11, Drew ran a 10⅖-second 100-yard dash at Ames, Iowa, for first place, an 18⅘-second 120-yard hurdles for first place, and he won both the 220-yard hurdles and the 220-yard dash. He topped off perhaps the best one-man performance in track history by running the anchor leg of the half-mile Drake relay team, winning in 1 minute 36⅖ seconds. Other relay teammates were Quint, Merboth, and Ervin.

In a meet in Des Moines on May 18, Drew won the 100-yard dash in 10⅕ seconds, the 220-yard hurdles in 27 seconds, and the 220-yard dash in 23 seconds.

Howard Drew was eighteen years old in his first year in high school. He then left school before graduation and carried bags at the Springfield Railway Depot, his natural speed enabling him always to beat the other aspiring bag-toters in the race to prospective customers. Although out of school, he was a member of an amateur club and still running in track events.

On February 2, 1908, he made his first appearance in New York. As an unknown novice he was given a handicap, but when he won against seasoned veterans, his handicap was scratched.

In 1910, the twenty-year-old Howard P. Drew returned to high school. He promptly won the New England titles in the 100-yard dash in 10 seconds and the 220-yard dash in 21⅘ seconds. In Pittsburgh, he became the 1910 Junior National Champion. He repeated that feat in 1911.

He was now attracting national attention and was invited to try out for the upcoming 1912 Olympics.

When on June 8, 1912, he beat Ralph C. Craig in the 100-meter dash in 10⅘ seconds, Howard Porter Drew was assured of a place on the Olympic squad. After his unfortunate injury at the Olympics, Drew, then only twenty-two, started in earnest his preparations for the 1916 Olympics. On November 16, 1912, he set a new record at the Twenty-third Regiment Armory in Brooklyn, in the 100-meter dash. His time was 10⅕ seconds.

On Monday, August 25, 1913, Drew equaled the world's record in the 100-yard dash at Charter Oak Track at the Connecticut Fair. His time was 9⅗ seconds. Three stop-watches caught his time as 9⅗ seconds, and two stop-watches caught his time in 9⅖ seconds. In 1913 he entered the University of Southern California.

On Tuesday, February 2, 1916, at the Twenty-second Regiment Armory in New York, he and Ray Morse, a Negro sprinter, finished 1–2 in the 100-yard dash.

But the war dashed Drew's hopes. There were no 1916 Olympics.

In 1918 the war was foremost on everyone's mind, and it finally nudged the athlete from center stage.

A combination of manpower shortages, travel restrictions, bad weather, and sickness virtually wrecked the Dubuque Germans' 1918 football schedule. However, some colleges had canceled football altogether. And then on November 11, 1918, newspapers around the world dug out the boldest type that they had to declare:

"THE WAR IS OVER."

On April 4, 1919, Sol Butler competed in the Pentathlon at the Penn Relays in Philadelphia. This event consisted of the running broad jump; hammer, discus, and javelin throws; and the 1500-meter race. Butler broke the Pennsylvania Pentathlon broad jump record of 22 feet 2½ inches that was set by Worthing of Dartmouth in 1915. He jumped 22 feet 4½ inches. Sol Butler finished fourth in the overall point totals for the pentathlon.

On May 4, Butler won five starts in a dual meet of Dubuque-Coe. However, Coe won the meet, 84–52. But Butler's five firsts, two seconds, and one third, was good enough for thirty-two points, five points for a first, three points for second, and one point for third. His achievements follow:

100-yard dash, 10⅖ seconds. First place
120-yard hurdles, 17⅗ seconds. First place
Shot-put, 37 feet 11 inches. First place
220-yard hurdles, 27⅕ seconds
Broad jump, 20 feet 11 inches
High jump. Second place
Discus throw. Second place
Javelin throw. Third place.

On May 17 Butler won five events and set three Iowa Conference marks. He tied the conference record of 10 seconds for the 100-yard dash, that had been jointly held by Charles Hoyt, of Grinnell, and Wilson, of Coe College. He broke the broad jump record of 21 feet 4½ inches, that Lighter of Coe had set. Butler's new mark was 21 feet 6 inches. He won the 220-yard dash in 22⅗ seconds, the 220-yard low hurdles in 26⅖ seconds, and the shot put, with a throw of 38 feet 7⅜ inches.

Meanwhile, on the same date, a Saturday, Gourdin, at New Haven, won the broad jump with a leap of 20 feet 6⅛ inches. The next year, 1920, he would jump 22 feet 8¼ inches. In 1921 he would jump, on June 14, 24 feet 4 inches, and on July 23, 1921, he would leap 25 feet 3 inches.

But now it was still June 1919. Sol Butler was in France. He had been selected as a member of Uncle Sam's team to compete in the Inter-Allied meet in Paris, France. On June 28, Butler won the running broad jump, with a leap of 24 feet 9½ inches, and stepped upon the world stage. The young man from the small college in the Northwest smiled shyly as King Nicholas of Montenegro congratulated him and bestowed upon him a medal of the Fourth Class of the Order of Danillo. Three United States bands blared patriotic music as thirty

The 1919 Harvard University track and field squad. Edward Orval Gourdin, class of 1921, is in first row, fourth from left.

thousand people cheered. Butler wept unashamedly. The young lad who had been shining shoes in Rock Island in 1915 had traveled a long way.

After he had graduated, Butler left the following school marks for future generations of Dubuque athletes to break:

May 28, 1916	220-yard hurdles, 25⅗ seconds
August 28, 1916	Shot put, 38 feet 10 inches
April 28, 1917	Running broad jump, 23 feet 5 inches
May 5, 1917	Discus throw, 104 feet
June 9, 1917	100-yard dash, 10 seconds
June 9, 1917	200-yard dash, 22 seconds

A year later, Sol Butler was in Antwerp, Belgium, as a member of the United States Olympic squad.

In 1920 Butler went into YMCA work, directed the Washington Park in Chicago, and also kept in shape by playing baseball, tennis, football, and basketball.

In 1921 Butler played with an amateur football team out of Chicago called the Lincoln Athletic Club. It was under the management of William Bottoms, who owned a nightclub, called "Dream Land," in the Windy City. The team was coached by Fritz Pollard. The *Chicago Defender* of December 3, 1921, headlined:

BUTLER AND BLUEITT STAR AS LINCOLN
A. C. WINS, 29–0

Butler's team, all black, had beaten the all-white team, the Portage Athletic Club. Butler had an eighty-yard run for a touchdown in the first quarter; and he later "scooped-up" a fumble and ran fifty-five yards for another score.

In 1920 Brown University, in Providence, Rhode Island, had an outstanding track season. One of its luminaries, Jaye Mayo "Inky" Williams, would in several years become a teammate of Butler's. Another outstanding Negro track athlete on that 1920 Brown team was Joseph E. S. Carter. Both Williams and Carter were sprinters.

In 1922 Butler joined the *Chicago Defender*'s basketball team. The headquarters of the *Defender*, of course, was in Chicago, but this team was the eastern branch, playing out of New York.

The charge of professionalism loomed against Butler. He was accused of playing a basketball game in Pittsburgh in 1921 and getting paid. Butler pleaded ignorance to any wrongdoings. He also main-

Sol Butler, in "tryout" sprint race, prior to the Inter-Allied championships at Paris, France in 1919. Left to right: Charles Paddock, University of Southern California; E. A. Teschner, Harvard University; Butler, Dubuque University; E. A. Torkelson, Phillips Exeter Academy; and H. B. Lever, University of Pennsylvania.

tained that he had served a sixty-day suspension for this alleged infraction.

The Lincoln A.C. and the *Chicago Defender* teams were supposed to be amateur clubs, but they had been known to schedule games against semipro and pro teams. Meanwhile, Butler was still competing in track, with an eye toward the 1924 Olympics.

On June 24, 1922, Butler had won the broad jump at Bridgeport, Connecticut. He jumped 23 feet 2½ inches. Even earlier, he had won a meet on June 3, as he jumped 23 feet 3 inches.

Finally, Butler walked into AAU headquarters, at 290 Broadway, in New York City, and handed in his AAU card to Frederick W. Rubien, president of the Metropolitan Association. An outstanding amateur track career ended with one hundred and eighty-six medals, twenty-five cups, eight gold shields, and four watches. It was noted that: "Sol at present is in business with his brother, Benjamin, and represents several auto concerns in the City."

In 1923 Sol Butler was playing professional basketball in Xenia, Ohio, for the John Roan Post American Legion team. The New York *Amsterdam News*, on February 21, picked up the action:

CUM POSEY'S LOENDI TEAM DEFEATED IN THRILLING BATTLE
POSEY ALLOWED ONLY ONE FIELD GOAL DURING THE ENTIRE GAME, BE-
ING LOCKED UP TIGHT BY THE WELL KNOWN SOL BUTLER

The Loendi Big Five was thought to have one of the best teams in the country, and Posey was regarded by sportswriters as the "best colored" basketball player in the nation. But now, thirty-two years old, Posey may have lost a step or two in foot speed against the twenty-eight-year-old Butler.

It was still 1923. April. The Penn Relays. Charles West would win the pentathlon for Washington and Jefferson. He would repeat this victory in 1924. The *Chicago Defender* of November 23, 1923, reported:

SOL BUTLER SOLD TO HAMMOND PRO FOOTBALL
TEAM FOR $10,000

Shortly after turning in his AAU card, Butler had signed with the Rock Island Independents football team. Another black player, Fred "Duke" Slater, was also a member of the Rock Island team. Later, the *Chicago Defender*'s reporter learned that Butler had been sold to the Hammond Pros for the balance of the season for $10,000.

In 1924, Butler also played with the Hammond Pros. In 1925 he was with an independent professional football team, the Toronto (Ohio) Tigers. He again returned to the Hammond Pros in 1926, and among his teammates was a Brown alumnus, J. M. Williams, at end.

When J. M. Williams was at Brown, John Shelburne was in the Eastern College Athletic Conference, at Dartmouth, in 1920. In June, at the Dartmouth-Columbia dual meet, he was a standout. He was about to put the shot, after winning the hurdles, when the starter called him to the 220-yard dash. He won the 220-yard dash, and then calmly came back and tossed the ball 43 feet 11½ inches for his third win of the meet. His coach, Harry Hillman, told him then that he had done his day's work.

John Shelburne would precede Butler into the pro ranks at Hammond, Indiana, in 1922.

On Sunday, December 27, 1931, Sol Butler was in Los Angeles. The *Chicago Defender* of January 2, 1932, reported:

SOL BUTLER SPRINTS 20 YARDS TO SCORE

Butler was a member of the Fritz Pollard Stars, which also included Fred "Duke" Slater and Joe Lillard. A semipro team, the Stars beat the Duffield Coast Stars, 20–6, before eight thousand fans. Butler's score was on a pass reception from Williams. And Lillard thrilled the crowd with a forty-five-yard touchdown run.

Always intrigued with "show business," Sol Butler lingered in the movie town. The *Chicago Defender* of January 30, 1932, probably revealed why:

SOL BUTLER SPRINTS 20 YARDS TO SCORE

Supposedly, Butler was "being considered for a part in a film to be

Left: The multi-talented Frederick Douglas "Fritz" Pollard in track attire. A 1916 member of Brown University track team, he ran the 120 high hurdles in 16⅗ seconds, the 220 low hurdles in 26 seconds, and broad jumped 21 feet, 4 inches. Right: De Hart Hubbard as the camera records his winning broad jump of 24 ft. 5⅛ in. at the 1924 Paris Olympics.

made by one of Hollywood's largest companies. Earl Dancer, former manager of Ethel Waters, suggested the former Dubuque ace for the spot. Just now the movie colony is overrun with athletes, but few race actors are included, there being a shortage of suitable subjects."

Butler was tapped for parts in African jungle movies. He played in several Tarzan pictures before packing for Chicago.

Back in Chicago, Butler briefly wrote for the *Chicago Defender*. He then played on the paper's basketball team. About this time he also became enthusiastic over a young Golden Gloves boxing champion, Altus Allen, and was his manager, but Allen's talents proved to be something less than championship caliber.

Always reticent and unassuming, Butler never discussed his past feats unless questioned. When he became the manager of a nightclub in Chicago, no one knew about the medals and awards at his South Parkway residence.

He later managed Pappy's Lounge, and was on duty Wednesday night, December 1, 1954. According to the police report:

Mr. Solomon Butler was shot in Pappy's Lounge at 4700 S. Cottage Avenue while he was on duty as a bartender. Jimmy Hill, age 52, had come into the tavern and was molesting a female patron. Mr. Butler escorted Hill out of the tavern and Hill returned a short while later with a gun and shot Mr. Butler. The manager of the tavern shot Jimmy Hill. Both Hill and Butler were hospitalized, and on December 1, 1954, Solomon Butler expired; Jimmy Hill was charged with murder.

Edward Solomon Butler was taken back to Wichita, Kansas, the soil of his birth fifty-nine years earlier, accompanied by his sisters, Mrs. Anna R. Gardner and Miss Josephine Butler.

One star flickers, diminishes, and recedes. And another one glows. Life goes on. Sports go on. In June 1921 Edward Orval Gourdin graduated from Harvard College. He was born in Jacksonville, Florida, in 1898. In Stanton High School, in 1916, he won the 100-yard dash, 220-yard hurdles, broad jump, and was second in the pole vault.

The Gourdins moved to Cambridge, Massachusetts, and the young Gourdin prepared for Harvard at the Cambridge High and Latin School.

On Saturday, July 30, 1921, Gourdin attracted national attention when he jumped 25 feet 3 inches, thereby breaking Sol Butler's American mark of 24 feet 8 inches, and Peter O'Connor's leap of 24 feet 11¾ inches, that had been set in 1901.

On October 21, 1921, Gourdin won the pentathlon of the National Amateur Athletic Union. This meet was held under the auspices of the New York Athletic Club. Gourdin scored twelve points to defeat Joseph Erbol by a single point. He won first place in three events: the broad jump, 21 feet 9½ inches; the javelin throw, 129 feet 9¾ inches; the 200-meter dash, 23⅕ seconds.

Edward O. Gourdin, left, shown narrowly winning the 100-yard dash at the Oxford-Cambridge vs. Yale-Harvard meet in 1921.

It was in the 1920s that meets comparable to those that had been held in the white colleges started in the black colleges.

On May 14, 1921, the first big college meet by the Colored Intercollegiate Athletic Association was held at Howard University. Howard won the meet that was held before three thousand enthusiastic spectators. And despite a heavy track that was rain-soaked, some adequate times were run. The summaries follow:

100-yard dash, Branch, Hampton, in 10⅕ seconds. Second place, Rozler, Howard. Third place, Trigg, Hampton.
440-yard run, won by Hallstolk of Lincoln, in 53 seconds. Second place, Robinson, Howard. Third place, Wynder, Lincoln.
220-yard low hurdles, won by Fannin, Howard, in 24 seconds. Second place, Young, Virginia Normal. Third place, Minyard, Howard.
880-yard run, won by Watley, Howard, in 2 minutes 6 seconds. Second place, Wynder, Lincoln. Third place, Hallstolk, Lincoln.
One-mile relay, won by Howard, in 3 minutes 36 seconds.
Running broad jump, won by Taylor, Howard, 20 feet 10 inches. Second place, Sayles, Howard. Third place, Green, Howard.
Pole vault, Johnson, Howard, 9 feet 3 inches. Second place, Redmond,

Lincoln. Third place, Daker, Virginia Normal.

12-pound shot put, won by Williams, Howard, 39 feet 7 inches. Second place, Law, Lincoln. Third place, Moore, Howard.

Javelin throw, won by Kent, Howard, 134 feet 7 inches. Second place, Williams, Howard. Third place, Law, Lincoln.

Running high jump, won by Redmond, Lincoln, 5 feet 6 inches. Second place, Luke, Howard. Third place, Sayles, Howard.

Discus throw, won by Law, Lincoln, 98 feet 4½ inches. Second place, Williams, Howard. Third place, Moore, Howard.

The black colleges, off to a slow start in track and field, were now running fast to catch up, and some said they were never behind but only needed a chance to compete. The outstanding black athletes from Negro colleges who wound up in white schools seemed to corroborate this.

The Negro track athlete in the black college was beset with problems that had nothing to do with his prowess. Meets were seldom attended by AAU officials, participation in white meets was limited, and Olympic selections were for the most part centered upon the large colleges and universities.

In 1935 the officers of the AAU, under whose auspices the Olympic trials were conducted, were told that Negroes could not compete in the annual meet that was scheduled for New Orleans. Had the officials

Gourdin, on the 1921 Harvard track and field squad. Third from right, second row.

yielded to these demands, the results of the 1936 Olympics would have been very different.

In the 1920s, the black track athletes who had national stature were found on the white, not the Negro, college campus, not because the white colleges attracted superior athletes, but because they offered more exposure. Meanwhile, the Negro had found forms of expression beyond sports.

In the middle and late twenties, in the East, black literary voices were being heard. *Opportunity*, a monthly magazine for Negroes—which regularly ran literary contests—speculated that a Negro renaissance was flowering in the arts.

Negro actors were appearing in such serious dramas as *The Emperor Jones*, and *All God's Chillun Got Wings.* A young former athlete named Paul Robeson played the lead in *The Emperor Jones.*

In fiction, in 1928, Claude McKay wrote *Home To Harlem*; Rudolph Fisher wrote *Walls of Jericho*, and Julia Peterkin published *Scarlet Sister Mary*. Nella Larsen scored with *Passing* and another book, *Quick Sand.*

In the salons and taverns of Harlem, Negroes were discussing Countee Cullen, a black poet and NYU undergraduate. His poems were appearing in black periodicals such as *Opportunity, The Crisis, The Competitor*, and also in the paper of a fiery young radical, A. Phillip Randolph's *The Messenger.* Cullen's verse was also beginning to appear in white periodicals.

There was talk around this period of the young promise of Langston Hughes, of E. Franklin Frazier, of Zora Neale Hurston, and her successful novel *Jonah's Gourd Vine.* Even Dr. Edward B. DuBois had turned his hand to fiction and created *Dark Princess.*

Roland Hayes, a Negro tenor, packed Carnegie Hall, singing with equal ease spirituals and French songs.

Along with an artistic renaissance in the twenties, there was a rededication to win an Olympic gold medal in an individual category. John Baxter had already been part of an Olympic relay team in 1908.

Prior to the 1924 Olympics, several Negroes had failed, but that year, De Hart Hubbard would start the resurgence.

Hubbard began his career in 1919 as a fifteen-year-old high school student. On the University of Cincinnati's track and field team, he won three events, the 100-yard dash; the broad jump; and the hop, step, and jump.

The next year, as a high school junior, Hubbard jumped 22 feet 6 inches in the broad jump. As a senior, he jumped 23 feet 1 inch, and as a University of Michigan freshman, he jumped 24 feet 6 inches. His steady advancement culminated with his jump of 24 feet 5½ inches, which won him an Olympic gold medal in the 1924 games. He had jumped 24 feet 7¾ inches in 1923, and in the running, hop, step, and jump, 47 feet ½ inch. He was still not satisfied. He had wanted to be the first to smash the world's broad-jump record, but instead he had to read about Gourdin's record-smashing victory. Even his Olympic win was not enough to console him. Although Hubbard finished ahead, the record still belonged to Gourdin.

On Saturday, June 13, 1925, at Chicago's Stagg Field, De Hart Hubbard would compete in his final race as a collegian. It was fitting that Sol Butler, then living in Chicago, was in the stands.

Hubbard had already won the 100-yard dash in 9.8 seconds, and wanted to set the world mark in his specialty, the running broad jump. He was down to his fourth and last try. Butler called him aside and told him to forget everything except that when he hit the takeoff board he should be sure to "get up into the air" as high as possible.

As Hubbard took his position before five thousand suddenly hushed and expectant fans, he seemed preoccupied, as if turning Butler's words over in his head. On his takeoff he knew immediately that he had it. He soared higher than he ever had before. The crowd's roar assured him that he had set a new mark. Hubbard had indeed achieved a new world's record in the running broad jump at 25 feet 10⅞ inches, breaking Edward Gourdin's mark of 25 feet 3 inches, set in 1924.

Strangely, this was not Hubbard's first world's record. He had set a world's mark in the running broad jump at a Negro meet. It was not recognized, however, because AAU officials had refused to attend.

One of the big eastern meets, the Penn Relays, held at Philadelphia's

Franklin Field, welcomed Negro colleges.

Lincoln University, of Oxford, Pennsylvania, won the one-mile relay in 1922, 1923, and 1924. In 1924, tiny Lincoln, with virtually no training facilities, won the one-mile relay in 3 minutes 38⅘ seconds, beating CCNY and Temple University. The members of Lincoln's team were R. S. Jason, R. K. Jones, F. M. Gordon, and W. H. Strickland.

It was not only the Negro colleges in the South, but Negro colleges throughout the country had established track athletics by the 1920's. The *Chicago Defender* of May 31, 1924, reported:

WILBERFORCE WON ALL THE FIRST PLACES WHITE COLLEGES
TRAIL FORCE TRACK MEN

Wilberforce was entered in the Fifth Annual YMCA Track and Field Meet at Zimmerman Field, Springfield, Ohio. The other competing schools were Antioch College and Wittenberg University.

On a cold, unseasonable, wet day, Wilberforce scored seventy-one points out of ninety. The results follow:

100-yard dash, won by Cornelius Thompson, Wilberforce, in 10⅖ seconds. Second place, Griffith, Wittenberg. Third place, John Clark, Wilberforce.
220-yard dash, won by Cornelius Thompson, Wilberforce, in 23⅘ seconds. Second place, Harry "Wu Fang" Ward, Wilberforce. Third place, Otis Freeman, Wilberforce.
880-yard run, won by Otis Freeman, Wilberforce, in 2 minutes 22⅗ seconds. Second place, Truman Safford, Antioch. Third place, Cornelius Thompson, Wilberforce.
One-mile run, won by Gaston Lewis, Wilberforce, in 5 minutes 21 seconds. Second place, Stuart Pool, Antioch. Third place, Robert Leader, Wittenberg.
Running broad jump, won by Gaston Lewis, Wilberforce, at 19 feet 9½ inches. Second place, Harry "Wu Fang" Ward, Wilberforce. Third place, Wilbur Griffith, Wittenberg.
Running high jump, won by Benjamin Hill, Wilberforce, at 5 feet 4 inches. Second place, Gladden Ronemus, Antioch. Third place, Carl Brown, Wilberforce.

Shot put, won by Harry "Wu Fang" Ward, Wilberforce, at 39 feet 6 inches. Second place, Gaston Lewis, Wilberforce. Third place, Morgan Evans, Wilberforce.

Pole vault, won by Charles Sedwick, Wilberforce, at 10 feet. Second place, Gladden Ronemus, Antioch.

Discus throw, won by Harry "Wu Fang" Ward, Wilberforce, at 87 feet 9 inches. Second place, Edward Lewis, Wilberforce. Third place, Morgan Evans, Wilberforce.

50-yard dash, won by Cornelius Thompson, Wilberforce, in 6⅖ seconds. Second place, Harry "Wu Fang" Ward, Wilberforce. Third place, Wilbur Griffith, Wittenberg.

In 1925 Hampton Institute won the coveted Abbott Trophy, but Lincoln University finished first in points with 49 to Hampton's 36½. Virginia Union College was second with 26; Virginia State College, third, with 5½; Fort Valley Industrial School, fourth, with 5 points; and Tuskegee Institute, fifth, with 4 points. The summaries follow:

100-yard dash, won by Booker, Virginia Union, in 10 seconds. Second place, Curry, Virginia State. Third place, Bost, Lincoln.

200-yard dash, won by Collins, Fort Valley Industrial Normal College, in 22⅘ seconds. Second place, Breaux, Virginia Union. Third place, Webb, Virginia Union.

440-yard dash, won by Baldwin, Hampton, in 51⅘ seconds. Second place, Derry, Lincoln. Third place, Benthorne, Hampton.

880-yard run, won by Silvera, Lincoln, in 2 minutes 4.3 seconds. Second place, Dyer, Lincoln. Third place, Curry, Virginia State.

One-mile run, won by Mitchell, Lincoln, in 4 minutes 39 seconds. Second place, Robinson, Virginia Union. Third place, Smith, Hampton.

Two-mile run, won by Mitchell, Lincoln, in 10 minutes 22⅗ seconds. Second place, Robinson, Virginia Union. Third place, Bradley, Lincoln.

220-yard low hurdles, won by Whitehurst, Hampton, in 27.9 seconds. Second place, Smith, Tuskegee. Third place, Baker, Lincoln.

120-yard high hurdles, won by Williams, Hampton, 17⅕ seconds. Second place, Coles, Hampton. Third place, Norris, Lincoln.

Shot put, won by Bryant, Lincoln, of 40 feet 7½ inches. Second place, Robinson, Hampton. Third place, Thompson, Virginia Union.

Discus throw, won by Bryant, Lincoln, of 120 feet 6 inches. Second place, Moore, Hampton. Third place, Tadlock, Tuskegee.

Javelin throw, won by Bryant, Lincoln, of 157 feet 6½ inches. Second place, Jeruay, Hampton. Third place, Tobin, Virginia Union.

Broad jump, won by Booker, Virginia Union, of 24 feet 1 inch. Second place, Ruff, Hampton. Third place, Johnson, Virginia State.

High jump, won by Sydnor, Lincoln, of 6 feet 1 inch. Second place, Young, Lincoln. Third place, Curry, Virginia State, and J. Williams, Hampton—tied for third.

Pole vault, won by Robbin, Hampton, of 10 feet. Tied with Boyd, Virginia Union. Second place, Lee, Lincoln.

In a track-and-field meet in May 1926, two hundred athletes from twenty different institutions converged at Hampton Institute's Armstrong Field.

Hampton won in the college division with eighty-seven points. Virginia Union finished with twenty-five points. Both St. Paul Normal College and West Virginia College scored twelve points.

Other Negro colleges were starting track-and-field meets. The *Chicago Defender* of May 7, 1927, reported:

TUSKEGEE WINS FIRST RELAY GAMES ALTHOUGH MOREHOUSE COPS
MILE AND HALF MILE TITLE

Before three thousand fans at their home grounds, Tuskegee rolled up thirty-eight points. The summaries follow:

100-yard dash, won by Collins, Fort Valley Industrial School, in 10⅖ seconds. Second place, Campbell, Fisk. Third place, Stevenson, Tuskegee.

Shot put, won by Tadlock, Tuskegee, of 35 feet 7½ inches. Second place, Stewart, Tuskegee. Third place, Harrison, New Orleans University.

Broad jump, won by Whitlow, Tuskegee, of 19 feet 7¾ inches. Second place, Blythewood, Claflin College. Third place, Harrison, New Orleans.

Discus throw, won by Tadlock, Tuskegee, of 112 feet 9¼ inches. Second place, Briston, Tuskegee. Third place, Simmons, Talladega College.

Javelin throw, won by Moore, Tuskegee, of 168 feet 9¼ inches. Second place, Stewart, Tuskegee. Third place, Fowkles, Atlanta University.

High jump, won by Roberts, Clark College, of 5 feet 5⅞ inches. Second place, Lambert, Morehouse College. Third place, Blythewood, Claflin College.

One-mile relay, won by the Morehouse College team: Archie, Lee, Anderson, and Alba. Time: 3 minutes 43.1 seconds. Second place, the Tuskegee team: Harris, Wilye, Cole, and Richardson. Third place, the Morris Brown team: Robinson, Nolan, Harrison, and Richardson.

Half-mile relay, won by the Morehouse College team: Christler, Archer, A. Stewart, and Garrison. Time: 1 minute 38 seconds. Second place, the Alabama State Normal College team: Burns, Jones, Conwoll, and Polle. Third place, the Atlanta University team: Ramsey, Ford, Blackburn, and Fowkles.

The *Chicago Defender*, on May 21, 1927, reported on the Colored Intercollegiate Athletic Association's meet held on May 14 at Hampton Institute.

HAMPTON WINS CIAA TRACK MEET

The point totals of five CIAA members (Howard University was not present):

Hampton Institute, 79 points
Virginia Union College, 29 points
Lincoln University, 13 points
St. Paul Normal College, 1 point
Shaw University, 1 point

The complete summaries follow:

100-yard dash, won by Breaux, Virginia Union, in 10 seconds. Second place, Booker, Virginia Union. Third place, Browne, Hampton.
One-mile run, won by Cole, Hampton, in 4 minutes 41½ seconds. Second place, Merritt, Hampton. Third place, Robinson, Virginia Union.
400-yard run[4], won by Baldwin, Hampton, in 51.7 seconds. Second place, Strickland, Lincoln. Third place, Grasty, Lincoln.
200-yard low hurdles, won by Harris, Hampton, in 26 seconds. Second place, Jackson, Virginia Union. Third place, Whitehurst, Hampton.
120-yard high hurdles, won by Baker[5], Hampton Institute, in 26.9 seconds. Second place, Walker, Hampton. Third place, Thatcher, Hampton.

[4] For this race, a *Chicago Defender* special trophy was awarded in honor of the newspaper editor and publisher, Robert S. Abbott, a graduate of Hampton Institute and the president of Hampton's alumni association.

[5] Williams, of Hampton, actually won, but was disqualified because he had knocked over too many hurdles.

220-yard dash, won by Breaux, Virginia Union, in 23.4 seconds. Second place, Bouker, Virginia Union. Third place, Scott, Lincoln.

880-yard run, won by Smith, Hampton, in 2 minutes 6.4 seconds. Second place, Derry, Lincoln. Third place, Travis, St. Paul College.

One-mile relay, won by the Hampton team: Snowden, Clark, Gray, and Baldwin. Time: 3 minutes 29 seconds. Second place, won by the Lincoln team: Stratton, Derry, Fletcher, and Strickland. Third place, won by the St. Paul team: Eastman, Harrison, Patterson, and Travis.

Shot put, won by Bryant, Lincoln, of 38 feet 11 inches. Second place, Moore, Hampton. Third place, Robinson, Hampton.

Pole vault, won by E. Baker, Hampton, of 10 feet. Second place, F. Baker, Hampton. Third place, Lee, Lincoln.

High jump, won by E. Baker, Hampton, of 5 feet 8 inches. Second place, Renfroe, Hampton. Third place, Goode, St. Paul Normal College.

Broad jump, Breaux, Virginia Union, of 20 feet 8¾ inches. Second place, Ruff, Hampton. Third place, Weatherford, Hampton.

Discus throw, won by Moore, Hampton, of 110 feet 3¼ inches. Second place, Jackson, Virginia Union. Third place, Hughes, Shaw.

Javelin throw, won by Williams, Hampton, of 138 feet 10½ inches. Second place, F. Baker, Hampton. Third place, Booker, Virginia Union.

Howard University had been conspicuously absent from the CIAA meet, because on the same day, Saturday, May 14, 1927, it was holding an "exhibition" meet. The university's track team had little trouble winning the meet despite a continuous drizzle. Among Howard's competition were the Washington YMCA, the Baltimore YMCA, the Baltimore Vocational School, and the Stampede Club of Washington, D.C.

Howard amassed ninety-one points in a meet that was kept from being a complete fiasco by the appearance of big-name Negro athletes from white colleges in the East: J. Ottley, V. Ottley, Charlie Majors, Augustus Moore from St. Bonaventure College, in New York, and Cecil Cooke from Syracuse University. Cooke was the National Amateur Athletic Union's 440-yard run champion. They all gave "exhibitions."

Track is international. Phil Edwards of British Guiana was elected captain of NYU's track team. He competed for Canada in the 1932 and 1936 Olympics as an American-educated British subject. Jack

London, also of British Guiana, competed for England in the 1928 Olympics, and Silvio P. Cator, a Haitian, was the first man to leap 26 feet in competition.

The Negro track and field athlete existed as a paradox. NYU track captain Phil Edwards ran on the relay team of Edwards, Walmsley, Viet, and David Myers.

Myers, also black, held a javelin meet record of 196 feet 3¾ inches. Black track athletes competed on mixed or all-black teams at the Penn Relays and at the Drake Relays in Des Moines, Iowa, and occasionally at invitational meets held in the South.

But Myers, who had set a record throwing the javelin at Franklin Field in April 1929, before forty-six thousand fans, was discriminated against on the football field.

NYU had left Joe Washington, a black member of its baseball team, at home when the squad played in the South in 1923.

J. L. Hart, a halfback-quarterback at Colgate in 1929, was not allowed to sit with his team when Colgate played Vanderbilt University, in Nashville. When University of Georgia officials advised NYU that they would not play against a Negro, NYU was not setting a precedent when it complied.

A perplexed Myers asked his coach, John F. "Chick" Meehan, where he should sit during the November 9, 1929, game. Meehan replied that he could "sit on the bench, or in the stands, or not come to the game at all if he did not want to."

Myers was the team's star player. He had earned the quarterback post from Vic Conner, Al Gandet, and O'Herin, who had each tried the position. Myers had also played a line position.

The *Chicago Defender* of November 16, 1929, reported:

MYERS 'LOST' DURING GAME WITH GEORGIA——FANS
CAN'T FIND STAR AS NYU WINS

NYU had won without the banished Myers 27–19. William O'Shields, another Negro player on the NYU team in the end position, was in uniform and much in evidence—on the bench.

Track athletes race against records—and the clock. Records are impersonal. And there is no physical contact. A Lincoln University one-mile-relay team that comes to the Penn Relays and wins in 3 minutes, 31⅗ seconds, has not really beaten Morgan College and Villanova, the second and third place finishers. It has beaten—or failed to beat—a meet record, an AAU record, an American record, or a world's record.

Almost from the beginning, black raced against white—or with white. For the Negro, the problems of track and field were generally of a different sort than those of team sports such as football. For example, Eugene Beatty of Michigan Normal College had won the 400-meter hurdles at the Penn Relays for three straight years. However, when he and Muncie Walton tried to enter the Paramount Hotel with their teammates, while competing in the Millrose Athletic Club Games, in New York, they were ordered to use the freight elevators and the back stairs.

The Negro colleges were participating in an increasing number of meets. On May 4, 1929, some two hundred twenty-five athletes from twenty-five schools gathered for the Third Annual Tuskegee Relays, at Tuskegee, Alabama. The turnout exceeded all expectations. Over four thousand spectators cheered the high school and college athletes as they went through their paces.

The summaries in the college division follow:

110-yard hurdles, won by Baker, Clark College, in 17⅕ seconds. Second place, Randolph, Tuskegee. Third place, Parker, Tuggie Institute (high school).
Pole vault, won by Baker, Clark, of 9 feet 10 inches. Second place, Buggs, Morehouse College. Third place, Randolph and Gordon, of Tuskegee, tied.
Shot put, won by Champion, Tuskegee, of 38 feet 3½ inches. Second place, Coger, Alabama State Normal College. Third place, Simmons, Talladega College.
100-yard dash, won by Collins, Fort Valley Industrial Normal College, in 9⅘ seconds. Second place, McCarthy, Tuskegee. Third place, Lewis, Alabama State Normal.
Two-mile relay, won by the Tuskegee team: Dotson, C. Wylie, F. Wylie,

and Grant. Time: 8 minutes 38⅘ seconds. Second place, the Fort Valley Industrial Normal School team: Dantley, Hill, Scantling, and Moon.

220-yard dash, won by Smith, Tuskegee, in 27⅖ seconds. Second place, Randolph, Tuskegee. Third place, Woods, Tuggie Institute (high school).

Broad jump, won by Sam Houston College, of 23 feet 4 inches. Second place, Roberts, Clark. Third place, Moon, Atlanta University.

Discus throw, won by Britton, Tuskegee, of 106 feet 9 inches. Second place, Wingo, Howard Academy (high school). Third place, Huffman, Morehouse College.

220-yard dash, won by Collins, Fort Valley Industrial Normal College, in 22.3 seconds. Second place, Pearson, Talladega. Third place, Wilson, Claflin College.

Javelin throw, won by Moon, Atlanta University, of 162 feet 11 inches. Second place, Moore, Tuskegee. Third place, Alba, Tuskegee.

Four-mile relay, won by the Tuskegee team: C. Wylie, F. Wylie, Lawson, and Wilson, in 20 minutes 26 seconds. Second place, the Morehouse team: Brown, Mosley, Davis, and Crawford. Third place, the Fort Valley Industrial Normal College team: Dantley, Hill, Scantling, and Moon.

Half-mile relay, won by the Fort Valley Industrial Normal College team: Brown, Dillard, Bostic, and Collins. Time: 1 minute 35 seconds. Second place, won by the Tuskegee team: Harris, Stevenson, Rose, and McCarthy. Third place, won by the Atlanta University team: Fowlkes, Jones, Moon, and Blake.

Sprint medley relay, won by the Tuskegee team: Dotson, Johnson, Hill, and T. Harris. Time: 2 minutes 37.9 seconds. Second place, won by the Claflin College team: Arnett, Martin, Johnson, and Knight. Third place, won by the Morehouse College team: Christler, Smith, Jones, and Brown.

Quarter-mile relay, won by the Fort Valley Industrial Normal College team: Fuller, Bostic, Dillard, and Collins. Time: 46⅖ seconds. Second place, won by the Alabama State Normal College team: Lewis, Webb, Frazier, and Poole. Third place, won by the Tuskegee team: Randolph, Stevenson, Rose, and L. Smith.

One-mile relay, won by the Tuskegee team: Dotson, Grant, C. Wylie, and L. Smith, in 3 minutes 38⅗ seconds. Second place, won by the Talladega College team: Garrison, Hayes, A. Robinson, and Walden. Third place, won by the Atlanta University team: Reed, Moore, Barnes, and Martin.

Tuskegee Institute won the meet easily.

On May 18, 1929, eight new CIAA records were set at Hampton's Armstrong Field. The host college topped the totals with sixty-one points. The other totals follow:

Lincoln University, 38 points
Virginia State College, 15 points
Virginia Union College, 14 points
Morgan College, 8 points
West Virginia College, 2 points
Howard University, 1 point
St. Paul College, 1 point

The meet attracted nine colleges and eight high schools. The college summaries follow:

100-yard dash, won by Tull, Hampton, in 10 seconds. Second place, Breaux, Virginia Union. Third place, Baskerville, Lincoln.
220-yard dash, won by Breaux, Virginia Union, in 22⅖ seconds. Second place, Luke, Lincoln. Third place, Tull, Hampton.
440-yard run, won by Baldwin, Hampton, in 51.7 seconds. Second place, Sterling, Morgan College. Third place, Lloyd, Lincoln.
880-yard run, won by Smith, Hampton, in 2 minutes 4.9 seconds. Second place, Curry, Virginia State. Third place, Wood, Morgan.
One-mile run, won by Byrd, Lincoln, in 4 minutes 34.4 seconds. Second place, Bradley, Lincoln. Third place, Haskett, St. Paul College.
Two-mile run, won by Bradley, Lincoln, in 10 minutes 15.9 seconds. Second place, Mitchell, Lincoln. Third place, Coles, Virginia Union.
120-yard high hurdles, won by Coles, Hampton, in 16⅕ seconds. Second place, won by Walker, Hampton. Third place, Cotton, Morgan.
220-yard low hurdles, won by Harris, Hampton, in 26⅖ seconds. Second place, Longshore, Lincoln. Third place, Larry, Howard.
Javelin throw, won by Williams, Hampton, of 161 feet 11¾ inches. Second place, Hawkins, Hampton. Third place, Lee, Lincoln.
Discus throw, Clapp, Virginia State, won at 123 feet 8 inches. Second place, Moore, Hampton. Third place, Warren, Hampton.
Shot put, won by Clapp, Virginia State, at 39 feet 7⅛ inches. Second place, Davis, Cheney College. Third place, Perkins, Hampton.
Broad jump, won by Breaux, Virginia Union, at 21 feet 11 inches. Second place, Sydnor, Lincoln. Third place, Preston, Lincoln.

High jump, won by Williams, Hampton, at 5 feet 11⅝ inches. Tied for first place, Sydnor, Lincoln. Second place, Preston, Lincoln.
Medley relay, won by the Hampton team in 3 minutes 40.7 seconds. Second place, the Lincoln Team. Third place, the Morgan team.
One-mile relay, won by the Hampton team in 3 minutes 27.2 seconds. Second place, the Morgan team. Third place, the Lincoln team.

In February 1930, Eddie Tolan, Gus Moore, and Edward Gordon were named National AAU champions in their specialties.

In May of that year, Tolan was leading the University of Michigan to track wins. In June Gordon defeated Edward Hamm in the broad jump, and a youngster named Ralph Metcalfe was finishing his prep career in track.

Metcalfe was born in Atlanta, Georgia, on May 29, 1910. When the family moved to Chicago, he attended Tilden Tech. Later, at Marquette University, he was unanimously elected captain of the track and field team.

Standing 5 feet 11 inches, and 180 points, Metcalfe was a power runner with a bursting finish. In the 1930s his best times were:

Distance	Metcalfe's Time	World's Record
40 yards	4 3/10 seconds	4 2/5 seconds
60 yards	6 1/10 seconds	6 1/5 seconds
60 meters	6 7/10 seconds	7 1/5 seconds
70 yards	7 seconds	7 seconds
100 yards	9 2/5 seconds	9 2/5 seconds
100 meters	10 1/5 seconds	10 3/10 seconds
200 meters	20 3/10 seconds	20 3/5 seconds
220 yards	20 2/5 seconds	20 3/5 seconds

In 1931 Sol Butler was playing semipro football and basketball. De Hart Hubbard was a recreation park supervisor in Cincinnati, and he and Harry "Wu Fang" Ward were on the amateur basketball team, the Cincinnati Lion Tamers. Meanwhile, Wesley Long, a columnist on the *Chicago Defender*, was writing about "The Attitude of the Public Toward Radio."

Paul Robeson had completed a highly successful twelve-week

engagement in England, playing the lead role in *Othello*. The baritone began an American concert tour at New York's Carnegie Hall, on January 10, 1931.

Playwright Marc Connelly's *Green Pastures* was in its hundredth-week run on Broadway. The Pulitzer Prize winning play, starring Richard B. Harrison, depicted the despair and pathos of the Negro in the South. The play enjoyed an unusually long run. (It played so long that the children in the cast outgrew the cornstalks, behind which they were supposed to hide, and taller cornstalks had to be ordered.) But *Brown Buddies*, starring Bill "Bojangles" Robinson, folded after only a few months.

The Civil Service was advertising jobs for policemen at $2,000 to $3,000 a year, "age 21 to 29 years," and Clarence Darrow, the noted criminal lawyer, gave six lectures at the Howard University School of Law in January 1931.

Duke Ellington was playing at Harlem's Cotton Club. Jimmy Lunceford and his band, the Tennesseans, were playing an engagement at the Arcadia Ballroom.

And seventeen-year-old Jesse Owens was a Cleveland high school junior in September 1931.

Black track and field stars in competition with whites continued to run well.

Before six thousand fans, Gus Moore of the Brooklyn Harriers Athletic Club won the two-mile race in Boston on February 12, 1931, in 9 minutes 20⅘ seconds.

The Penn Relays was the mecca for America's greatest track and field talent. In 1931 invitations went out to 82 colleges, 51 preparatory schools, 197 high schools, 43 junior high schools, 58 grammar schools, and 9 parochial schools. And on Saturday, April 29, 1931, they converged on Franklin Field, Philadelphia.

The Negro colleges, although small, and in many instances, without adequate athletic facilities, made their presence felt.

Before twenty-five thousand fans, George D. Williams of Hampton Institute hurled the javelin 197 feet 1½ inches, a new Penn Relay meet record.

Lincoln University's one-mile-relay team—P. Lloyd, M. Moultrie, U. B. Duke, and J. Byrd—won their event in 3 minutes 37.1 seconds.

Everett Utterback of the University of Pittsburgh won the hop, step, and jump at 45 feet 4⅜ inches. Eugene Beatty of Michigan Normal College won the 440-meter hurdles in 54.7 seconds.

On May 10, 1931, a sixteen-year-old sophomore at Cleveland's East Tech High School established a broad jump record of 22 feet 2¾ inches. People were saying that if Jesse Owens did not "burn himself out" he was certain to be a star in the future. His times, even in Fairmount's Junior High School, were so phenomenal that his coach, Charles Riley, often thought his stop watch must be wrong. A boy that young just could not possibly run that fast.

The Negro college meets continued. The *Chicago Defender* of May 23, 1931, noted:

FOUR COLLEGE RECORDS FALL AT HAMPTON—GEORGE WILLIAMS
THROWS JAVELIN OVER 200 FEET

Williams had performed an astounding feat. In 1931 no more than ten American athletes had thrown the javelin in competition for more than two hundred feet. Hampton won the meet with thirty-two points, followed by:

Lincoln University, 28 points
St. Paul College, 22 points
Tuskegee Institute, 22 points
Virginia State College, 15 points
Morgan College, 15 points
West Virginia State College, 8 points

In May 1932, at Hampton Institute's Armstrong Field, St. Paul Normal College scored forty-four points to win the 11th Annual Intercollegiate Track and Field Meet. Hampton, the reigning CIAA champion, had thirty-six points. Howard University, twenty-three points.

Later in May, St. Paul Normal College, located in Lawrenceville, Virginia, won the CIAA track championship with forty-one points. The other college scores follow:

Morgan College, 35 points
Hampton Institute, 33 points
Howard University, 27 points

In the Midwest, also in May 1932, Wilberforce University amassed fifty-two points to win a meet before one thousand five hundred fans at Wilberforce, Ohio. Runners-up were West Virginia College, Alabama State Teachers College, and Kentucky State College.

In July 1932, James Johnson was one of twelve Negroes at the final tryouts for the Olympic team at Palo Alto, California. A controversy arose over the fairness of the selection committee. The *Chicago Defender* of July 30, 1932, reported:

JOHNSON OUT OF OLYMPICS: FANS PROTEST

Illinois State Normal fans are up in arms over the action of the Olympic committee in striking the name of Jimmy Johnson, star sprinter of State Normal, from the 400-meter relay list. . . . Johnson was entitled to run on the relay team by his showing at the recent try-outs on the Pacific Coast, but the committee displaced him and reversed their first decision by selecting Bob Kiesel and Hec Dyer.

The fifth and sixth place finishers in the 100- and 200-meter relays usually made up the 400-meter relay squad. Johnson had finished fifth in the 100-meter-dash finals. The winning U.S. 400-meter-dash relay team in the 1932 Olympics consisted of Robert Kiesel, Emmett Toppino, Hecter Dyer, and Frank Wykoff.

On May 4, 1933, in Cramton Bowl, in Montgomery, Alabama, Tuskegee Institute won thirteen first places, eight second places, and three third places, in a dual meet against Alabama State Teachers College. Tuskegee Institute finished with ninety-seven points, to Alabama State Teachers College's seventy-seven points.

Later in May, some four thousand spectators gathered to watch the Tuskegee Institute Relays, at Tuskegee, Alabama. There were three hundred fifty athletes from three hundred fifty colleges, universities, and high schools.

Tuskegee finished first in points, followed by Alabama State Teachers College.

In May 1933 Morgan College, handicapped by a lack of appropriate track and field facilities, nevertheless scored forty-one points to win the Twelfth Annual CIAA Track Meet, at Hampton's Armstrong Field.

The points garnered by the other colleges follow:

St. Paul Normal College, 40 points
Hampton Institute, 27 points
Lincoln University, 25 points
Virginia Union College, 14 points
Virginia State College, 3 points
Miners Teachers College, 1 point

On Saturday, April 28, 1934, Virginia State College defeated Hampton, 72–56. The summaries follow:

Discus throw, won by Jones, Virginia State College, at 115 feet ½ inch. Second place, Moore, Hampton. Third place, Jordan, Virginia State.
Shot put, won by Courtney, Virginia State, at 36 feet 4⅞ inches. Second place, Jeter, Virginia State. Third place, Weatherford, Hampton.
Pole vault, won by Courtney, Virginia State, at 10 feet 9 inches. Second place, Murphy, Hampton. Third place, Hooker, Hampton.
High jump, won by Borican, Courtney, and Brown of Virginia State. All tied at 5 feet 6 inches.
Broad jump, won by Courtney, Virginia State, at 22 feet ¼ inch. Second place, Weatherford, Hampton. Third place, Carroll, Virginia State.
Javelin throw, won by Courtney, Virginia State, at 138 feet 8 inches. Second place, Payne, Virginia State. Third place, Borican, Virginia State.
100-yard dash, won by Sullivan, Hampton, in 10.3 seconds. Second place, Coefield, Virginia State. Third place, Jeter, Virginia State.
120-yard high hurdles, won by Courtney, Virginia State, in 16.3 seconds. Second place, Johnson, Hampton. Third place, Madden, Virginia State.

Eddie Tolan shown winning the 200-meter dash in 21 seconds at the 1932 Olympics and becoming a double winner. Time: 21.2 seconds.

220-yard low hurdles, won by Payne, Virginia State, in 26.7 seconds. Second place, Johnson, Hampton. Third place, Thomas, Virginia State.

Opal C. Courtney had four first-place wins and a tie for a fifth first-place win, but he would not be eligible to participate in any more meets. Courtney had been on the track team at Kansas State Teachers College, in Pittsburgh, Kansas, in 1933. When he transferred to Virginia State College he was disqualified in line with section three of the CIAA Constitution:

No student who has participated in any branch of sport in one institution in the association shall be eligible for the same sport in another institution of the association until one year has elapsed since his participation in the first institution.

Eddie Tolan, one of the best hopes for the 1932 Olympics, graduated from the University of Michigan in 1930. Many feared he would "turn pro" before the games; however, the *Chicago Defender,* on January 16, 1932, eased these fears:

EDDIE TOLAN ENTERS WEST VIRGINIA INST.—WORLD'S SPRINT
CHAMPION WILL STAY AMATEUR—HOPES TO BE
READY FOR OLYMPIC TRIALS

Tolan, Metcalfe, and others left to participate in the Olympics, taking with them hopes of their fellow Negroes that the dreaded jinx against "their boys" would end.

Meanwhile, Henry Owens was beaming with parental pride over his son.

James Cleveland Owens was born in Dansville, Alabama, on September 12, 1913. In 1928 the family moved to Cleveland, Ohio. At Fairmount Junior High School, James Cleveland was shorted to "JC," which his southern drawl pronounced as "Jesse." A teacher misunderstood, and so James Cleveland Owens became Jesse Owens.

In the eighth grade at Fairmount, Jesse Owen's physical education teacher suggested he participate in track. When the youngster beat the other boys by some fifteen yards, the teacher looked at the stop watch in disbelief. The year was 1930, and Jesse Owens was seventeen.

In 1932, at Cleveland's East Tech High School, young Owens continued his assault upon scholastic records. When he graduated, twenty-eight colleges offered him scholarships. He chose Ohio State University, at Columbus, Ohio.

One of eight children of a day laborer, Owens' chances for a university education would have been extremely limited were it not for his amazing athletic talent. But even with scholarship help, he worked in a gasoline station during his freshman year at Ohio State. In the winter, he was a page boy in the State House of Representatives in Columbus.

On Saturday, May 25, 1935, Jesse Owens stepped upon the world stage. The setting: the Western Conference Outdoor Track and Field Meet, at Ann Arbor, Michigan.

In forty-five minutes, Owens put on the greatest one-man performance in the history of track athletics. He broke three world records and tied a fourth.

At 3:15 Owens tied the 100-yard dash world's record in 9⅖ seconds. At 3:25 he leaped 26 feet 8¼ inches to break the world's broad-jump record. At 3:34 he broke the world's record in the 220-yard dash in 20.3 seconds. At 4:00 P.M., Jesse Owens won the 220-yard low hurdles in 22⅗ seconds, establishing a new world's record in this event.

The *Cleveland Plain Dealer* gave Owens' feat front-page coverage:

JESSE OWENS BREAKS 3 WORLD MARKS

Owens' broad-jump record broke the 1931 mark of 25 feet 2⅛ inches by Japan's Chuhei Nambu. His 9.4 second 100-yard-dash mark tied the mark set by Frank Wykoff of USC. Jesse Owens' 220-yard dash mark had broken the 20.6 second mark set by Roland Locke of the University of Nebraska, and Owens' 220-yard low hurdles record had beaten the 23-second record of C. R. Brookins, of Iowa State University.

The news flashed around the world to London, Stockholm, Berlin, Rio de Janeiro. And there was much rejoicing by the Owens family at 2178 East 100th Street, Cleveland, Ohio.

Like Tolan, and others in 1932, Owens looked forward to the 1936 Olympics and his special role. The *Cleveland Plain Dealer* of July 16, 1936, reported:

GOODWILL AMBASSADOR

The United States may or may not distinguish itself at the Olympic games in Berlin this summer, but whatever happens the nation will be fittingly represented in more ways than one by the colored star, Jesse Owens. Not only is he expected to compete in three track events, but he has been named Ohio's Ambassador of Goodwill by the House of Representatives at Columbus, which body he served during the winter as a page.

On and off the track, Owens comported himself with maturity far beyond his years.

He was not only the State of Ohio's goodwill ambassador, but America's, and was the most talked-about black athlete since Jack Johnson, but without the controversy that always seemed to surround Johnson.

When Owens returned home, he forced the New York Giants, led by Mel Ott, and the New York Yankees, led by Lou Gehrig—who were to clash in the World Series—from center stage in the sports world.

Track athletes do not start at the college level but in grade schools. School yards reverberate with pounding feet and bold challenges. Unorganized school-yard sprints come first. Boy against boy. Boy against girl. Girl against girl.

Then comes organization. No more impromptu races, snatching off a cap and surging forward with all one's energy. It is now class against class.

The first Negro track and field meets were at the grade and high school levels; meets at black colleges were simply added attractions.

Track coaches, sociologists, physiologists, anthropologists, geneticists, sportswriters, and others have studied, debated, and written endless theories as to why black athletes have been so outstanding in sprint events, but not long-distance races.

Perhaps one simply had to look at the small-sized playgrounds of the past—at the Howard Academy, the M Street School, the Commercial High School, the Armstrong Manual Training High School, the Thaddeus Stevens High School, and the Baltimore Colored High School.

The black boy who had raced his chum in the school hallway, the schoolyard, and the sandlot, was now at the white university. There he had the best of coaching and facilities—and space to run.

The first Negro track and field athletes at the collegiate level were quarter-milers, and half-milers.

When the Negro college meets started, the racers' times were not too different from those of their white counterparts.

In the 1920s big meets, such as the Penn Relays, began. Tiny Lincoln, Howard, and Morgan raced against large Temple and NYU. The Negro track and field athlete stepped out of the shadows onto the pages of the metropolitan dailies. But still the august AAU did not beckon. No invitations to try out for the Olympics were tendered to the Negro colleges.

Jackie Robinson, on May 7, 1938, broad-jumped 25 ft. 6½ inches to break the standing record of 25 ft. 5½ inches set earlier by Matthew "Mack" Robinson, his brother. Robinson is shown in 1940 at UCLA, competing in the broad jump competition.

Poage, Taylor, Drew, and Butler carried the hopes and aspirations of an entire ethnic group. The burden metamorphosed into ailments, possibly psychosomatic, even before "psychosomatic" was a recognized medical term.

Then suddenly the Negro track athlete was at center stage.

A 5-foot 7-inch, 155-pound football star, Frederick Douglass "Fritz" Pollard, came running and landed on page one. Multitalented Paul Leroy Robeson joined Pollard.

They eased the way. For then De Hart Hubbard finally won the gold medal. Then they came. Running. The black auxiliaries. Tolan! Metcalfe! Gordon! And, finally, the incomparable James "Jesse" Cleveland Owens. Owens went to Berlin in 1936 as a national track and field star. And returned as an international hero.

We were not there. But we all saw him:

> Lithe, light-footed and straight-up stance.
> He ran, he jumped, as beautiful as the dance.
> We saw in him our own backyard.
> Two boys lined-up by a tree to start.
> "Come on man les race."
> Track and Field, speed and grace.

8

Black Olympians

According to Greek mythology, the first Olympics in the ninth century B.C. were started by an eccentric king of Elis, named Oenomaus. Oenomaus had a beautiful daughter, Hippodamia, who was the most sought-after young lady in Greece. But King Oenomaus would only offer his daughter's hand in marriage to the suitor who could kidnap her in his (the suitor's) chariot, eluding Oenomaus, who had the lightest chariot and the fastest horses in the land. As time went by, thirteen prospective suitors tried to kidnap Hippodamia. All were caught by Oenomaus and subsequently decapitated with one swift stroke of his sword.

Finally Pelops, a brave and highly intelligent young man, bribed the king's charioteer to weaken the axle on the royal vehicle. Then Pelops abducted Hippodamia, and the king chased the couple as usual. But just as he approached them and raised his sword to smite the fatal blow to the young suitor, the royal chariot crashed and collapsed, killing the king. The couple chose a green valley near the Alpheus River for their wedding celebration, at which they also staged religious festivals and athletic contests.

The valley was called Olympia, and the festival became the Olympic games. Other myths, legends, and fables have been woven by poets and historians about the origins of the oldest of all athletic competitions. But one fact is certain, the first recorded Olympic games were in 776 B.C. And thereafter the Greeks began to reckon time by Olympiads—the four year intervals at which the games were held.

341

History and legend merged. Archeologists have found evidence in the ruins of Olympia that many great buildings within the enclosure for games and religious celebrations were constructed as early as 1200 B.C.

The games were conducted on a high moral and religious level. But over a thousand years they deteriorated because of professionalism, scandals, discord, and political intrigue. The games became a battle-field instead of wholesome, peaceful, amateur athletic contests. The games were still the exclusive property of the Greeks until after 146 B.C., at which time Greece was conquered by the Romans. In A.D. 394, the games were suspended by the Roman emperor Theo-dosius I. Thirty years later, the Temple of Olympia was destroyed and lay buried for fifteen centuries.

Baron Pierre de Coubertin, a French diplomat, was primarily responsible for the revival of the Olympics in 1896. He was obsessed with the idea of the ancient games after visiting the ruins, which were being uncovered by a group of German archeologists. Coubertin then started campaigning for a revival of the Olympics in earnest. He called an international sports congress in Paris in 1894. He then presented his Olympic plan. The delegates voted unanimously to hold the first "modern" Olympiad in Athens in 1896.

The 1896 Olympics involved eleven European countries and the United States. The American team consisted of thirteen athletes, ten in track and field, one in the swimming competition, and two revolver marksmen.

The first Negro American to compete in Olympic competition was George Poage, in the 1904 games, which were held in St. Louis, Missouri, where they played second fiddle to the World's Fair held in that city the same year.

The American Selection Committee had decided on Chicago as the locale for the 1904 games, but at the last minute, the organizing committee for the St. Louis World's Fair exerted pressure to have the games moved. Because of these late preparations, only nine overseas countries were represented, and even for the most exciting events, there were less than two thousand spectators. Of the twenty-six athletic competitions in track and field, only three were won by non-Americans.

The games opened on Monday, August 29, and closed on Saturday, September 3. President Theodore Roosevelt was the honorary chairman of the Fair, and David R. Francis was the president of the Olympic games.

On August 30 the 400-meter hurdles were run. This event consisted of ten hurdles, 2 feet 6 inches high. Harry Hillman of the New York Athletic Club finished first in 53 seconds. F. Waller of the Milwaukee Athletic Club was second, and George Poage, also representing the Milwaukee Athletic Club, finished third.

Harry Hillman made a sweep by also winning the 200-meter hurdles in 24⅗ seconds. F. Castleman finished second, and George Coleman Poage again finished third.

The 1908 Olympics were held in London, England. There were eighty-five Americans among the two thousand athletes. John Taylor, a graduate of the college and school of veterinary medicine at the University of Pennsylvania, was the second American Negro to compete in the Olympic games.

Dr. Taylor was a member of the Irish-American Athletic Club. The club subsequently dropped the "Irish" when other Negroes joined and it was obvious that members other than Irish belonged.

The Olympics opened on Monday, July 13, 1908, with His Majesty King Edward VII arriving in a four-horse landau, driven by scarlet-coated postillions and accompanied by outriders. Queen Alexandra was by his side as he officially gave the signal for the games to begin at 3:30 P.M.

Taylor was scheduled to run in heat four on Tuesday. He won by twelve yards in the 400-meter run over Italy's R. Penna. His time was 50⅘ seconds. The Olympic record was 49⅕ seconds.

The next day, Wednesday, July 15, J. B. Taylor was in heat three, the semifinal trial. He won by five yards in this heat, with a time of 49⅘ seconds, to advance to the finals with two teammates, J. C. Carpenter of Cornell and W. C. Robbins of Harvard. The fourth to qualify was Wyndham Hallswelle of Great Britain.

The race produced a controversy that has existed to this day. The Americans accused the British, and the Englishmen accused their U.S. visitors, of unsportsmanlike conduct.

The London *Times* of Friday, July 24, 1908, reported:

A SENSATIONAL FINISH

J. C. Carpenter and W. C. Robbins, the two white Americans, were off at once with the lead in front of the Englishman, with the Negro runner from the States lying last. Round the far end of the track Hallswelle was fast catching the two leaders who were on the inside of the track . . . soon after Hallswelle turned the bend he was forced very nearly on to the bicycle track. . . . The interference with Hallswelle appeared to them (judges) so palpable that they broke the tape while the race was still in progress before the runners reached the winning post. . . . It was not as if Carpenter, the one who forced Hallswelle to run wide, and elbowed him severely as he tried to pass him, had himself taken a wide curve at the bend and the run straight on. He appeared rather to run diagonally, crossing in front of the Englishman so that he was obliged to lose several yards, and finally could only run on the extreme outside edge of the track. . . .

After a long consultation, the judges declared the race void. And it was announced that it would have to be run again on Saturday, July 25, at twelve o'clock. The judges disqualified Carpenter and announced that Robbins would run in a lane with strings. The London *Times* asserted that the judges had consulted "medical men" about the race and they had examined Hallswelle and found his "chest sore and bruised where he had been elbowed."

The London *Times* reporter was convinced that, with J. C. Carpenter on the inside, Hallswelle next, then W. C. Robbins, the two Americans were out to box in the Englishman. Taylor was on the outside, but the reporter speculated that he was blameless:

No one who saw what happened could come to any other conclusion than that it was deliberate and prearranged, though Taylor had apparently elected to keep out of it. . . .

The Americans were incensed. Michael C. Murphy, trainer and coach of the team, saw no reason for Carpenter's disqualification and would not allow another race to be run by Taylor and Robbins: "I don't care for the new date of this race. We are not taking part anyway. We consider Carpenter to be the Olympic champion, and for us the 400 meters flat is a closed story!"

Carpenter had run a fantastic 47.5-second 400 meters. This would not be bettered in Olympic competition until 1932. But it was Hallswelle's name that went into the record book.

Sándor Barcs, in his book *The Modern Olympics Story,* corroborated the *London Times* story:

The start was successful, and Carpenter immediately took the lead, with Robbins and Hallswelle close behind. Taylor started poorly and was out of the race all along. Then Hallswelle began the final spurt. Carpenter followed and wanted to pass Robbins and Hallswelle. According to objective onlookers, Carpenter in the height of the struggle, fouled Hallswelle. Those spectators who saw the incident from close range began to shout. "Foul! Foul!"

Perhaps as much a mystery as the race itself was Taylor's performance. He was the odds-on favorite to win and had run well in the heats.

The American 1600-meter relay team consisted of W. F. Hamilton, N. G. Cartmell, J. B. Taylor, and M. W. Shipp. The first two athletes in the 1600-meter relays each run 200 meters, the third athlete runs 400 meters, and the anchor man runs 800 meters.

Taylor, running 400 meters on the third leg, led by thirty meters when he passed the baton to Shipp, who won by twelve meters. The time was 3 minutes 29.4 seconds. Germany's relay team finished second.

The 1908 Olympics came to an end on Saturday, July 25. The first five winners' point totals were:

United States	115 points
United Kingdom	86⅓ points

Jim Thorpe as he easily wins the 1500-meter run in Stockholm, Sweden in 1912.

Sweden	11 points
Norway	9 points
Greece	8 points

The eighty-five members of America's track and field team, including its single Negro American, could well feel proud.

On Friday, June 14, 1912, the SS *Finland* of the Red Star line left the port of New York with 274 passengers on board—164 of them members of the American Olympic team. The destination was Stockholm, Sweden, for participation in the games there. Howard P. Drew, a Springfield, Massachusetts, High School athlete, was favored to win the 100-meter dash for the United States.

Drew entered the fifteenth heat and won in eleven seconds. In the first heat of the second round on Saturday, July 6, he again won in eleven seconds.

But Howard Drew did not start in the finals on Sunday, July 7. He had strained a sinew in one of his legs in the second-round win.

Ralph Craig of the U.S. was the eventual winner in the 100-meter dash in 10⅘ seconds. One of the officials lamenting Drew's misfortune was Michael C. Murphy, again the trainer of the American team. He said: "It was unfortunate that the little colored boy Drew broke down.

But for that unfortunate happening I believe he would have proven America's greatest sprinter since the days of Wefers. I say this without underestimating Craig's fine running."

Drew was courageous to the end. He had limped out to the field, trying to shake off the injury, but finally he had to be carried off.

The 1912 Olympics were also the scene of another poignant drama that was unfolding. James Thorpe was born on May 28, 1888, near Prague, in the Indian territory which is now Oklahoma. His twin brother, Charles, died at nine. Thorpe was a direct descendant of a Blackhawk chief of the Sac and Fox Indians. An Irishman named "Thorpe" married the granddaughter of the Blackhawk chief, so Jim Thorpe was part French, Sac and Fox, Potawatomie, and Irish.

At the 1912 Olympics Thorpe won the pentathlon and the decathlon. He won the pentathlon—which is based on the winning low score —with nine points. F. R. Bie of Norway was second with twenty-one points, and James Donahue of Los Angeles was third with twenty-nine points. Thorpe won the decathlon with a score of 8,412.96 points.

Jim Thorpe put on an amazing demonstration of speed, strength, agility, and stamina. Czar Nicholas of Russia presented him with the model of a silver Viking ship. King Gustavus V of Sweden proclaimed to the young Indian: "Sir, you are the world's greatest athlete." Thorpe's records were:

Decathlon	*Pentathlon*
100-meter dash. third place. 11 2/10 seconds	Broad jump. first place. 23 feet 2 7/10 inches
400-meter run. fourth place. 52 2/10 seconds	Javelin throw. third place. 153 feet 2 19/20 inches
1500-meter run. first place. 4 minutes 40 1/10 seconds	Discus throw. first place. 116 feet 8 4/10 inches
110-meter high hurdles. first place. 15 6/10 seconds	1500-meter run. first place. 4 minutes 44 8/10 seconds
High jump. first place. 6 feet 1 6/10 inches	200-meter dash. first place. 22 9/10 seconds
Shot put. first place. 42 feet 5 9/20 inches	
Discus throw. third place. 121 feet 3 9/10 inches	

Decathlon
Pole vault. third place.
10 feet 7 19/20 inches
Broad jump. third place.
22 feet 2 3/10 inches
Javelin throw. fourth place.
149 feet 11 2/10 inches

All Thorpe's records were expunged from the books; his victories were given to the runners-up. It was several years after all the pomp and tinsel of the Olympic pageantry that a sportswriter reported to the AAU that Jim Thorpe had played professional baseball in Rocky Mount, North Carolina, in the Carolina Association in 1910. Later that same season, Thorpe had been transferred to Fayetteville, North Carolina, in the Eastern Carolina Association.

The six foot, 185-pound Indian's records were awarded to runners-up H. Wieslander of Sweden (decathlon) and F. R. Bie of Norway (pentathlon).

Thorpe admitted his guilt in a letter he wrote to the Olympic committee. But he blamed his naiveté more than any conscious intent as the reason he never informed the committee that he had played baseball for money.

His medals were never returned.

Howard Porter Drew never participated in another Olympics, but continued to compete until he was well into his thirties. The First World War spoiled his chances in 1916. By 1920 his best years were behind him and he failed to qualify in the tryouts.

The eleven-thousand-ton U.S. Army transport, *Princess Matoika*, sailed from New York on July 26, 1920, for Antwerp and the Olympics.

One hundred twenty-four track and field members were on board including two Negro Americans. Benny Ponteau, a 135-pound Negro boxer, representing the St. Christophers Club of New York, was taken along as an alternate. On July 13 Benjamin Ponteau had advanced to the finals in the tryouts by defeating Sergeant Daniel J. Twomey in three rounds, but in the finals he lost to Frank Cassidy of the Ozanam Athletic Association of New York.

Howard Porter Drew finishing first in a sprint race in 1914.

R. Earl Johnson, representing the Morgan Club of Pittsburgh, finished second in the 10,000-meter run in the tryouts at Harvard Stadium on July 17. And five qualifiers were off for Antwerp in the 10,000-meter run: Fred Fallen, George Cornetta, Sherman Landers, R. L. Templeton, and R. Earl Johnson.

At the tryouts Sol Butler set a new American record of 24 feet 8 inches in the running broad jump on his fifth and last leap. The world's record of 24 feet 11¾ inches had been set by Patrick O'Connor of England in 1901. Butler's mark broke Myer Prinstein's 24 feet 7¼ inches American record set in Philadelphia on April 28, 1900. The two other running broad jump qualifiers were J. M. Merchant and H. Polltzer.

The ship landed in Antwerp on August 8. And on August 14, three thousand athletes representing twenty-seven nations passed in review before King Albert and Queen Elizabeth. The king gave a brief speech. Later, Cardinal Mercier pronounced the benediction, and seven cannon shots announced the beginning of the Seventh Olympiad.

Earl Johnson was running in third position when he was stricken with cramps. Only fifteen of thirty-nine runners in the 10,000 meters crossed the finish line. Butler pulled a leg muscle in his first qualifying jump and was lost for the rest of the competition.

Sol Butler, like Howard Porter Drew eight years before, tried mightily to force his injured body to perform, but he had to retire. He stood aside, a lonely and dejected figure, with tears drenching his face.

Butler was at the top of his form and was the odds-on favorite to bring Uncle Sam a victory in the running broad jump, and perhaps even break A. L. Gutterson's 24 foot 11½ inch 1912 Olympic broad jump record.

W. Pettersson of Sweden eventually won the 1920 Olympic running broad jump with a leap of 23 feet 5½ inches.

It was not quite a complete shutout for black athletes in the 1920 Olympics. Harry F. V. Edward, a black West Indian running for England, finished third in the 100-meter dash. The dash was won by H. M. Abrahams of England in 10⅗ seconds.

R. Earl Johnson returned home and continued to compete as he looked toward the 1924 Olympics.

On Sunday, July 6, 1924, the Eighth Olympiad opened in France in the Colombes Stadium located outside Paris.

Forty-five nations were competing in the twenty-six track and field events. The American track and field team had 110 members, including three Negroes.

On Tuesday, July 8, De Hart Hubbard and Edward O. Gourdin finished one-two in the running broad jump. Hubbard's winning leap was 24 feet 6 inches, and Edward Gourdin's second place leap was 23 feet 10⅞ inches. Hansen of Norway finished third.

R. Earl Johnson had again qualified for the 10,000-meter run. Now representing the Edgar Thompson Steel Works of Pittsburgh, he was the third American Negro in the 1924 Olympics.

Since Johnson's last Olympic appearance, he had won the AAU's 10-mile championship, and the 5-mile championship.

Other 10,000-meter finalists with Earl Johnson on the American team were Verne Booth, John Gray, and Wayne Johnson. The 10,000 meters was set for the first day of competition on Sunday. The track was heavy. It had rained all morning, and as the race began, the rain still pelted down. The *Boston Globe* of July 7 reported: "Earl Johnson, Pittsburgh, the Negro star, showed occasional bursts of speed. He passed Booth twice, but dropped back toward the finish."

Willie Ritola of Finland won in 30 minutes 23⅕ seconds. Wide of Sweden finished second. Booth was the closest American runner in twelfth place.

The games came to a close on July 27. Clarence Houser of the University of Southern California, and the shot put and discus champion, carried the Stars and Stripes as he led the American contingent out. The United States' point total was 255, with Finland, 166, Great Britain, 85½, Sweden, 31½, and France, 26½.

The 1928 Olympics were held in Amsterdam, Holland. One hundred and fifteen thousand fans showed up for the available forty thousand stadium seats. The eighty-six members of the American track and field team sailed from North River pier in New York on July 11, at 11 A.M. aboard the U.S. liner, *President Roosevelt*. Major General Douglas MacArthur had succeeded the late William C. Prout as head of the American Olympic committee.

Three American Negroes were members of the 1928 track and field team. De Hart Hubbard, the defending Olympic running-broad-jump champion, was now twenty-five, and a public recreation supervisor in Cincinnati. Edward Gordon, also competing in the running broad jump, was a freshman at the University of Iowa. John Lewis, a Detroit High School youngster, was entered in the 1600-meter relay.

On June 30, at the Midwest sectional Olympic tryouts in Detroit, Michigan, a nineteen-year-old University of Michigan freshman had achieved a surprise win in the 200-meter dash. Eddie Tolan, the national scholastic sprint champion for the past three years, won the event in 21.2 seconds. He defeated Fred Alderson of the Illinois Athletic Club.

At Cambridge, Massachusetts, the following week, Eddie Tolan finished first in the first heat of the 200-meter dash tryouts. But in the semifinals Tolan ran behind Tom Sharkey, Henry Cumming, Howard Jones, and Frederick Alderman. And in the 100-meter dash on July 6, in the second trials of the second heat, Tolan ran behind Claude Bracey, Rice Institute; Jackson Scholz, New York; Francis Hussey, New York; and Don Bonnett, Toledo.

Five athletes qualified for the broad jump: Edward Hamm, Georgia Tech; 25 feet 2⅜ inches. (Second) Alfred Bates, Penn State; 24 feet 2½ inches. (Third) De Hart Hubbard, Cincinnati, 23 feet 11½ inches. (Fourth) Edward Gordon, Iowa City, 23 feet 6⅜ inches. (Fifth) Charles Ansen, Ohio State.

Hubbard had been having ankle trouble, and said: "I hope my ankle doesn't prevent me from going to Amsterdam. But if it does I think that Ed Hamm will bring the Olympic championship to America."

Edward B. Hamm won the running broad jump at the 1928 Olympics with a leap of 25 feet 4¾ inches. Silvio P. Cator of Haiti was second with 24 feet 11½ inches. And Alfred H. Bates of the United States was third with a leap of 24 feet 4½ inches. Both Hubbard and Gordon failed to make the finals.

One Negro American athlete was shut out of the red brick stadium located in the southwestern outskirts of Amsterdam. John Lewis was listed as a member of the 1600-meter relay team, but was replaced by Ray Barbuti.

Two Negroes, running for Britain and Canada, had some success. Jack London, running for Britain, finished second in the 100-meter dash. Phil Edwards, who was educated at NYU and captained its track team, finished fourth in the 800-meter run for Canada.

The 1932 Olympics were held in Los Angeles. In July, twelve Negro track and field finalists, including two Negro female athletes, met at Palo Alto, California. They included James Johnson of Illinois State University at Normal; Louise Stokes of Malden, Massachusetts; Tydia Pickett, a seventeen-year-old Chicago athlete representing the Board of Education playgrounds; John Brooks of the University of Chicago; Eugene Beatty of Michigan State Normal College; Edward Gordon of the University of Iowa; Howard Spencer of Geneva College; Cornelius Johnson of the Los Angeles High School; George Williams of Hampton Institute; Ralph Metcalfe of Marquette University; and Eddie Tolan and Willis Ward of the University of Michigan. George Williams was the first athlete from a Negro college to try out for the Olympics.

On July 2, at Dycke Stadium, Evanston, Illinois, Eddie Tolan equaled the Olympic record of 10⅗ seconds in the 100-meter dash. Ralph Metcalfe also ran a 10⅗ seconds 100-meter dash. James Johnson won the 200-meter dash in 21 3/10 seconds, bettering the Olympic record by 3/100 seconds.

In the final qualifying tryouts at Palo Alto, Tolan ran in the first heat of the 100-meter dash with Emmett Toppino, Loyola University of New Orleans, Stewart Wilcox, Wesleyan, and Hudson Hellmich, Illinois.

James Johnson was in the second heat of the 100-meter dash with Frank Wykoff, USC; George Simpson, Columbus, Ohio; W. P. Carr, Milrose Athletic Association, New York; and Ralph Montague, Olympic Club, San Francisco.

Ralph Metcalfe ran in the third heat of the 100-meter dash with Don Bennett, Ohio State; Nat George, West Coast Athletic Club; Earl Wedmyer, Maryland; and Richard Hardy, Cornell University.

The 100-meter dash (109.3 yards) finalists who would go on to Los Angeles were Metcalfe, Tolan, Simpson, and Toppino, finishing in that order.

The finalists in the 200-meter dash (218.7 yards) were Metcalfe, Tolan, Simpson, Kiesel, and Dyer, in that order.

In the running broad jump, the top three qualifiers—Dick Barber, Edward Gordon, and Lambert Redd—were selected. John Brooks was fourth.

In the high jump there was a triple tie for first place at 6 feet 6⅜ inches among Robert Van Orsdel, USC; George Spitz, New York Athletic Club; and Cornelius Johnson, Los Angeles High School. In a triple tie for fourth were Walter Marty, Olympic Club; Parker Shelby, Los Angeles Athletic Club; and Willis Ward, the University of Michigan, at 6 feet 5⅗ inches.

On July 30, 1932, Vice President Charles Curtis, representing President Herbert Hoover, opened the Tenth Olympiad.

One hundred five thousand fans, the most ever to attend an Olympics, looked on under a blazing sun after Curtis's twenty-six word address, as two thousand athletes representing forty-two nations passed in review. These teams ranged from Haiti's two athletes to over four hundred on the United States team.

The two athletes on Haiti's team were both Negroes, Andrea Theard and Silvio Cator. Cator was competing in his second Olympics, having finished second in the running broad jump in 1928. He was born on October 9, 1900, in Cavillon, Haiti, and had paid his own way to both Olympics. On his sixth and last try on September 9, 1928, at the Colombes Stadium in France two months after that year's Olympics, Cator was the first athlete to jump 25 feet in competition.

In the high jump, Cornelius Johnson, a seventeen-year-old high school student, tied for first place at 6 feet 5⅜ inches with three others: Duncan McNaughton, Canada; Robert Van Orsdel, the United States; and Simon Toriobio of the Philippines. In the jump-off, Johnson finished fourth behind Toriobio, Van Orsdel, and McNaughton.

In the 100-meter dash finals six athletes lined up: Takayoshi Yoshioka, Japan; Daniel Joubert, South Africa; Arthur Jonath, Germany; and Eddie Tolan, Ralph Metcalfe, and George Simpson of the United States. The *Washington Post* of August 2 noted:

TOLAN WINS OLYMPIC 100 METERS FOR AMERICA
NEGROES FINISH ONE TWO AS METCALFE RUNS SECOND

The 1932 100-meter winners at Los Angeles: Ralph Metcalfe, USA, second place; Eddie Tolan, USA, first place; and Arthur Jonath, Germany, third place. Tolan's time was 10.3 secs.

In the 1932 Olympics, Eddie Tolan broke the tape first in the 100-meter dash, but Metcalfe (on Tolan's left) hit the tape almost at the same time. Both were timed in 10.3 secs.

Jonath was third in a race so close that it seemed that Metcalfe had won. However, an electrophotographic camera clock confirmed Tolan's victory. His margin was about two inches. His time was 10.3 seconds.

The five foot 7 inch, 165-pound Eddie Tolan ran the fastest 100-meter dash in the thirty-four-year history of the revival of the Olympic games. Ralph Metcalfe was clocked in identical time.

In the running broad jump, long lanky Edward Gordon, who had failed to qualify at Amsterdam in 1928, won with a leap of 25 feet ¾ inches. Lambert Redd was second with a leap of 24 feet 11⅜ inches. Chuhei Nambu of Japan was third with a leap of 24 feet 5¼ inches.

On August 3 Arthur Jonath; Carlos Luti of Argentina; William Walters of South Africa; Tolan, Metcalfe, and Simpson lined up for the 200-meter dash. The next day, the *Washington Post* front-paged:

TOLAN WINNER IN 200 METERS BEFORE 85,000

Eddie Tolan set a new Olympic record in the 200-meter dash of 21⅕ seconds. He ran two races in two days and set two world Olympic records. George Simpson finished second, and Ralph Metcalfe was third.

The black Olympians finally made their mark. Tolan, Metcalfe, and Gordon all won medals—and Cornelius Johnson narrowly missed.

But there was still grumbling in some quarters. Except for George Williams, all the Negro competitors were from white colleges. Williams had finished a distant fifth in the javelin throw with 206 feet. The winning throw, by Matti Jarvinen of Finland, was 238 feet 7 inches.

Williams, whose mark was made at the tryouts, failed to qualify for the Olympics. Thus nearly all the black Olympians were from white colleges. In addition, rumors abounded about what had happened to the two Negro female athletes.

In 1928, women were first admitted to track and field competition in the Olympics. In 1932, Tydia Pickett and Louise Stokes, both entered in the sprints, would have been the first black female Olympians, and they had apparently qualified.

The *Chicago Defender* noted that they had run "fourth and fifth in a field that allowed six to qualify, but they were replaced by two white athletes. And black women athletes had to look toward 1936—and Berlin.

When the tryouts were completed in 1932, four Negroes were on their way to Los Angeles. After the 1936 tryouts, ten Negroes were on their way to Berlin: Jesse Owens (100- and 200-meter dash, broad jump, and 400-meter relay[1]); twenty-six-year-old Ralph Metcalfe

---

[1] Owens was not originally scheduled for the 400-meter relay, but after his sensational performances the public demanded that he compete.

The 1932 Olympic broad jump winners at Los Angeles, California. Left to right: Lambert Redd, USA, second place; Edward Gordon, USA, first place; Chuhei Nambu, Japan, third place. Gordon jumped 25 ft. ¾ in.

(100-meter and 400-meter relay); Frederick "Fritz" Pollard, Jr. (110-meter hurdles); Mack Robinson (200-meter run); Archie Williams (400-meter run); James LuValle (400-meter run); John Woodruff (800-meter run); John Brooks (running broad jump); David Albritton (high jump); Cornelius Johnson (high jump).

Shirley Povich observed on July 13, 1936, in the *Washington Post:*

It would seem from the final American Olympic trials, in which ten colored lads have won first places, broken two Olympic records, and won 12 berths on the United States team, that the American Negro is peculiarly fitted for track and field sport.

The American Olympic team sailed for Berlin on July 15, 1936. The track and field team was led by the peerless Jesse Owens from Ohio State University. The lithe, lightfooted son of a former Alabama sharecropper was then at his peak.

On August 2 in the new Olympia Stadium at Berlin, the Eleventh Olympiad opened before one hundred ten thousand fans. The weather was unseasonably cold and windy, with ominously threatening skies. Owens was not scheduled to run in the first qualifying trials until the twelfth heat—about noon, but he arrived early to get "the feel" of the track. When he was finally called for his heat in the 100-meter dash, the clock read 12:10. He balanced himself first on one leg and then on the other as he stripped off his warm-up suit. Fifteen hundred reporters, representing the world press, saw him nearly fall several times. They must have wondered if a case of nerves were setting in for the young black athlete, for he had been constantly followed and interviewed ever since arriving in Berlin and had patiently and courteously answered all questions and fulfilled every interview request, often to the consternation of the coaches.

In the 100-meter heat, Owens ran a 10⅕ seconds dash that set a new world's record (later disallowed because of a "following wind"). The fans knew they were in for a spectacle.

In the 100-meter dash finals the next day the field consisted of Martin Osendarp of Holland, Erich Borchmeyer of Germany, Hans

Strandbirg of Sweden, and Frank Wykoff, Ralph Metcalfe, and Jesse Owens of the United States.

Owens got off to a jack-rabbit start. Metcalfe was slow off the blocks but was soon abreast of Owens as the tape loomed ahead. However, Owens hit it first in 10.3 seconds, tying Tolan's 1932 Olympic record. Metcalfe was second in 10⅖ seconds.

On Tuesday, August 4, Owens ran in the 200-meter heat. His time was 21.1 seconds, a new Olympic and world's record, but he had no time even to accept congratulations, for he had another qualifying event scheduled.

They were waiting for Jesse at the jumping pits, where the others had already made their qualifying jumps. As he pranced through the runway and into the pit to measure his stride and test road conditions, the red flag indicating a foul went up. Jesse stopped in disbelief and stood uncertainly, not knowing what to say.[2]

Still wearing his jersey pullover, Owens stood momentarily stunned. Now grimly serious, not testing the track this time, Owens sped down the runway as fast as he could, and took a mighty leap. But he was off stride and had overstepped the takeoff. The red flag again waved. One qualifying jump was all that remained before possible elimination for the world's greatest broad jumper.

Lutz Long, the German broad jumper, put his arms around Owens to console him. Other athletes gathered round in a genuine show of camaraderie.

Showing no outward emotion, Owens calmly walked the spring path to the takeoff board, then retraced his steps. Running full speed, he took off a full foot behind the takeoff line. Jesse Owens qualified for the running broad jump.

The field in the running broad jump finals included Maffei of Italy; Naoto Tajima of Japan; Lutz Long and Ieichun of Germany; and Robert Clark and Jesse Owens of the United States. Lutz Long was in the lead at a mark approaching 26 feet but Jesse Owens leaped 26

---

[2] Joseph N. Bell, *Olympic Thrills* (New York: Julian Messner, 1965), p. 103.

Jesse Owens soaring to a new world's running broad jump record at the 1936 Olympics in Berlin. Distance: 26 ft. 5 5/16 in.

Jesse Owens (on right) and Germany's Lutz Long, relaxing after finishing their broad-jump heats at the 1936 Olympics held in Berlin.

feet 5 5/16 inches. Another Olympic and world's record!

Lutz Long finished second with a leap of 25 feet 9 27/32 inches, the longest jump ever made by a European, second only to Owens' prodigious leap as the longest in Olympic history. Tajima finished third with 25 feet 4 47/64 inches. Maffei and Leichun tied for fourth with 25 feet 4 21/64 inches. Robert Clark finished sixth with 25 feet 1 31/32 inches.

Clark's sixth-place leap would have won any other Olympiad except 1928, when Edward Hamm cleared 25 feet 4⅜ inches.

Long was the first person to shake Owens' hand when he cleared the broad-jump pit. The young German had a look of obvious admiration in his eyes.

Later, over coffee in the Olympic Village, Jesse Owens wondered aloud at Lutz Long's unbridled enthusiasm over his victories.

Long replied: "I am here to struggle to win, but the first one I wish to beat is always myself."[3]

Incredibly, Owens had won the 100-meter dash and the broad jump. The next day, Wednesday, August 5, he would be trying for his third gold medal in three days. He had tied one Olympic and world's record (the 100-meter dash) and broken another Olympic and world's record (the running broad jump).

The 200-meter dash finalists were Wynand van Beveren of Holland; Lee Orr of Canada; Paul Haenni of Switzerland; Martin Osendarp of Holland; and Mack Robinson and Jesse Owens of the United States.

Mack Robinson's seventeen-year-old brother, John "Jackie" Roosevelt Robinson, awaited word of the outcome as eagerly as anyone else.

While the runners waited, poised for flight, Harold Whitlock of Great Britain, leading the 50,000-meter walk, was finishing at the very point where the 200-meter dash would end. Other walkers were also coming into view. As the runners waited, the threatening clouds burst and rain pelted them.

The walkers finally cleared the track, and the 200-meter dash got under way. Owens, off like a shot, was racing as his grade school

---

[3] Jesse Owens with Paul Neimark, *I Have Changed* (New York: William Morrow Company, Inc., 1972), p. 134.

teacher, Charley Riley, had taught him; as if he were running on red-hot coals. He established still another Olympic and world's record in 20.7 seconds. Matthew Robinson's second-place finish of 21.1 seconds was a tenth of a second below Eddie Tolan's 1932 Olympic record.

Italy had an outstanding 400-meter relay team favored to win. America's team was composed of Sam Stoller, Marty Glickman, Foy Draper, and Frank Wykoff.

But Owens had created such a sensation that many wanted him—and Metcalfe—to run in the relays as well. Owens, who doted on competition, also wanted one more medal. The *Cleveland Plain Dealer* of August 6 reported:

OWENS' REQUEST TO RUN IN RELAY DENIED

The head coach of the American team, Lawson Robertson, who had competed in the 100-meter dash in Athens, in the 1906[4] Olympics, informed the press: "Owens has had enough glory and collected enough gold medals . . . to last him a while. We want to give the other boys a chance."

But no precedent would have been set by allowing Owens to compete in a race for which he was not originally scheduled; Lawson Robertson had been the head coach of the 1928 Olympic team when John Lewis was replaced with Ray Barbuti.

Public opinion and pressure from the higher echelon of the American Olympic establishment caused Robertson to relent. He replaced Sam Stoller and Marty Glickman with Jesse Owens and Ralph Metcalfe, a move that made nearly everyone happy, except perhaps Italy and its partisans.

Owens, Metcalfe, Draper, and Wykoff, running in that order, set a new world's record in the 400-meter relay in 39.8 seconds. Italy's team of Mariani, Caldana, Ragni, and Gonnelli finished second in 41.1 seconds.

When the American team mounted the winning platform, Metcalfe

---

[4] The first Panhellenic games in 1906 were not officially a modern Olympiad, but have come to be listed with the modern Olympics.

The 1936 winning 400-meter relay team at Berlin. Left to right: Jesse Owens, Ralph Metcalfe, Foy Draper, and Frank Wykoff.

signaled for Owens to stand on the highest step, but Owens insisted that Metcalfe (who had placed second in the 1932 and 1936 Olympics in the 100-meter dash) mount that place of honor. Owens was giving Metcalfe his last chance to breathe the rarefied air from the top of the heap.

The United Kingdom had a great 1600-meter relay team. America's team consisted of Harold Cagle, Robert Young, Eddie O'Brien, and Al Fitch; a good, but certainly not a great team. However, Coach Robertson had a fast runner available, James LuValle, who had finished third in the 400-meter run in 46⅘ seconds, tying with William Roberts, who was clocked in the same time. LuValle's third-place mark was the third fastest run in Olympic history. And Archie Williams, who won the 400-meter race, ran the second fastest 400-meter race in Olympic history at 46.5 seconds.

That England had a strong team could be readily seen. William Brown had finished fourth in the 400-meter run, but had been clocked in the same time as James LuValle. And A. G. Brown had been barely beaten by Archie Williams, coming in second in the 400-meter run in 46.7 seconds. Frederick Wolfe and Godfrey Rampling were the other members of Britain's team.

Robertson stayed with his scheduled 1600-meter relay team, and the United States possibly gave up a gold medal. England finished first in the 1600-meter relay in 3 minutes 9 seconds and the U.S. finished second in 3 minutes 11 seconds.

But still America's "black auxiliaries," as the German press referred to the Negro athletes, came home toting a bagful of medals. Of the ten black athletes on the track and field team, nine won either a gold, bronze, or silver medal:

100-meter dash, Jesse Owens, 10 3/10 seconds. Tied world record. Gold medal. 10 points

100-meter dash, Ralph Metcalfe, 10 2/5 seconds. Silver medal (second place). 5 points

200-meter dash, Jesse Owens, 20 7/10 seconds. World record. Gold medal. 10 points

400-meter run, Archie Williams, 46 5/10 seconds. Gold medal. 10 points

400-meter run, James LuValle, 46 4/5 seconds. Bronze medal (third place). 4 points

800-meter run, John Woodruff, 1 minute 52 9/10 seconds. Gold medal. 10 points

200-meter dash, Matthew Robinson, 21 1/10 seconds. Silver medal. 5 points

110-meter hurdles, Frederick Pollard, Jr. 14 2/5 seconds. Bronze medal. 4 points

400-meter relay, Owens, Metcalfe, Draper, Wykoff 39 4/5 seconds. Gold medal. 10 points

High jump, 6 feet 7 15/16 inches. Cornelius Johnson. Gold medal. 10 points

High jump, 6 feet 6 3/4 inches. David Albritton. Silver medal. 5 points

John Woodruff winning a relay race. Woodruff was the 1936 Olympic 800-meter winner in Berlin, Germany. His time: 1 min. 52 9/10 secs.

Running broad jump, Jesse Owens, 26 feet 5 21/64 inches.
World record. Gold medal.   10 points

Phil Edwards, an American-trained Negro running under the colors of Canada, won a third-place bronze medal in the 800-meter run. His time, 53⅗ seconds.

World lightweight champion Joe Gans had been implored by his mother many years before the 1936 Olympics to "bring home the bacon" at the time of his championship fight with Battling Nelson in Goldfield, Nevada. From Berlin, in 1936, the black athletes brought home the entire hog.

Of course Jesse Owens was the number-one topic of conversation as the *Queen Mary* docked on August 25, 1936. He was engulfed by the news media. Edsel Ford, the automobile magnate, Helen Hayes and her husband Charles McArthur, who were also on board the *Queen Mary*, were virtually ignored. A proud nation saluted its Olympic heroes in general, and James Cleveland Owens in particular. It was thought that to the victor would go the spoils. The *Cleveland Plain Dealer* of November 17, 1936:

Jesse Owens returned from Berlin on the steamship Queen Mary, on Monday, August 24, 1936. On Friday, August 28th, a police motorcycle escort led his open automobile in a parade to the State House in Columbus, Ohio (shown here). He was greeted there by Governor Martin L. Davey and other dignitaries.

OWENS LEADS IN RACE FOR SULLIVAN AWARD

The Sullivan Award was started in 1930 to honor James E. Sullivan, one of the organizers and driving forces behind the AAU, who died in 1914 and who had been instrumental in spreading the doctrine of amateurism throughout the land. The recipient was supposed to be the "American sportsman who by his performance, example, and influence, as an amateur, and as a man, had done most to advance the cause of sportsmanship."

Modest, unassuming, and polite, Owens had been a model of perfect decorum at the Olympic games. And he was even his state's (Ohio) official "Ambassador of Goodwill." The Cleveland *Plain Dealer* of December 31, 1936, reported:

OWENS LOSES IN RACE FOR MEDAL
AAU PICKS MORRIS OVER JESSE BY 93 VOTES

Typically, Owens took it in stride. His only response was: "That's funny. But I'm glad the best man won."

The six hundred "experts" had given Morris 1,106 votes to Owens' 1,013 votes. And who was Glenn Morris? Glenn Morris was the Olympic decathlon champion. He was an unknown in 1932, as he sat in the stands at the Los Angeles Olympics and watched Jim Bausch win the decathlon.

The nineteen-year-old Glenn Morris had remarked: "I can do all the things that he can do, and I can do most of them better than he can."

Under a revised scoring system for the 1936 Olympics, Morris's total exceeded Bausch's.

Morris was an outstanding athlete. In the grueling decathlon, one has to be. However no athlete—before or since—has ever equaled the fantastic display of sheer foot speed put on by Jesse Owens. He was clearly the people's champion.

And awards or no awards, the 1936 Olympics was the year of the black Olympian.

Index